Daily Life SERIES 13

DAILY LIFE IN SPAIN IN THE GOLDEN AGE

MARCELIN DEFOURNEAUX

DAILY LIFE
IN SPAIN
IN THE GOLDEN AGE

Translated by Newton Branch

London
GEORGE ALLEN AND UNWIN LTD

FIRST PUBLISHED IN 1970

This translation © George Allen and Unwin Ltd 1970

SBN. 04 946003 X

Translated from the French
LA VIE QUOTIDIENNE EN ESPAGNE AU SIÈCLE D'OR
© Hachette, Paris, 1966

PRINTED IN GREAT BRITAIN
IN 10 ON 12 PT BASKERVILLE TYPE
BY BUTLER AND TANNER LTD
FROME AND LONDON

FOREWORD

Time-honoured even in Spain, the expression 'Golden Century' (*el Siglo de oro*) can be interpreted in two ways. It can cover that long period which lasted from the time of Charles V until the Treaty of the Pyrenees. During this period, gold, and more important silver, coming from America, enabled Spain to launch great ventures abroad and to gain military ascendancy over the whole of Europe. Yet, by the end of the reign of Philip II, signs were manifest in the homeland that Spain was suffering from economic exhaustion.

On the other hand, 'The Golden Century' can mean that period which was made illustrious by the genius of Cervantes, Lope de Vega, Velazquez, and Zurbaran. During this time, Spain, although politically enfeebled, was able to impose some of her cultural brilliance on the world of letters, especially in France, where her example provided the pattern from which was born that country's 'Great Century'.

To attempt to give a picture of daily life during the whole of the sixteenth century and the next fifty years would be to risk anachronism, not only in the description of the material aspects of existence, but also, what is more important in our view, in the proper understanding of them.

The sum total of the actions and behaviour which make up the daily life of individuals is inseparable, not only from the social framework of their lives, but also from their beliefs and ideals, which themselves constitute the spirit of an age.

Between the reigns of Philip II (1556–1598), Philip III (1598–1621), and Philip IV (1621–1665), there was evolution both in politics and morals, whose influence was seen in the life of the nation and in the literature which is a reflection of it. The death of the 'prudent king' gave the aristocracy an important place in the government and enhanced its place in society. The expulsion of the Moriscos meant that the last vestiges of Islam were erased from medieval Spain. The economic decline helped to accentuate the differences between social classes, and the slowing down of creative activity was accompanied by an increasing taste for ostentation and formalism. Thus, by a paradox, whilst the genius of her culture was felt throughout Europe, the country seemed to become increasingly introspective and, in a way, more purely 'hispanic' than in the previous century.

Clearly one must challenge the innumerable literary documents which show us both sides of the coin and one must suspect that often they distort the truth by describing as normal and 'everyday' things which in fact were remarkable only because they were singular. Their use is possible only if we constantly compare them with other documentary sources. Among these, the accounts of foreign travellers are of particular interest; for, despite their multiplicity and the uneven intellectual qualities of their authors, their similarity is, in some measure, a warranty of truth.

We should not forget that in the first half of the seventeenth century the 'Spanish Tour' had become fashionable for writers, and remained so up to the time of Théophile Gautier, Alexandre Dumas, and beyond, with all that it implied in the systematic search for the picturesque.

These travellers' tales, however, do illuminate certain material and moral aspects of the Golden Century, which, looking back over three hundred years, we might be tempted to regard as singular and untypical of the era. Checking them with other contemporary texts, we discover that Spain was already endowed with a marked originality both in her people and in her countryside which had made a striking impression on travellers from other parts of Europe.

These accounts finally allow us to correct the inaccurate impression gained from a consideration of the more superficial and frivolous accounts of life in Spain. We are put on our guard against an illusion, arising from our knowledge of subsequent history, that an impoverished Spain was in some way beaten in advance in her duel with France. For there is hardly a traveller in Spain during the first part of the seventeenth century who is not amazed by the might of 'Spanish Monarchy' – a term meaning all the possessions under the direct authority of the government in Madrid. This was the monarchy which Richelieu, up to the time of his death several months before Rocroi, never ceased to fear for its skill in both political and military enterprises.

These are the reasons which have led us to entrust to a few foreign travellers, mostly French, the task of writing an imaginary 'Letters from a Journey in Spain'.

CONTENTS

'Blue stockings'. Clothes and feminine fashions. 'Outings'. The 'Tapado' and the carriages.

ILLUSTRATIONS

CHAPTER ONE

'LETTER ABOUT A JOURNEY
IN SPAIN'

The journey: customs, transport, inns – Diversity of the Spanish country-
side. Expulsion of the 'Moriscos' and its consequences. The economic
decline and its causes. Decadence of the towns. The part played by
foreigners. The Spanish temperament and provincial independence –
The kingdom of France and the kingdom of Spain.

Having studied the Castilian language for a long time in order
to explore the excellent works in which so many able minds have
revealed to us the characters and the customs of their country, I
sought a more personal knowledge of that proud and prudent
nation which seems unwilling to go abroad except to dominate
others and to extend her empire over other peoples.

Though I have learnt much from travel in a foreign land, I did
not have enough time in Spain to be enlightened about everything.
I did not fail to ask trustworthy people about the things which I
could not see for myself, for they alone know those who live there.
Everything here, therefore, will appear as I saw it. Dealing with so
many diverse matters, it will not be surprising if I tell untruths
without meaning to lie and others in which I may err, not knowing that I am astray.[1]

I entered Spain by the easiest way, crossing the Bidassoa, a
river, or rather a torrent, which separates the two kingdoms. The
inhabitants on both banks speak a language which is understood
only by the people of those parts. There is constant communication
across this frontier even when there is a state of war between the
two countries.

At Irun, the first township belonging to the king of Spain, a
quarter of a league away, you are not asked for a passport nor the
reason for your coming, and there appears to be no fear or mistrust.
An agent of the Inquisition merely asks if you have in your luggage
any literature banned by the Holy Office (nearly all of which is
the work of heretical theologians), and, for this inspection, makes
you pay an obol which they claim as a due to the Inquisition.[2]

13

The first royal custom-house is not reached till one leaves the mountains of Vascony and approaches the town of Vitoria. It is here that the 'kingdom of Castille' begins, which includes the whole of Spain, save for the kingdoms of Navarre, Aragon-Catalonia, and Valencia. These, nevertheless, are part of the Spanish monarchy and owe allegiance to the King. But they retain their *fueros*, which are certain privileges, one of which is extremely inconvenient to the traveller, as I have several times found to my cost. Between Castille and the other kingdoms – or, to be more precise, provinces – there are 'toll-houses', or control points, where there are customs officers and guards, and you are not allowed to enter or leave a province, under the threat of a severe penalty, unless you register your apparel, merchandise and money, and pay for everything even if it is a little used. Moreover, one has to have a passport. The possession of one, however, does not prevent the functionary from questioning it, saying that it is not in order, and pretending to check whether there is more in your trunks and valises than you have declared in your papers. The fact is they want to hold you to ransom for a few more pistoles before they let you go on your way.

One day I complained to a Spanish nobleman about the importunities of these gentry who, like harpies, await the traveller, especially a foreigner, in order to play all sorts of dirty tricks on him. He replied that one tolerated these blackguards because the King's main revenue comes from customs dues of this type. In consequence one allows a bit of thievery in order that they may produce more income. These tax-farmers are nearly all Portuguese Jews (although they pretend to be Christians). Moreover, when they have done well by their robbery and are gorged with silver and gold, one tries to catch them in the Inquisition's net by disclosing the fact that they only claim to be nationals in order to be accepted in Spain, despite the fact that they belong to the race that blasphemes against the name of Jesus. Then they are forced to disgorge, and are slowly tortured until they have paid for all the wrongs and injustices they have done to the king and his subjects.[3]

Apart from the inconvenience of the customs, there are other things which delay the traveller, above all the small use which is made of horses. Yet there is no country in the world where the postmen have better mounts and, since the relay stages are only two to four leagues apart, these horsemen can go at full speed and cover up to thirty leagues in a single day. But the Royal Mail is used only for letters and special dispatches which are sent from Madrid to the principal towns and frontiers of the kingdom, whence they go to Flanders and Italy (when war with Spain does not prevent it).

Although Philip II has permitted certain private individuals to use this service, people rarely do so because mule transport is generally preferred. Persons of quality who wish to travel comfortably, hire a litter which is carried by two mules. But, in addition to being very slow, this mode of travel is also extremely costly. Ordinarily one travels on muleback and I had to come to an agreement at St Sebastian with a *moco de mulas* (a muleteer) for me to hire two of his animals and for him to serve as guide on the way to Madrid.[4]

As far as food is concerned, I also learnt to travel according to the custom of the country, which is to buy what one wants to eat here and there; for it is impossible to find along the way, as one can in France and Italy, inns which provide both board and lodging. Here is the daily procedure: as soon as you arrive at an inn you ask if there are beds; having taken care of that, you hand over the raw meat which you have brought with you, or else you search for a butcher or give some money to the innkeeper's varlet to buy it for you, as well as other necessities. But as – and this usually happens – they swindle you, the best thing is to carry your victuals in your own saddle-bags and to make provision each day, wherever you are, for the needs of tomorrow, such as bread, eggs, and oil. It is true that on the road you sometimes meet hunters who have killed partridges and rabbits, which they will sell at a reasonable price.[5]

It is very strange that one cannot find in a tavern anything that one has not brought oneself. The reason for this is that taxes, called *millions*, are imposed on everything that one eats and drinks. In each town and village the right to collect these taxes is granted to tax-farmers, and meat and other comestibles can be sold only by those who have bought the concession.

It is pitiful to see these inns. You are put off your food as soon as you have seen their filth. The kitchen is a place with a fire in the middle under a big pipe or chimney, from which the smoke belches back so thickly that you often feel you are in a fox's earth in which the beast has hidden itself and from which they are trying to smoke it out. A woman or a man looking like a wretched

15

vagabond and dressed in rags will pour you a measure of wine from a goatskin or a pigskin, which serves instead of a cellar (it is only in Catalonia and in the kingdom of Valencia that wine barrels are used). All this makes choice wine, plenty of which is produced in that country, stink of hide and pitch and it becomes a very disagreeable beverage. But if you are travelling during the fruit season you can get figs, grapes, apples, and also oranges of marvellous flavour.

Since the table set in the dining-hall is communal, masters, servants, and muleteers all eat their own food together before retiring to rest – some on piles of straw, others in beds, which are worse than the straw because it would be a miracle if the fleas and bedbugs allowed you a wink of sleep.

Listen to Guzman d'Alfarache. He was a native of the country and, having passed a night in a *venta* (an inn) in Andalusia, he said, 'If I had been placed on my mother's doorstep, I do not think she would have recognized me, such was the strength of the fleas which attacked me. It was as if I had measles when I got up in the morning and there was not an inch on my body, my face, or my hands where there would have been room for another bite.'[6]

A slight consolation for this ill-treatment is that it costs little. You pay in accordance with a tax marked on a board called *el arancel*, which the landlord must exhibit so that it can be read by all, and on this are displayed the prices which are fixed by royal decree. These are moderate. One generally pays a real (which is worth four of our sols) for a bed, a real for the meal, and a real for the candle and service. But the *ventoros* (the innkeepers) are sometimes just as thieving as highwaymen and, in the morning when you mount your mule, you should not fail to check your gear, otherwise something is bound to be missing.

The elder Mariana says in his *History* that the soil of Spain can be counted as among the best in the world and that no other country has a better climate or greater fertility.[7] But it has to be admitted that nature has not heaped on Spain the natural advantages of France, and, apart from the Biscay area and the regions of the Asturias and Galicia, the dryness of the climate, and the starkness of the mountains, together with the indolence of the people, leave a great part of the country uncultivated and wild. The mountains which cross Spain on every side are neither cultivated nor embellished with villages as in France. They consist of high, bare, and jagged rocks which are called *sierras* or *penas*. If they are smaller and covered with trees, the people call them *monts* and pasture their cattle on them. Between them are plains of very even ground, like those in Castille; for the most part, however, these are not cultivated except around the big towns and for a league or half a league around the villages. The villages are so far apart that one can sometimes ride a whole day without seeing a living soul, except perhaps an occasional shepherd tending his flocks. The greater part of Aragon is even more arid, without trees or vegetation, except for thyme and other plants on which sheep can graze. I am told that more than two hundred thousand of these sheep come from France each year.[8]

It is true that not all of Spain has this hard and desolate aspect. A man can easily draw water from the earth or use streams to irrigate beautiful gardens in the middle of these deserts. In the flat open country of the Mancha – one of the driest areas – I saw a great number of wells, which are called *norias*. Over them people erect wheels to which earthenware pots are tied. Mules turn the contraption to raise the water in the pots to the top of the well. The water then falls into a reservoir, from which it flows through small channels to irrigate the soil, thus making it possible to produce all sorts of cereals and vegetables.[9] But it seems as if nature has confined these most fertile and agreeable parts to the perimeter of the country. As one reaches Andalusia one's eyes marvel at the innumerable olive, orange, and cypress trees, which spread out like forests.[10] The most admirable area is around Granada, where the Moors for a long time occupied the kingdom. They brought water from the snow-capped Sierras, by means of canals and tunnels, to fertilize the plains and the blossoming hills which surround them to make it one of the most beautiful sights in the world.

Another delightful part is to be found in the kingdom of Valencia, which is so lush that they call it *regalada* (which means 'the offering'), as if it were a gift from heaven. It seldom rains, but the people use spring water which they channel through narrow brick troughs into their gardens. The place is everywhere green with trees, grass and vines, and they grow rice in the marshes. There are palms, lemon and orange trees, mulberry trees (for they breed silk-worms), and a kind of cane, from which they extract a sweet liquid which they make into sugar.[11]

But this beautiful Spanish garden lost most of its richness and splendour when, in 1610, the late King Philip ordained the expulsion from his kingdom of all the Moriscos, who had been living there in greater numbers than in any other province. This extraordinary severity, which deprived the King of a large number of good and faithful subjects, has caused much discussion and mixed feelings. Some deplore the inordinate cruelty which drove a whole people from their native country. Others praise an action which not only showed the piety of their Catholic King but also rid Spain of these false Christians, whose ancestors had been masters of Spain for several centuries while continuing to have secret dealings with Africans, Turks, and other enemies of the monarchy.

I wished to learn more about this, but there is still such a division of opinion among even the most learned and discreet people that one can only let them continue to argue their case.

Those who condemn the decree of Philip III and his counsellors hold that for centuries the Spaniards have allowed the Moors to live in a land which they have reconquered and to practise their Mohammedan faith. Moreover, obsessed as they were with the desire to wage war, the Spaniards allowed the Moors to cultivate the land and carry on various trades to which Christians had become unaccustomed.

When Ferdinand and Isabella seized the realm of Granada, thereby putting all Spain in their power, they promised to respect the religion of the Moors. But the promise was soon broken and all Moors were deported unless they consented to be baptized.

The great king Philip II, moreover, perceiving that the Moors secretly kept to their Islamic faith and openly continued to speak their own language and to retain their own clothes and customs, ordered that they should be dispersed throughout Spain so that, being integrated with the Christians, they would forget their ancestors, and the power which their great numbers gave them would be substantially weakened. Thus the Moriscos – the name given to converted Moors – would cease to be a danger to the Faith and to the security of the realm, even though many in their hearts would certainly still cling to their false religion.

Let us say that those who are of this mind maintain that it is a greater virtue to convert the miscreants and to educate the depraved than to kick them out of the house. It is not sound policy, unless there is a very good reason, to inflict such widespread punishment on a state that it emerges from it more weakened than corrected.

But far more numerous are those who applaud a decree which they consider both prudent and heroic and, while admitting the evil that it may inflict on Spain, consider that this is not to be compared to the general harm and danger which menaced them so long as the Moriscos went on living in the kingdom. How can one hope to lead to the way of Christ a people so stubborn that for a century they have resisted both the preaching of the Cross and persecution, and still remain as devoted to their Koran as the Moors in Africa? The priests who had been charged to teach them Catholic doctrine knew well that, even if the Moriscos made the ritual gestures of Christianity, these were mere mummery inspired by the fear of the Inquisition. For example, when they were obliged to go to confession at Easter they presented themselves in most orderly fashion but they confessed no sins. Never did they go to priests for help when their people were sick; from fear that the priests might come in an official capacity, they hid their maladies. So they all had sudden deaths—or so the family slyly pretended.[12] Furthermore, far from diminishing in number, they increased after Philip II had chased them out of the ancient kingdom of Granada: for none of them joined the army or even the Church, and they had numerous children whom they brought up to hate Christianity.

Of these Moriscos, there were about 70,000 families assembled in the kingdom of Valencia, facing the coasts of Barbary. From these shores there often came pirates, who, coming ashore at night from their brigantines, seized men, women, and infant Christians to enslave them in Algiers and other towns. And, since the king of Spain had a continuous war with the Moors and Turks of Barbary, their kinsmen in Spain could give their aid against him. All things considered, it was a wise move to expel them from the country.

Whatever the reasons may be, it is certain that the kingdom of Valencia has since remained in a state of ruin, that many of the villages where the Moors lived have not yet been rehabilitated and that the land remains untended. Spain has not been able to recover from this huge loss of population, which some have estimated at several million people. But I do not think it can have been so great, because, apart from Aragon in which an equal number of Moriscos had transformed the valley of the Ebro into a garden, the other parts of the kingdom had not contained so many of them.[13]

Above all, several other things have weakened Spain, a fact admitted by certain of her authors. The discovery of the Indies and the need for emigrants to populate them continue to attract many people each year who want to settle there. They think the new country is better than the one they have left and hope to find new fortunes. But the treasures of Peru have only given Spain a false wealth, and the conquest of the Indies should be called much more a scourge from heaven above than an act of grace.[14]

In fact, the Spaniard, the master of these treasures, has used them not only to finance vast wars in the name of Charles V and his son Philip, but also to buy from other nations the many things of which they were in need. As a result, Spain is merely a channel through which passes the gold of the Indies which will be discharged into the seas of plenty in other countries. If we may liken the world to the human body, we can compare them in this respect: the mouth receives all sorts of meats, chews them and digests them, and then sends them to other parts of the body. The mouth gets nothing but the simple taste of those morsels which, perchance, get caught in its teeth.[15]

Spain therefore cannot do without trade from other countries, even when she is at war, which applies to France, a country which trades not only with Biscay, Navarre, and Aragon, where it was always more or less allowed, but even with the whole of Spain, despite attempts to forbid it, since Provence has always had a commercial relationship with Valencia for the sheer necessity of exchanging their goods. The same applies to Brittany and Normandy and other oceanic provinces and their relations with Bilbao and Cadiz. I am not speaking only of wheat and the materials which are exported from these countries, but of all sorts of manufactured goods from hardware to steel blades. I thus learned that it was an error to believe that all good swords were forged in Toledo.

It follows that the handicrafts of Spain, formerly flourishing, are almost ruined today. For instead of working on their products, such as wool and silk, as she used to do, Spain sends the raw materials to foreign parts, and in Holland, France, and England materials which fetch a high price are manufactured. Since the major part of Spanish commerce is controlled by foreigners, towns which until quite recently were active with artisans and the trade in their goods have wasted away and are no more than shadows of their former selves. Thus Burgos, formerly opulent thanks to its trade in Castillian wools, has lost nearly all its markets; and Segovia, which made beautiful cloth, is today half deserted and very poor.[16]

All the same, there remain some great and lovely towns. But all except Madrid are outside Castille. Saragossa, built on the Ebro, looks more like Toulouse than any other town in France that I have seen, having the same great houses made of brick. I was shown an old castle, called *Aljaferia*, which had been a palace of the ancient kings and now belongs to the Inquisition. Barcelona, almost as big as Lyons, is enclosed in a stone wall which separates it from its suburbs, in which there is a harbour and a mole which were built at great cost because in former times ships had to hold off from this roadstead in the open sea, and were often seized by the corsairs of Barbary. In the centre of the ramparts, the streets are very narrow but full of life. Near the cathedral there is a palace called the Deputation, where their Estates-general deal with the country's affairs. Around the walls of the chamber one can see portraits of the ancient counts of Barcelona right up to the reigning king. Our own Charlemagne and his son Debonnaire have their proper places. There is also a Chamber of Deputies in Valencia, which is governed in similar fashion. But here the most beautiful building is the merchants' Lodge, or *Lonja*, situated in the main square and approached by flights of stone steps. I will not mention Seville, which is so well known throughout the whole world on account of its immense trade with the West Indies.[17]

What is most extraordinary about these towns is the prodigious number of Frenchmen to be found there. Some have a variety of trades and others go there to sell merchandise which they bring from France. I was assured – though it is hard to believe – that there were more French in Catalonia than natives: that there were an estimated 15,000 in Valencia and, in Saragossa, more than 10,000 from Gascony and the Auvergne. Of the latter, the less fortunate came from Gévaudan and this is why the Spaniards call them 'Gavaches'. The reason why the French, and many other nationalities, are so numerous is the chance of a sudden change in their way of life; those who arrive poverty-stricken soon find themselves comfortably well off and sometimes even go home rich men.[18]

In fact, since all labour is very dear in Spain, the foreign artisans earn a lot, especially since they have more application than the Spaniards, who despise all occupations which they class as 'lower trades'. Masons and carpenters are mostly aliens who earn three or four times as much as they would in their own countries. In Madrid you will not see a single water-carrier who is not a foreigner; and most of the tailors are also foreigners. Even the land is not culti-vated by the natives: in Aragon during the seasons for ploughing, sowing, and harvesting, great numbers of peasants arrive from Béarn to earn high wages for sowing wheat and harvesting it.

As for businessmen, in addition to the profits they make on their merchandise, they try to smuggle into France copper coins, like the *liard*, or half-farthing, to exchange it against silver. Since King Philip raised the price of copper, silver is cheaper in Spain than in France, and hence there is a profitable market.[19] The difficulty is getting the silver out of Spain, a traffic which is prohibited by law. All the same, as I saw at Pampelune at the end of the fair where there were a number of French merchants, who had their ways of smuggling their gains over the mountains. If they could not get a permit (which is seldom granted), they find peasants who undertake to make the transaction at a rate of 1 or 2 per cent at St-Jean-Pied-de-Port, the first township in Navarre which remains French. These peasants are known to be trustworthy; to evade the guards they walk by night or pick their way over the crags and wastelands where there are only goats and shepherds.[20]

It is not long ago that mendicants came from every country to seek their fortunes here. The Germans came in bands each year, and one hears that on leaving their homes they promised to bring back dowries for their daughters from the alms they would receive in the villages and all along the way. It is as if Spain, for them, were the West Indies of Castille. Many pilgrims from France also go to Saint-Jacques-de-Galice, some through devotion, others because they are rogues and vagabonds. I have met many in Biscay carry-ing staffs and begging-bowls, and with the cowrie-shell badge on their cloaks. Even in the towns you see beggars who are maimed or blind (or pretending to be blind) so that, to quote one of their authors, it seems that there cannot be anywhere else for them to go, and that all the filth of Europe had been poured into Spain.[21]

It is strange that so many go to Spain to seek their fortune when, as I have said, most of the country is poor and wretched. But, apart from those who imagine that all the gold of Peru has been tipped into the country and hope that some small portion of it may come their way, the Spaniards are also to blame. They never stop cursing aliens who, they claim, live off them and take the bread out of their mouths. But if there is such poverty, it seems to me that it is not caused by the nature of the country but by the temperament of its inhabitants. Their minds are clouded with dreams of grandeur and they prefer misery or service for a grandee rather than turning their hands to some craft or industry. A cobbler, when he leaves his last and his awl, and sports a sword and dagger at his hip, will scarcely raise his hat to a customer for whom a moment before he was working in his shop.[22]

Thus, though the Spaniards are often admirable in misfortune, facing the failures and successes of their lives alike with the patience of a strong spirit, and though many are courteous, affable, and brave without boastfulness, one is not wrong in saying they are arrogant to a man. They despise the rest of the world, which they think is merely there to serve them: added to this is their ignorance of other countries, a curious but real aspect of a nation which has subjugated so many others. But the noblemen and the grandees seldom leave Madrid and do not go to war unless they are ordered and are given full expenses. As for the others who have never left their own homes, they do not know if Amsterdam is in the Indies or in Europe! The ordinary bourgeois and the poor peasant can scarcely believe in the existence of countries beyond Spain or of kings other than their own.[23]

It is a fact that one finds no less scorn for each other between Spaniards who live in different parts of the kingdom. Each thinks himself superior and each puts the blame on the other for the vices and disgrace of their provinces. I take no part in the quarrels of the Aragonese, Catalans, Valencians, and Castillians, but I would say that pride and gravity were the more particular virtues of the Castillians, and that the people of Aragon are no less proud, but are haughty and obstinate as well. Their character is not tempered with an equal kindliness. The Catalans are more industrious than others and less different from us French, both because of the climate, which is like ours, and also because a great number of the French have established themselves in this province, raised families, and mixed their blood with the natives. The temperament of the people of Valencia and Andalusia is thought to be

23

more volatile than that of other Spaniards, who do not consider them to be good soldiers because they have too much delicacy and are over fond of their pleasures.

These jealousies and disputes make up a large part of ordinary conversation when people from different provinces meet. But when a Castillian arrives, all the others combine and turn on him like so many watch-dogs at the sight of a wolf. They complain about Castille's tyranny, which prevents their having a fair share of honours and rewards, despite the fact that they have done just as much, and more, than the Castillians to increase the power of the Crown. But Castille, they say, keeps boasting about the role she has played, though her political supremacy came to her only by chance. They maintain that if Ferdinand, King of Aragon, had had a son by Isabella, Queen of Castille – not a daughter like Jeanne, who married Philip of Austria and was the mother of Charles V – their son would have had the name of Aragon. His sceptre would have reunited Spain. The Castillians retort that it was thanks only to Charles V and his son Philip II that Spain has won among other nations the renown which she now enjoys: and that it is Castille which has added the rich and vast territory of America to those parts previously colonized by the Moors. Hence the jingle:

> *A Castilla y a León,*
> *Nuevo mundo dio Colón.*

In other words, Christopher Columbus acquired the West Indies to benefit the kingdom of Castille, even though the profit has been spread throughout the whole of Spain. They add that Castille has always been the brain and heart of the country and deserves recognition because of the loyalty with which Castillians have always served the king, whereas others are always in revolt.[24]

It seems to me that the Castillians have a just grievance in this debate. There is no other place in Spain which pays heavier taxes. This is the reason why so many of its people go to other provinces and why half the country has been deserted. On the other hand, Biscay and Navarre, which in themselves are not in any way richer, are far more densely populated and more highly cultivated because they are not so overburdened with taxes. The reason is that only in Castille did the king have absolute power. Others who joined the Crown in the days of the Catholic kings have retained, as I have said, their customs and privileges almost as if they were foreign enclaves in the heart of the monarchy.[25] Each of these ancient kingdoms has maintained its State Assembly, called the *Cortès,* on which the king calls from time to time to ask for subsidies. But, whereas Castille votes the supplies he requires, the assemblies of Aragon, Catalonia, and Navarre generally refuse or make only token contributions.

Even though Philip II, in the last century, took the opportunity after the revolt in Saragossa to curtail the independence of the Aragonese, he did not dare do away with their liberty, to which they are so attached that they are ready to risk all to defend it. The king's writ does not run in the whole of Spain. The borders of the old kingdom are marked by stones which the sheriffs, the police officers, and other justiciaries can cross only after placing on the ground their *varra* or insignia of office.[26]

There is in Aragon a supreme Judge who is the guardian of their *fueros;* to him anyone who has a grievance either as to his person or his goods can bring a complaint against any jurisdiction in order that the judge who has made a bad judgement may be punished. Furthermore, the citizens claim the right to forbid any armed forces, except Castillians, to enter and quarter themselves on their territory. As a result the king has each time to ask for a permit, which is only accorded on all sorts of conditions. The people of Catalonia are no less jealous of their rights, especially the burgesses of Barcelona who govern the city and its territory through their Council. They do not gladly suffer the passage of royal troops through their country, fearing that the king may use them to restrict their freedom. Moreover, the king gets little benefit from these two provinces, certainly not more than he receives from Navarre, from which he gets nothing more than the security of a frontier along the Pyrenees, the real and natural barrier which God has placed between France and Spain. But the fear that the Navarrese might return to the dominion of their ancient and lawful princes, for whom they still have a certain regard, makes it risky to overcharge them by way of taxes.

As for Portugal, which Philip II, as heir to the ancient principalities, united to his own states, the advantages are all on the side of the Portuguese and the burdens are shouldered by the Castillians. It is a fact that Philip had to vouch that he would never allow any Castillian to take part in its government; but the gentlemen of Portugal are given positions of dignity and trust in Spain.

Finally there came from Portugal numbers of false Christians who had obtained leases on certain forms of tax and revenue of the Castillian kingdom; they render to the king only a part of their gains, enriching themselves at the expense of the poor. But, in spite of this, the Portuguese hate the Spaniards and the king has had to maintain garrisons in all the principal towns of that country for fear of revolt.

Thus, in order to defend this vast realm, which includes Naples, Franche Comté, and Flanders, the Spanish king is aided and sustained only by Castille and by the treasure which her galleons bring back from America. Nor does he get more than the smallest share. First, even before it is unloaded in Seville, silver from the Indies has to pass through the hands of traders and extortionists who have gained concessions from the king in return for money lent to him for the upkeep of his troops and to meet other expenses. The so-called 'services' are more a cause of ruin than a means of support for the state. The traders, who are nearly all foreigners (they used to be Genoese but are now mostly from Portugal), not only lend money at a high rate of interest but also 'wangle' permits to allow them to take their profit out of the country. They are like suction-pumps which remove all the silver and gold from Spain.

Therefore, if you compare the two great monarchies of Spain and France, even though the former is larger and enriched (as people imagine) by all the treasure of the Indies, the latter is in fact the stronger of the two. This is because of the divisions between Spain's various kingdoms and possessions and the disinclination of the people for trade and other useful arts. By contrast the king of France has only one realm; but it is a single unit, and his subjects, submissive and obedient, give him a greater and more certain treasure than all that could come from Peru.

In returning to France, I passed over the great plain of Roncevalles, where Charlemagne fought the Saracens and lost the battle. I came to the top of a mountain and paused to ponder the Spain I was quitting on one side and the France I was about to enter on the other.

Spain appeared to me like a scorched country whose bald and rocky mountains did not conceal the fact that few of its plains and valleys were green or attractive. By contrast, France looked to me like a garden, in which nature had landscaped the heights and depressions, the soil, the plains and valleys: and this countryside that I could see – not the most beautiful in France – seemed to me to be astonishing and extremely agreeable as I compared it to the place I had left.

But I must add that the difference between these two countries does not stop me from esteeming Spain or admiring her wisdom, her temperance, her prudence, and so many of her moral and political virtues which for the most part shine in the men she produces.

The most celebrated Greek was born among the rocks of Ithaca; and there is a place in Provence called Crau, which is also littered with boulders. But the people who live there would not exchange it for a region full of flowers and orchards, because in these sterile fields a herb grows, so excellent and of such virtue that one leaf is worth more than whole bunches grown in a fatter land. The moral is that the choicest plants often grow in lean places: and if Spain is dry and arid, this does not stunt her robustness and vigour. Moreover, even though Spain may be poor in produce, she has never lacked great men who have excelled both in literature and in the arts of politics and war, and men equally admirable and redoubtable to their neighbours.

CHAPTER TWO

THE CONCEPTION OF LIFE

*The Catholic Faith – Honour – The honour of being Christian and of
'pure blood' –* Hidalguism *and the passion for nobility – Reaction: anti-
honour as a social attitude. Idealism and realism.*

'We surpass every nation in the world in our ability to incur the
hatred of one and all. What is the reason? I simply do not know.'[1]
This question was asked by Mateo Aleman in *Guzman de
Alfarache*; other nations were not slow to answer it, and an Italian
travelling in Spain at the beginning of the seventeenth century
flings back the most virulent reply:

'Beautiful countryside of red sand which produces nothing but
rosemary and lavender: beautiful plains where you will come across
only one house in a whole day: beautiful mountains of bare rock:
beautiful hills without a blade of grass or a drop of water: beautiful towns made of wood and mud. . . . From this Eden, from this
haven of delights, have come several legions of knights errant.
These, accustomed to eating bread baked in the earth, onions, and
roots, and to sleeping in the open: these people, wearing shoes
made of old rope and the cast-off clothes of shepherds, come to our
country playing the duke and expecting to sow fear in it.'[2]

This is the reaction of a man whose country, far richer from the
heritage of centuries and the gifts of nature, has almost entirely
fallen under the sway of a nation of soldiers, uncouth, proud,
arrogant – and often in rags and tatters. The French are not slow
in denouncing the 'Senor Espagnol', who is shown in contemporary
caricatures as a figure wearing a cape full of holes over a long *épée*
and uttering preposterous rodomontades.

> I am the terror of earth's brave men,
> And every nation to my rule must bow.
> I'll have no peace, for war's my only love,
> Mars is not valiant 'til I show him how.[3]

Insult and mockery are the price paid for the fear aroused by
a nation which has, for a century, cast its shadow over the whole

of Europe. There are not a few Spaniards who congratulate themselves on this involuntary homage paid to their country: 'Oh unhappy Spain,' one of them said, 'the day she ceases to have enemies
who stimulate her greatness.'[4]

To the accusation of being haughty and arrogant, another
can be added, which was already expressed in the *Satire Ménippée*
at the end of the sixteenth century. This accusation was repeated
by most French travellers in the following era and one of them, the
Provençal poet, Annibal de l'Ortigue, put it into verse:

> Carry your beads to pray to God Eternal
> Be prodigal of vain and empty words
> And use the church for your rendezvous;
> Fear Hell itself less than the Inquisition:
> Such is the way of the Spanish court.[5]

Without doubt a satirical portrait; but as with all caricature it
only exaggerates by burlesque and malice the features of the model.
False pride, fanaticism, and even hypocrisy are but a sneering
deformation of the real values deeply rooted in the soul of Spain.
The qualities which animate all personal and social life are honour
and faith.

'Saints and Sinners'; in these antinomic but complementary
words people have summed up the characteristics of Spanish
religiosity in the seventeenth century.[6] The Catholic faith appears
to be of one substance with the Spanish soul, but its sincerity and
even the manifestations of its fervour seem to be a denial of
Christian morality. This apparent contradiction, which foreigners
denounce as hypocrisy, still puzzles us, to say the least, because it
seems to lack any logic, but we find evidence of it in innumerable
documents.

But to be precise, logic – that is, reason – is in Spain far more
than in any other country estranged from faith, partly because of
the historical conditions under which it asserted itself, and partly
because of a basic irrationality in the Spanish spirit which has a
peculiar quality that explains all contradictions.

Spain was forged during the long *reconquista* against the Moors.
It is certain that this war of reconquest which lasted for seven
centuries was not a crusade aiming to extirpate Islam, since the
advance of the Christians was followed neither by the extermina-
tion nor the forcible conversion of the Infidels. Yet tolerance

towards the Muslims incorporated in the Christian kingdoms (*mudéjares*) – very considerable up to the fourteenth century – was soon to diminish. The restrictive measures taken against religious minorities – Muslim and Jewish – in the last two centuries of the Middle Ages appeared to be the prelude to a unification under the sign of the Cross brought about by the Catholic kings and their successors. But as soon as the Jews and Moors were, at least officially, converted to Christianity, there was a new menace. This stemmed from Erasmus and Luther – the questioning of the Catholic dogma and certain practices pertaining to it. In Spain, the Crown and the Inquisition, closely united, easily overcame this danger by uprooting certain centres of heresy which had appeared in the peninsula. Facing a Europe divided by religious doubt, Spain now stood out as the champion of Catholicism. But the role of the 'Soldiers of God' in the service of the counter-Reformation was not assured only by the companions of St Ignatius but also by the Spanish soldiers fighting in Flanders and France and on the battlegrounds of the Thirty Years War. Could God abandon – not only in mundane matters, but also in the great question of ever-lasting salvation–those who had fought and suffered, those who were always ready to die for His Cause? Was not Spain assured of a fund of grace which would pay dividends to all those who held fast to God?

The cause of God is defined in the dogma which the Council of Trent reaffirmed in defiance of Protestant heresy: to adhere to the cause is to travel on a road surely to salvation; to refuse is to commit the greatest of crimes – heresy. 'I would prefer not to reign at all than to reign over heretics,' Philip II once said, and the hatred of heretics was still one of the dominant characteristics of Spanish religion and explains its fanaticism. As against this unforgivable crime, the weaknesses of the halting sinner were of relatively small account: they arose from his earthly condition, and divine mercy, through the intercession of the saints and the Church militant, will wipe out all the stains of sin, especially if the sinful soul has put itself right with God in the last hour by means of confession and absolution. In public 'notices' and 'news bulletins' which reflect the agitated life of the Spanish capital in the seventeenth century, similar announcements of assassinations and murderous affrays recur constantly: 'Tonight, Fernand Pimentel was killed by a sword thrust before he had time to grasp his own weapon. . . .

He cried out loudly for confession and died with every sign of repentance for his sins; and saying aloud the *Miserere mei Deus*, then amid floods of tears: "*In te, Domine, speravi*", he expired' (August 8, 1622); then: 'At eight o'clock in the evening certain gentlemen waited for Diego de Avila to come out of a house to kill him. They jumped on and slaughtered him; he cried out loudly for confession' (December 1, 1624); or: 'Christopher of Bustamante was killed in Parades Road *before he had time to make confession*' (October 3, 1627).[7]

But this faith, which came from true belief and was confirmed by the sacraments, might sometimes end in covering up moral deviations which were hardly compatible with the spirit of Christianity and with the commandments of the Church. 'Sin, do penance, sin again' seemed to be the programme of life for a section of Spanish society, especially among the upper class, in which extreme religious fervour was sometimes reconciled with a singular slackening of moral principles.

Thus, in contrast to the mysticism which reached its pinnacle in St Teresa and St John of the Cross, and to the anguish for salvation which led many a warrior or great lord to end a hectic and brilliant career in severe self-mortification, for many Spaniards religion tended to a formalism which placed a special value on outward appearances and was quite different from the spiritual values which it sought to express.

When Philip IV required the nuns of the convent in Agreda to do penance for the sins of his insatiable sensuality, the abbess, Sister Maria, reminded him in vain that penance requires first an effort from the sinner. At the other end of the social scale, the criminals locked up in the prison of Seville were men of exemplary devotion. Each night, after curfew, they assembled for prayer. One of them, acting as sacristan, made them kneel. The prayer was said in a loud voice: 'Jesus Christ our Lord, who shed Thy precious blood for us, have pity on me, a great sinner'. Then he continued, 'Each returns to his own occupation. One is a sinner, one denies God, and another is a robber.'[8] But there are worse things than the alternation between crime and the contrition which redeems a man. 'How many thieves,' Quevado asks, 'tell their beads not to save themselves from the sin of stealing but for protection from the law and punishment when they are stealing!' Hypocrisy? Certainly not. But the Spaniard seemed to be readier to die for God than, in His name, to curb his own aspirations and instincts.

There is another value which surpassed life itself: honour. Like faith, honour plunged its roots deep in medieval traditions and clung to the belief which, throughout the Christian world of the west, held that the ideal of men of noble birth should be the doing of courageous and heroic deeds. But honour – *la honra* – had its own particular colour and a pervasive place in Spanish life, which grew to become a paroxysm in the period of the Golden Age.

In the words of the Castillian code of the *Partidas* (thirteenth century):

'Honour means the repute which has been earned by his rank, by his noble deeds, and by the worthiness which is manifest in him. . . . There are two things which balance each other: killing a man and sullying one's reputation, *for a man who has lost his good name, even through no fault of his own, is deprived of all worth and honour: better for him to be dead than alive.*'[9]

Thus there was a double conception of honour: an expression of a man's personal worth, and his social standing which could easily be destroyed by others.

In the first instance, honour was tightly bound up with personal qualities, especially courage. The Spaniards had lived in this heroic atmosphere for centuries. Following the great feat of the Reconquest, the prodigious exploits of the *conquistadores* gave Spain an immense empire overseas, while her armies overran Europe from Sicily to Flanders and from Portugal to Germany; and her fleets crushed the Turks at Lepanto. Why should the honour of belonging to this nation of conquerors not be a matter for pride? Lope de Vega puts these very significant words in the mouth of Garcia de Paredes, one of the most famous warriors of the Italian campaigns:

'I am Garcia de Paredes, and then . . .
But it is enough to say "I am a Spaniard".'[10]

However, there is more honour in gaining a victory over oneself, in knowing how to be master of one's fate, whether good or bad. This *sosiego* – this serenity with which heroes meet their fate

32

1. La Plaza Mayor de Madrid

2. Fiesta of horsemen in the Plaza Mayor

and which softens their arrogance in triumph – was typical of Philip II when he received disastrous news of the *Invincible Armada*. In a different sense, the brush of Velazquez has given the face of Ambrosio Spinola an unforgettable expression at the moment when he receives the keys of the city of Breda from his vanquished adversary. In this painting, 'Spinola bows to his enemy and, with a hardly perceptible gesture, spares him the humiliation of kneeling at the feet of his conqueror.'[11]

Such an attitude can degenerate into a more refined sort of pride in which the graciousness of the gesture is an end in itself and so becomes worthless. The impression that this formalism made on the spirit of Spain is more significant than that made by the death of Don Rodrigo Calderon and the events which followed. Victim of the reaction against those who had so scandalously enriched themselves in the reign of Philip III, Rodrigo Calderon, Marquis of Siete Iglesias, was brought to justice by the Duke of Olivares, the new favourite of Philip IV. His too rapid rise in society, his arrogance, and his ostentatiousness made him the most unpopular man in the realm. This is why he became a scapegoat at the beginning of the new reign. Accusations and evidence piled up against him. Fantastic allegations such as sorcery were added to the real crimes and abuses which were attributed to him. The trial was followed with passionate interest, and, as soon as the death sentence was pronounced, a scaffold was erected in the Plaza Mayor de Madrid, with a *mise en scène* calculated to make the maximum dramatic impression on the public. But Rodrigo Calderon arrived at the base of the scaffold calm and scornful; '. . . he treads the steps with ease, throwing the skirt of his cloak over his shoulders, retaining even in this terrible extremity, great dignity and a *grand seignior*'s mastery of himself'. Since then his trial, his crimes, his unpopularity, and the peoples' hatred of him have vanished, wiped out by the nobility of his bearing. Spain remembers only the supreme elegance with which Calderon came face to face with death. Moreover, he became a sort of idol, with people fighting over his relics, even over bits of cloth stained with his blood. 'Brave as Rodrigo on the scaffold' has been a proverb in Spain ever since October 21, 1621: 'The most glorious day,' a contemporary said, 'in the whole of our century. . . .'[12]

However, no man is entirely the master of his honour, and the theatre of the Golden Age – like the code of the *Partidas* four

c

33

centuries before – keeps reminding us that honour can always be tarnished by others. Thus the dictum of Lope de Vega:

> No man attains to honour by himself,
> For it is in the gift of other men.
> A virtuous and well-deserving man
> Need not attain to honour: so it is thus
> That honour stems from others, not oneself.[13]

This obsession with honour as a social value is the mainspring of the dramatic play which, with mystical literature, constitutes what is most typically native in the literary heritage of the epoch.

'For the Spanish dramatists, honour plays the same part as the Fates in Greek tragedy. They represent it as a mysterious power, looking down on everyone's life, forcing people to abandon their feelings and natural inclinations, sometimes forcing them to acts of sublime self-sacrifice, at others to the commission of crimes or terrible atrocities. But these must be regarded in the light of the provocation which caused them and the dire necessity of which they were the consequence.'[14]

Since honour is worth more than life itself, there is only one way to wash away an affront: kill the culprit. 'A Spaniard will never delay the death of one who has insulted him,' Tirso de Molina proclaims, and revenge for outraged honour is the theme of the greatest dramatic creations of Lope de Vega and Calderon de la Barca. The confusion between *honra* and *fama* (renown), that is between the social and the personal aspects of honour, appears clearly in the plays, in which dishonour arises from the infidelity of a woman or from slurs on her virtue. The whole family group is dishonoured – not only the husband but the father, the brother, the uncle – and each has the duty to take vengeance. Moreover, honour having an absolute value in public opinion, mere suspicion even though unjustified can bring upon a man an inexorable punishment; because:

> Honour's a clear, transparent glass;
> A breath's enough to cloud it over.[15]

In *The Doctor and his Honour* (*El Médico de su Honra*), by Calderon, the protagonist compels a surgeon to bleed his wife – wrongly suspected – to death:

> Love adores thee
> But honour abhors thee.

In this hypertrophy, which is almost pathological in its interpretation of real honour, one detects, as in former times, a tendency on the part of the writers to go beyond the limits of plausibility. Is this really the expression of the state of mind of a particular class? It would be difficult to explain the success, throughout half a century, of the 'comedies of honour' of Lope de Vega and Calderon if there were not a certain identity between the sentiments expressed on the stage and the feelings of people in real life. Was it not Lope de Vega himself who declared in his *Art of Writing Comedies* that 'Questions of honour are best because they affect all manner of people'?

Moreover, it is clear that, quite apart from the theatre, questions of honour played an important part in everyday affairs and even more in the whole spiritual life of the Spanish. Barthélemy Joly comments acidly at the start of the century: 'This insistence on what they call *sustentar la honra* (the maintenance of honour) is honour without profit and is partly the reason for the barren state of Spain.' Forty years later, Balthazar Gracian, author of *The Hero*, among other works, condemns the misuse and abuse of the word:

'One hears of a man who tried to persuade another to forgive and make up a quarrel with a friend; he replies, "But what about honour?" Another has been told to leave his mistress and put an end to years of scandal. The man replies, "But what of my honour then?" From a blasphemer, advised to give up his blaspheming and swearing, came the answer, "But where lies honour?" A prodigal, dreaming only of tomorrow, says, "No, it's a question of honour." A man of good position who was warned not to compete with ruffians and assassins, said, "My honour does not lie there." And each of them is surprised to learn where the other places his honour. . . .'[16]

Thus, as the concept of honour becomes exasperating, it begins to turn into a jumble of mechanical reflexes and verbal extravagances, and to lose that fundamental conception of being tightly bound up with individual worth which nurtured the heroism of Spain in the Middle Ages.

There were two elements in the soul of Spain, the Catholic faith and the concern for one's honour, and these combined in a single entity: the honour of being a Christian, which was affirmed in the doctrine of the 'purity of blood' (*limpieza de sangre*). This created a gulf which cut across a Spain insisting on being entirely and uniquely Catholic. It is a deep gulf that kept alive and exacerbated the memory of the religious conflicts which were characteristic of Spain in the Middle Ages.

This schism was apparent even before the Catholic kings took their stern measures – the expulsion or enforced conversion of the Jews in 1492 and of the Muslims in 1502 – and it widened with the expulsion of the Moriscos under Philip III into a veritable chasm in the first half of the seventeenth century, creating all sorts of pitfalls both moral and social. It originated in the times when great tolerance of religious minorities came under pressure from the public and was more and more replaced by vexatious restrictions. These restrictions induced certain people of the Jewish faith and *mudéjars* (Muslims living in a Christian land) to be baptized. That many of these conversions were sincere is evidenced by the fact that certain *conversos* (converts) became true believers in their new faith and were elevated to high rank in the Catholic hierarchy. For example, Salomon Halévy, the rabbi in Burgos, became a bishop in the same town under the name of Pablo de Santa Maria.

But these conversions, even if sincere, did not wipe away the stigma of the converts' origin, and at the beginning of the fifteenth century there appeared the first of 'the purity of blood laws', the work of corporations and lay and religious bodies, which refused to accept these 'new Christians' and forbade them from holding certain offices. The most notorious – but not the first – of these laws was passed in 1449 by the magistrates of Toledo, despite opposition from the Castillian king, John II, and from Pope Nicolas V. It read as follows:

'We declare that the so-called *conversos*, offspring of perverse Jewish ancestors, must be held by law to be *infamous and ignominious, unfit and unworthy to hold any public office or benefice within the city of Toledo or land within its jurisdiction,* or to be commissioners for oaths or notaries, or to have any authority over the true Christians of the Holy Catholic Church.'

Thirty years later, in 1478, the Spanish Inquisition came into being. Whilst in no way confirming the bans imposed by these laws, it appeared at least to give them moral support. At that time Judaism and Islam were still 'legal' in Spain; but the purpose of the Inquisition was to watch and punish – for apostasy – those who had been baptized but secretly held to their ancient beliefs. Suspicion hovered over the 'new Christians', whose numbers notably increased in the period following the steps taken by the Catholic kings which forced Jews and *mudéjars* to choose between exile or conversion. The annexation of Portugal in 1580 re-introduced to the Spanish realm descendants of Jews who had sought refuge in the neighbouring country in 1492. These *marranos* (swine) aroused especially bitter hatred in the Spanish people. They were accused of 'Judaizing' in secret, and many of them presently figured in the *autos-da-fe*. On the other hand, being used to trafficking in silver, they were useful to the monarchy as money-lenders and tax-collectors, but were accused of putting pressure on small people and of ruining the state for their own personal gain.

As the number of 'the converted' grew, so did the statutes concerning 'the purity of the blood' increase between the end of the fifteenth century and the beginning of the seventeenth. Many municipalities followed the example of Toledo. The great military and noble orders (St Jacques, Calatrava, Alcantara) insisted on 'proofs' of purity from those who wished to enter their ranks. The chapters of certain cathedrals were closed to *conversos*. This was a paradox since the canon law recognized no such exclusions, and their bishops might well be 'new Christians'. As for the religious orders, they were divided. Some were liberal enough in the acceptance of 'impure' novices; others refused those who could not prove that at least a 'good part' of their blood was on ancient lineage. The example thus set by the most illustrious bodies, either by birth or because of their social status, was bound to increase the bias among the people at large. Not only pious brotherhoods, but corporations of merchants and craftsmen also demanded 'proof' of pedigree and would admit only 'old Christians' to their membership. This matter of 'purity of blood' became an obsession throughout Spain. The real evil, however, did not lie in the curtailment of civil rights which afflicted the 'new Christians', but in the discredit and even ignominy which were attached to them and could not be offset by their sincerity or their fervour for a new faith.

Here, as in other regions invaded by such notions of honour, a

37

breath of scandal could ruin the reputation of a family, dishonour-
ing and relegating its members to the status of pariahs who, in
the public eye, constituted the social classes of the *conversos*. A
Franciscan teacher of the university of Salamanca at the end of the
sixteenth century wrote on behalf of several colleagues:

'We came to Spain to avoid the doctrine that being a blasphemer,
a thief, a highwayman, or an adulterer, or being guilty of sacrilege
and any other vices, was better than having Jewish origin. Our
ancestors embraced the Christian faith two or three centuries ago.
But there remains an intolerable intolerance [*sic*]: suppose that
there are two candidates for a professorship, a benefice, a prelature,
or some other office. One is a gifted man who comes from a family
which once was Jewish but turned Christian ages ago. The other is
illiterate, ungifted, but, simply because he is an "old Christian",
he will be preferred to the other.'[17]

Thus the proof of pedigree became of the utmost importance at
that time. It became even graver for those under suspicion; for it
is easy to make accusations. It became especially so after 1530, when
the Supreme Council of the Inquisition ordered its tribunals to
record for future reference the names of all who had had dealings with the Holy Office over questions relating to their faith.
Even worse for their descendants was the practice of exhibiting in
Cathedrals placards bearing the names of reprobates. 'Thus,' said
the municipal magistrates of Tudela, in 1610, 'we can preserve the
purity of blood and distinguish the descendants of those people,
*so that time shall not obscure nor extinguish the memory of their
ancestors. In this way, we can tell men who have been truly born
and bred.*'[18] The churches still retained sanbenitos, the yellow
hoods which some were made to wear by the Inquisition as a
penance after confessing a heresy. Thus, 'He keeps his credentials
at church,' became a proverbial expression. It meant that a man's
pedigree was dubious in terms of the true faith.

If such records appeared to establish beyond doubt an 'impurity',
to refute them needed genealogical research into both the paternal
and maternal branches, which was hardly possible except for those
whose family trees were recorded in history or in the archives.
Again, the further one went back, the greater the risk of discovering a 'mixed marriage' in the very distant past. Moreover, the
existence of a malign public, always disposed to attack the

poderosos (the mighty), led to the appearance of the 'green books'. These contained family trees, some true, some false, which attributed to the great families ancient Muslim or Jewish roots. The most famous of these books, the *Tizón de España*, dated from the sixteenth century. It had a lasting success and was reprinted many times, for it appeared to prove that there was no great family in Spain which was not tainted by a few drops of 'impure' blood in its veins.

Even though the court had reacted, under Philip III, against such registers 'which produced and still produce irreparable and unjust harm', the industry of the *linajudos* flourished. These people fabricated false genealogies either to back a man's claims to an appointment to high office requiring 'purity' or, alternatively, to discredit him. They sometimes also resorted to pure blackmail, like that denounced in 1655 by the priest Barrionuevo:

'There was a group [in Seville] of about forty people. It had its own clerk of the court, its procurator, and other officers of the law. All genealogical enquiries had to be submitted to this court. Thus a candidate for a military order, a post in the Inquisition, or a place at the university, had first to be in the good graces of these people in order to get a "certificate" of pure blood and to have the necessary recommendations to those whom he wanted to approach. Anyone who refused to be swindled was accused of being a grandchild of Cazalla, or Luther, or even Mahomet. Some have been arrested, others condemned to death, or to the galleys, or have suffered other penalties.'[19]

For common folk, lacking 'ancestry', the situation was entirely different. If in the artisans' world a certain number of trades, which were reputed to have been formerly mostly in the hands of the Moriscos – tailors, blacksmiths, cobblers, for example – attracted suspicion against those who practised them, there was prejudice in favour of the peasants. Nearly all of them were puffed up with pride, more or less with good reason, in being 'old Christians'. Moreover, because of the desire to improve the social status, so characteristic of the times, there came the notion that 'purity of blood' in itself conferred a sort of nobility; no doubt inferior in the scale of social values to that which stemmed from illustrious birth, but, in another sense, of superior quality, since it was impossible for the ancient nobility to be entirely without a 'stain'.

A *Memoire* written in 1600 says that:

'There are two kinds of nobility: the greater is the *hidalguía*, the lesser the *limpieza*. Even though the former carries more honour, it is a great disgrace to be denied the latter; in Spain there is more esteem for a pure-bred commoner than for a *hidalgo* who lacks this purity.'

The theatre – the mirror of the concept of honour – does not fail to make use of this antithesis; to the sarcasms of the Commander of Calatrava who mocked the peasants of Fuenteovejuna for speaking about 'their honour', Lope de Vega replies through the lips of one of them:

> There's more than one of you who basks in the glory
> Of having won the accolade of knighthood
> That has no claim to boast such noble blood.

The virtues of Spaniards, in their greatness, their intemperance, and their differences, are typified by the *hidalgo*, the true symbol of society in the Golden Age. The *hidalgo* was placed on the lowest rung of the ladder of the nobility and, for this very reason, he was forced to be most punctilious about all questions of honour. Unlike the grandees, he did not have vast territories and vassals to govern; huge taxes and high command were not for him. He did not take part in palace intrigues, nor seek royal favours, and was not embarrassed by the need for compromise of those who wish to 'arrive'. His sole capital was his honour, inherited from ancestors who fought for their faith. But there were no Moors left to fight. . . . Some *hidalgos* went beyond the seas to seek new glories under the banners of Hernando Cortés, Almagro, and their like; but for the most part they remained on the soil where they were born. In some leather, iron-bound coffer they kept their precious *executoria* (letters patent), adorned with their escutcheons which attested their rank and guaranteed their privileges: exemption from direct taxation, immunity from the debtors' prison, and, in a case of capital crime, the dishonour of the gibbet. With even greater care they jealously maintained every form of outward appearance: in the eyes of the world this proclaimed their caste – whatever their personal fortune or misfortune might be – and their superiority over that 'vile' class of taxpayers (*pecheros*), peasants, artisans, and the *bourgeoisie*.

Doubtless there were some who led a fairly comfortable life on their small estates, in houses distinguished by an escutcheon engraved in stone, thanks to the revenues from the lands that they cultivated (for agriculture was not demeaning). Such a *hidalgo* drew the picture of his daily life for Don Quixote:

'I spend my days with my wife and son. My exercise is hunting and fishing. I possess six dozen books, some in Latin, the rest in Castillian. Some are works of devotion, the others of history. I more often finger the pages of those which are profane if they provide decent diversion, and do not weary me with their style, but interest and excite me by their invention. Sometimes I dine with friends and neighbours and I often entertain them. I go to mass every day. I give to the poor without making a display, so as to keep hypocrisy and pride out of my heart. I am a votary of the Holy Virgin and I enrust myself always to the mercy of the Lord our God.'

But this ideal image of a noble and rustic life must have been rare, for Sancho Panza wanted to kiss the feet of his host, judging him worthy of sainthood. The typical *hidalgo* tradition is more surely evoked by Estebanillo Gonzáles as he recalls his ancestry and his youth:

'My father was afflicted by a disgrace which he passed on to all his sons like original sin. He was a *hidalgo*. This is not unlike being a poet, for there are few *hidalgos* who escape perpetual poverty and continuous hunger. He possessed letters patent of his nobility so ancient that even he was unable to read them, and no one cared to touch them for fear of getting their fingers greasy from the bedraggled knots and ribbons of the tattered parchments. Even the mice took care not to gnaw them lest they were stricken with sterility!'

Hunger, 'the subtle hunger of the *hidalgo*', as Cervantes called it, was in fact the lot of many of those who, uprooted, came to the cities to find a living suitable to their rank. Some managed to slip into great households as equerries or 'chaperons' of ladies of quality, whom they accompanied in the street. But how many more were reduced to extreme poverty? One such was the *hidalgo* described by the author of *Lazarillo de Tormes*, who lived on alms and the scroungings of his 'lackey', and ate ravenously the crusts of bread which the latter brought back to his lodgings, all of which did little to moderate his anxiety for his personal honour. A fictional portrait, you say: and it is true that it is the original of the image of the *hidalgo* which reappeared half a century later in the picaresque novel.[20] But we cannot doubt that it was a reflection of current reality when the Bishop of León made it known to Philip III that there had arrived in his diocese,

'. . . a great number of impoverished men of good birth and of *pure and noble blood*. They come from the mountains of the Asturias and Galicia and have been quartered in ecclesiastical establishments, both secular and regular. In the greatest misery, they go about aimlessly, shoeless, half-naked, and sleeping on street corners in the bitterest cold, at great peril to their health and lives.'[21]

Why then did they leave their native countryside? Without a doubt to go and hide their poverty in the anonymity of the towns, far from the eyes of those who knew them – and sometimes colouring their departure with a nobler motive. The whole philosophy of the *hidalguía* is contained in the dialogue between the *hidalgo* and his lackey, Lazarillo, who asked the reason for his coming to Toledo:

'He said that he came from Old Castille and that he had left his country in order not to have to lift his cap to a certain gentleman, his neighbour.

' "It seems to me, sir, that I would not have worried about that, especially with a grander and richer man than me."

'He replied: "You are a child and you understand nothing about the demands of honour, which comprises the whole capital of an upright man. Now let me tell you that I am, as you see, a *hidalgo*; nevertheless, if I met the Count in the street and he did not raise his hat (by that I mean completely raise it) you can be sure that I, to avoid raising mine, would go into some house and pretend that I had some business there. *For a nobleman owes nothing to others, except God and the King. It is unseemly for a decent man to neglect his self-esteem for a single minute*." '

It is, then, this exaggeration of the sense of honour which here personified the *hidalgo*; an honour which was lacking as much in moral content as in material purpose. For he did not even boast of the past and future exploits with his sword 'which he would not exchange for all the gold in the world'. It was merely the visible symbol of the rank which he considered to be his by right.

Hidalguism might have been merely the product of a limited social group, fit only to provide ample material for satirical literature; in fact, the concept of honour which it implied tended to become a malady of the whole social system. It would doubtless be absurd to give too much credence to foreign travellers and to certain Spanish moralists who denounced it as an essential cause of the economic decadence of the Spain of the seventeenth century. But there can be no doubt that the 'passion for ennoblement' which affected Spain contributed to her decline by diverting men from certain forms of productive activity. The contempt for manual labour was shared even by the artisans who lived by it. Barthélemy Joly remarks about the artisans of Valladolid:

'As for the small handicraftsmen, unable to do anything else but work for their living, they do it as a matter of form. Most of the time they sit disdainfully outside their shops and, for two or three hours in the afternoon, they parade up and down wearing swords. If they manage to amass two or three hundred reals, they suddenly become noblemen. There is no reason for them to do anything until, having spent it all, they have to go back to work to earn some more money to enable them to show themselves off again.'[22]

Malicious evidence, certainly; but the state of mind it denounces is incontestable and was to be found in every class of society.

It is instructive to see the Order of Santiago returning, in the middle of the seventeenth century, to the tolerant attitude which formerly permitted its knights to take part in high commerce and in the dealings of the Bank of Seville, and even interpreting in the most restrictive sense the ban on trading by specifying that the term 'merchant' applies to 'whoever has a shop no matter what goods are sold, who personally resides there or is represented by employees or accountants as in a public bank, and engages in commercial transactions either on his own account or through his agents'. [23] The wealthy merchant also endeavoured to escape from his present social standing and to pass into the noble class or to identify himself with it by his style of living. There were various courses open to him. Lack of funds constrained the monarch to sell *executorias de hidalgo* which assured to the holder the same privileges as those of the *hidalgo* by birth: the purchase of *juros* (government bonds) issued by the royal treasury, and the establishment of *censos* (ground rents on peasant land-holdings), served the same end. These transformed the former merchants and their descendants into landlords, who then ceased to take a part in the active economy of the country. In default of a noble title, each tried to preface his name in official documents by the title *Don*, to which even the *hidalgos* had no legal right. But the practice became more widespread and tended to be used by all those who had reached a certain level in the social scale.

But voices were raised against the ills of that sort of dishonour which is attached to manual labour and the dangers which follow obsession with the desire for nobility. Saavedra Fajardo writes:

'In the country, agriculture is neglected, and the same applies to the exercise of mechanical skills, to business, and to commerce. *The spirit of the nation is so haughty and vainglorious that even the common folk are not satisfied with their natural state. They long for ennoblement and scorn every occupation which seems to be contrary to their aspiration.*'[24]

Others reacted more strongly against this formalist cult of honour and *hidalguism* and questioned its very principles. Only astonishment is expressed by Lazarillo at the attitude of his master, whom he prevents from dying of hunger, but who nevertheless loses none of his pride:

'Who would believe that this gentleman has sustained himself throughout yesterday on a scrap of bread which his servant, Lazarillo, had hidden close to his breast for a whole day and night, where it could not have greatly improved its cleanliness. Dear Lord, how weary you must be of this world if, because of this cursed so-called point of honour, you will suffer what it will not suffer for you!'

But criticism became sharper in denouncing the absurdity of a notion of honour, which, founded on the opinions of others, poisons everyone's life. Thus, says Guzman de Alfarache: 'What a heavy burden, this weight of honour . . . which is in no way enforced on the unfortunates who claim it! How difficult to acquire and keep it! How easy to lose it simply because of public opinion!' And Guzman contrasts this false honour with true honour, the 'offspring of courage', which, inbred in each individual, cannot be taken from him as long as he remains courageous.

'This is the honour which is worth seeking and keeping . . . for what is ordinarily called honour is nothing more than false pride and vainglory. Men exhaust and kill themselves because of their canine hunger for it, only then to lose it as well as their soul – and this is indeed a reason for regrets and tears.'[25]

From this reaction, pressed to extremes, arose what has been rightly called anti-honour, meaning the deliberate wish to trample on, to deprecate, and to parody all the values which people held so dearly: an attitude which furnished one of the major themes of the picaresque novel. From the very first, it meant the rejection of the weight of public opinion with a lack of deference amounting to cynicism: 'In all my misfortunes,' Guzman says, 'I had kept my assets but lost all sense of shame–a sentiment which is without profit for the poor because the less he has, the less a man suffers for his own faults.' Anti-honour, by contrast, exalts the basest actions and equates their glory. 'God be praised,' Guzman exclaims, as he reverts to robbery, a profession which he had abandoned for some time, 'that once I learn a thing, I never forget it. I was as proud of my skill as is a good soldier of his arms and a cavalier of his mount and harness.'

Anti-honour finally culminated in the complaisance with which it displayed its own despicable nature. An example is given by Estebanillo Gonzalez in an account of his 'high exploits', especially in military campaigns, in which he amuses himself by underlining his cowardice and making fun of the courage of his comrades-in-arms, and of all those high standards which had assured to Spain, even in the eyes of her foes, an incomparable prestige.[26]

This excessive reaction is explainable by its own counterpart. The difference is not merely one between two distinct attitudes towards life. It arose from two elements which were at the same time opposed to each other but intimately bound up together in the Spanish soul – idealism and materialism. This combination produced a paradox often manifest both in social and individual life and is perfectly illustrated by those inseparable characters, Don Quixote and Sancho Panza, in the greatest literary creation of the Golden Age.

CHAPTER THREE

MADRID. THE COURT AND THE TOWN

I. Madrid, the royal town – The court: The palace and the princely life. Etiquette. The buffoons. Gallantries in the palace – Royal fêtes. The 'Buen Retiro'. Splendour and poverty at court – The life of the grandees. Luxury and sumptuary laws. Fashion. Money and love. Moral decline of the nobility.

II. The town. Transformations and embellishments. Dirtiness of the streets. The water and air of Madrid. Provisioning and economic activity – The population of Madrid: Cosmopolitanism and insecurity. Social life: The 'mentideros' and public opinion. Fashionable life and the Prado. The life of the people. The Manzanares and the festival of the 'Sotillo'.

I

Solo Madrid es Corte (There is no capital but Madrid[1]). This saying, popularized at the beginning of the seventeenth century, reflected the proud satisfaction felt by the people of Madrid in living in the very heart of the Spanish monarchy; but it also expressed the fundamental peculiarity of their town – that it was a 'court' in the double sense of the Spanish word, a court which is both a princely and a political capital.

The ancient Castillian cities – Toledo 'the Imperial', Valladolid, and occasionally Segovia – in the previous epoch, enjoyed a very active civic life, independent of the royal presence. The Madrid of the seventeenth century, on the other hand, owed its essential traits and its specific character to a decision of Philip II which transferred the seat of his government to this city. Should one see in this decision the wish to make it the 'definitive' capital of all Spain? A more likely explanation is that he wanted to supervise the construction of the palace-monastery of Escurial, where he was to instal himself in 1571; moreover, when his son and successor, Philip III, resolved in 1601 to transfer both his court and his government to Valladolid, the people of Madrid, so they say, went

46

into mourning as they watched the long train of horses, wagons, and coaches making their way towards the north. The municipality addressed an appeal to the sovereign which attested to the symbiosis which had grown up between the court and the town.

'Deprived of the court, the town has suffered the greatest calamity that any locality has ever experienced, because everyone of every category found some way of making a living. Some were engaged in the important commerce arising from the sale of lingerie, linen, and silken materials, all woven locally. Others were employed at court and in the chancellery, also in trade and the transport of goods. . . . *To speak of Madrid is to speak of what she used to be, of what remains of her ancient glory but with nothing now to sustain her.*'[2]

Five years later the return of the sovereign, this time final, made Madrid the capital city: an artificial capital because its growth had not been properly grafted on to the state of which it was now the head, and because it owed its status to the arbitrary wishes of two monarchs. But, by this very fact, the whole being of the town was inextricably bound up with the presence of the king and his entourage. Far from there being any cleavage – such as that between Versailles and Paris in th edays of Louis XIV – court and town intermingled, living one with the other, and one for the other.

The sudden ascent of Madrid explains the difference of opinion between Spaniards and foreigners. The former were amazed at the extraordinary 'rise' of their city, the intensity of its social life, and the splendour conferred on it by the presence of the court. The 'Spanish Babylon', the 'World Metropolis', the 'Marvel of all Nations' – no epithet seemed excessive to describe it. On the other hand, the foreigner wondered at the drabness of its urban façade, the filth of its streets, and, through a natural reaction to the excesses of Spanish hyperbole, tended even more to emphasize the discomforts of the town and the hard, prosaic facts which were covered over by the brilliant veneer of city life.

Built on the edge of the plateau which dominates the Manzanares, the Royal Palace – the Alcazar – was an ancient fortress erected in the fourteenth century, restored and converted as a residence for Philip II but owing its main embellishments to his second successor, Philip IV. The palace was, however, far from being 'the most wonderful royal edifice in the world', which was a contemporary claim. It had a rectangular shape, flanked by four dissimilar towers facing the town. It was built of stone, and its marble balconies and ornaments lent it a certain majesty. But in other parts, brick, and, even, mud walls adjoined the stone in its construction.

One went through the main gate into courtyards, the larger ones being surrounded by porticos ornamented with busts. The chambers and offices of different councils opened on to these courtyards – the Council of Castille, the Council of the Indies, and the Council of Finance – in which decisions affecting the destiny of Spain and the whole world were made. A big crowd milled about all day, giving the royal courtyard the look of a public place, which was accentuated by its booths and hawkers. There one saw the great lords followed by their pages, side by side with the *lestrados* who were employed in various ministries, captains who had come to ask for a new command or a pension, and litigants (often accompanied by an *escribano* or notary), who awaited the appearance of some serious-looking council magistrate to beg a favour of him or quite simply a ruling on a case which had been pending for months or even years. The sluggishness of Spanish administration was proverbial. Someone once said: 'It is a shame that Death does not recruit his administrative officials from the Spanish ministries. They could provide humanity with a certificate of eternal life.'

The first and second floors of the Alcazar were occupied by the royal apartments and their suites, which comprised a multitude of rooms. Some were huge and well lit, others small and dark; they were all connected by narrow corridors and staircases. The public salons were covered with magnificent Flemish tapestries and graced with admirable paintings – Rubens, Titian, Veronese – and their numbers notably increased in the reign of Philip IV. In 1643, despite the penury of his treasury, the King sent his official painter, Diego Velazquez, on a mission to Italy, with the object of still further enriching his collection of paintings.

'But,' says Lope de Vega,'I would be sorry for the people depicted in the palace tapestries if they showed any trace of real feeling.' Within their imposing framework there was in effect a realization that all actions and movements are immutable and semi-mechanized, that life is subject to the most rigid etiquette. Counsellor Bertaut wrote: 'There is no prince who lives like the King of Spain.

3. The Infante Don Carlos

4. Queen Margaret of Austria, wife of Philip III

His actions and preoccupations never vary. They march forward with such a sure step, day by day, that he knows exactly where he is going every day of his life.' But all the same, this etiquette was not fashioned for the Spanish court. It is the same as that which governed the courts of the Grand Dukes of Burgundy in the fifteenth century, Philip the Good and Charles the Bold, and which their descendant, Charles V, introduced to the country over which he was called upon to reign. Perhaps the Emperor 'the greatest master of ceremonies of all times', as someone called him, had even increased this rigidity. In any case, it is a fact that every foreigner was struck by it. If one believes Madame d'Aulnoy, this sacrosanct respect for etiquette caused the death of Philip III. The king, at his desk on a winter's day, was incommoded by the fumes of a brazier which had been placed near him. But none of the gentlemen present dared remove it, for fear of encroaching on the functions of the Duke of Uceda, the 'Court Cellarer', who was then absent from the palace. During the following night the sovereign was seized with a violent fever, complicated by erysipelas, which carried him off a few days later.[3]

If Philip III's death was due to erysipelas it is probable that the story of the brazier is a fabrication. Nevertheless, it is not improbable that Madame d'Aulnoy clung to these details as a Spaniard who wished to underline the inflexible tyranny of etiquette and made a monarch a semi-sacred personage who was – or must at least seem to be – impervious to the uncertainties of the world. But it was Philip IV, not his father, who undoubtedly gave a regal stamp to this hieratic character, as if he wished by his bearing in public to compensate for the irregularities of his private life.

'He is invested,' Bertaut says, 'with such gravity that he behaves as he walks about just like an animated statue. Those who have approached him state that when they spoke to him there was never a change in his face or his posture; that he received them, listened and replied with the same expression. Nothing in the whole of his body moved, except his lips and his tongue.'

Even more than the sovereigns, brought up from infancy in the formal atmosphere of the court, queens of foreign birth felt themselves severely constrained by the iron collar of an etiquette which was strictly enforced by the *camarera mayor*, who never left their side. We know how Victor Hugo in *Ruy Blas* made use of the rest

D

of Madame d'Aulnoy's anecdotes. The Queen's 'household', like
that of the King, included a chief major-domo and a number of
ménins (young pages from the noblest families of the realm). She
was constantly surrounded by ladies-in-waiting and not even the
shadow of doubt could be cast on her. No man, other than the
King, could spend a night in the palace.

The King and Queen dined alone except on the rare occasions
when there was a celebration for the marriage of some lady of
the court, when she was invited to the royal board. Once a week,
the public – in effect, courtiers and people of distinction who had
earned this privilege – was invited to attend a royal repast. The
arrangements were like those of the French court – first at the
Louvre and then at Versailles – partly on account of the influence
of the two queens who came from Madrid: Anne of Austria and
Maria Theresa. The *aposentador* (steward) kneels and waits for
his master to come to the table. After the most senior prelate then
available at the court has said grace, the King seats himself. The
major-domo of the week stands by his side, holding a staff which
indicates his status. The carver, the butler, and the cellarman begin
to serve. They too are subject to strict protocol: each time the King
wants to drink, the cellarman fetches a goblet from a nearby
dresser, uncovers it, and presents it to the physician who is attending the royal meal; he then covers the glass and, accompanied by
two mace-bearers and a court footman, kneels and presents it to
the monarch; when he has taken his drink, the cup is carried back
to the dresser, and the cellarman brings a napkin with which the
king wipes his lips. A like ceremony accompanies the presentation
of each dish. The meal over, and after a chaplain has given thanks
to God, the carver approaches to remove any crumbs which may
have fallen on the King's clothes.

The Queen's repast had the same solemnity. Brunel, who had
the honour to be present, sitting in a corner, at a dinner of Marie-
Anne of Austria, the second wife of Philip IV, writes:

'Opposite [the queen], there is a lady who places each dish before
her and who is, as it were, her carver. On either side there are
others: on her right, there is one who samples the drink and, on
the left, another who holds a saucer and a napkin. She drinks little
but eats well enough. A lot of dishes are served to her but none of
them is very good, so far as one can judge. She has a jester who
50

talks all the while and tries to make her laugh and to divert her with his patter.'

However, in this life of public performance, there were moments exempted from the rituals of the court, when the sovereigns became, so to speak, human beings. For example, a Jesuit priest describes to one of his colleagues the visit made by Philip IV and Isabella of Bourbon to their monastery, in company with the little Infanta who was to become Maria Theresa of France:

'She arrived with her brother, without a wrap, wearing a tight-fitting jacket of red wool. She was so tiny, golden-haired, and fair of face, that she resembled the Infant Jesus. Her parents, the king and queen, said to her "Go on, little one". But she stood still, quite breathless at the sight of all the lights and the ornaments. Her mother almost swooned with delight as she watched her. One of the friars then asked of Philip IV permission to offer a small souvenir to the Infanta. "Yes," said the King, "give her what you will." Then the little girl stepped forward to receive – as everyone knew – a valuable reliquary, which was much admired. More vivacious and gay than when she first appeared, the girl was radiant as she contemplated the gift. Her mother said: "Say something to the friar". The girl said: "God be with you". A thousand blessings rained on her, *and her father covered his face to hide a smile.*'[4]

The fear of the monarch that he might lose the immutable gravity which stemmed from majesty even when he was with his children, was significant. This fear was even more surprising when one considers certain aspects of court life which seemed to be a contradiction in terms. The most striking example is the position held by the buffoons, the court jesters, in the royal *entourage*. Their importance is evidenced not only by the wages paid to them but by the fact that Philip IV commissioned his own artist, Velazquez, to immortalize them as if they were members of his own family. They lived on familiar terms with princes; and in the life of a court in which everyone's function was rigorously fixed one could see them everywhere – in the antechambers, in the royal apartments, in the reception-rooms. These 'pleasure-makers' (they were thus described in the palace account) had but one role – to make people laugh: by their monstrous physical deformities (most of them being dwarfs or hydrocephalics) which were emphasized by

their livery; by the contrast between the human misery which they
represented and the names with which they were dubbed (one of
the buffoons of Philip IV had the name of the victor of Lepanto,
Don Juan of Austria); and by their incessant patter, spiced with
pleasantries – in good or bad taste – which sometimes lifted the
grave and rigid masks protecting the king and his family. Antoine
de Brunel reports that Queen Marie-Anne, a young lady who had
recently come from Germany, was unable to restrain her mirth at
the antics and the ridiculous remarks of the buffoons.

'It was made known to her that this was not appropriate to a
Spanish queen and that her behaviour should be more serious. She
replied, quite surprised, . . . that she could not behave otherwise
unless one removed the jester, and it was not her fault if she were
not allowed to laugh at him.'[5]

But there was a deeper meaning in the role played by the
jesters. The physical deformities of some of them disguised a very
sharp wit, and, as the buffoonery gave them the right to say what
they pleased, it often happened that they did not mince their
words about stark realities in the sovereign's hearing. By echoing
murmurs which no one else would dare to repeat in a serious
manner the buffoons expressed public opinion to the monarch.

To leave this subject, there was another practice which seemed
to contradict the sacrosanct respect due to the Queen of Spain:
the *galanteo en palacio*, the art of publicly courting the ladies of
the palace. It was already an established custom at the austere
court of Philip II, as a member of the staff of the Venetian Ambassador indicates:

'Close to the Queen are ladies of the highest birth. Three of them
serve her with the greatest of respect at table: others, leaning
against the walls of the Queen's chambers, were conversing with
their admirers. *These gallants have the privilege of wearing their
hats in the presence of the sovereigns*, as they talk in lowered voices
to the young ladies to whom they are "attendant knights". These
men are princes or lords, distinguished because of their wealth or
birth. They court the ladies to pass the time and also to find a
wife. If they had any other intentions they would be disdained
because the rules of Her Majesty's palace are very strict in this
matter. . . .'

But the Venetian lessens the implication of this last remark by adding that several gallants can be in attendance on the same lady, 'even though she must listen *only to one at a time. . . .*'[6]

Thirty years later, Barthélemy Joly also records that public dinners given by the queen were frequented by gentlemen dancing attendance on their ladies. 'They have the right to remain covered during dinner to entertain each his own, without anyone overhearing, provided the Queen keeps an eye on them.' How had they earned this extraordinary privilege of remaining covered both in the presence of their lady and of the Queen? Bertaut explains it as a supreme refinement of courtesy:

'. . . they wish to demonstrate that the ladies to whom they devote themselves have the same right to their attention as the King has consideration for his subjects, in authorizing them to remain covered. And they explain this lack of courtesy by saying that they are so intoxicated, absorbed, and lost in the contemplation of their ladies that they never think to remove their hats any more than they would in the presence of the Queen.'

The opportunities to 'flirt' would have been too rare if they had been limited merely to the days when the Queen gave a public dinner. If deprived of murmured conversations with their Dulcineas, the gallants stationed themselves outside the palace and waited for their ladies to appear at windows or balconies in order to gaze at and converse with them 'by signs invented for this fine intercourse', says Councillor Bertaut with virtuous indignation. But the biggest stroke of luck came when the Queen emerged accompanied by at least some of her ladies-in-waiting:

'Then their paramours, always on the alert, follow on foot close to the doors of the coach to entertain them. When the Queen is delayed, the men carry in front of the coach where the ladies are, some forty or fifty white candles which often provide very beautiful illuminations: for there are often several carriages with several ladies in each. Thus [concludes the Countess d'Aulnoy, no doubt with considerable exaggeration], one often sees a thousand torches, not counting those for the Queen.'

Great events and the festivities which are held in celebration of them frequently relieved the monotonous routine of life at court.

53

They were never more numerous or brilliant than in the last half-century which marked the decline of Spanish might. Everything and anything was a pretext for those celebrations: a royal birth, a military victory, a pontifical election, the reception of an ambassador or a foreign prince. For the most part their character was that of a general rejoicing in which, at least as spectators, the whole population of the town could take part. The merry-making organized for the visit of Charles, Prince of Wales, who had come to ask for the hand of the Infanta, lasted for six months, from March to September 1623. Nearly every day there were processions, bull-fights, fireworks, banquets, and scenes of riotous splendour, with which the Catholic king hoped to dazzle and convert the young Protestant.[7]

Other festivals, arranged in the palace or in the royal residences near Madrid (especially in Aranjuez), still maintained a 'court' character. But it was to create a less formal atmosphere than that of the ancient Alcazar that Philip IV built the Buen Retiro, on the furthest side of Madrid. Planned and erected in a vast park (the present Madrilenian garden of the Retiro is only a small part of it), the new palace comprised sumptuous salons, which were adorned by paintings by Zurbaran and Velazquez. There was also a 'coliseum of the theatre', decorated by the Florentine, Como Lotti, who was also an expert in all the theatrical apparatus essential to the spectacular presentation of themes of mythology and chivalry. Even before work on the Bueno Retiro was finished, its pleasure gardens were enlivened by a permanent festival. An enemy of the King's favourite wrote that: 'The Duke of Olivares spent all his time at work on masquerades, balls, and farces, which were a waste of time, to the neglect of more important matters. This sort of life evoked rather the last days of Nineveh, or the time of Nero and the fall of the Roman Empire.' In 1637, to celebrate the accession as Emperor of Ferdinand III, cousin of the King, a hillock which had been in the park 'since the world was created' was rased to the ground, and in its place an improvised set was erected, requiring 80,000 wooden planks. Around this, galleries and theatre boxes were erected, all richly decorated, from which the courtiers could watch a brilliant mock battle in which the King, the Duke of Olivares, and the principal officers of the court all took part 'dressed in extremely expensive costumes'. The total expenditure rose to 300,000 ducats, and this debauchery of public funds by an impoverished monarchy so scandalized many people that it required an official explanation. 'It is held that a display of this importance had another purpose than as pure play-acting and a pastime. The reason for this ostentation was to make it known to Cardinal Richelieu, our very good friend, that there is still enough treasure to spend to teach his king a lesson.'[8]

The intellectual tastes of Philip IV, this royal patron of the arts, were manifest in the meetings at the 'Palace Academy', where courtiers and men of fine wit gathered, and in the presentation of works by Lope de Vega and Calderon de la Barca, at the 'Coliseum' of Buen Retiro. But here again one finds a strange contrast between the niceties of etiquette and certain diversions which do not seem to be in the best of taste. The Marshal of Gramont, who came to Madrid in 1659 to ask, in the name of Louis XIV, for the hand in marriage of the Infanta, Maria Theresa, attended one of these performances. He describes the Spanish king as, 'completely immobile throughout the whole performance. He never moved his hand, his head, or his feet nor exchanged a single word with his queen, and later retired with the same solemnity, after giving her a ceremonial bow'. Yet this is the same king who, a few years earlier it is true, actually envisaged the production of a play in which the ladies of the court would be impersonated and thus become its involuntary actresses. 'His Majesty,' says the priest, Barrionuevo, 'has ordained that only women shall go to this comedy, and without their farthingales. The king and his queen will watch through the screens of the royal box. Mousetraps have been prepared and more than a hundred well-fed mice will be released on stage, as well as in the pit and the balcony. If this takes place, it will be something well worth seeing and will be a fine distraction for Their Majesties.'[9]

By a contrast – a contrast to be seen throughout Spain at that time – in the middle of all these feasts and sprees, even the court felt the pinch; perhaps it would be more accurate to say that there was a lack of necessities when anyone exceeded the household budget. If they had not been paid, tradesmen sometimes refused to make deliveries. 'There are often days,' Barrionuevo wrote in 1654, 'when the royal households are out of everything, including bread.' The next year, in October 1655, Queen Marie-Anne complained that there were none of the pastries which she liked so much. The chronicler reports that the lady in charge of the matter told her that the pastrycook had cut off supplies because he was already owed too much money. Even the King, accustomed to eat fish on the eve of Marian festivals, 'eats nothing but eggs, then more eggs, because those in charge of the household haven't a penny left'.

Naturally, the wages of the king's servants were paid only in arrear, if they were paid at all. In a note, dated November 1657, filed in the archives of the royal palace, one can read this:

'Diego de Velazquez, *aposentador* (comptroller) of the palace [an office to which the great painter had been appointed in 1652] declares that apart from the ordinary wages of his office, he is owed a whole year's salary. This amounts to 60,000 reals. Furthermore, he is owed 30,000 reals for the year 1653. The sweepers and other servants had stopped work and, what is worse, there is not a real to pay for logs for His Majesty's apartment.'[10]

It is true that this happened during 'the terrible years' of the reign; but a long time before a contemporary chronicler, Novoa, had opposed the waste entailed by the building of Buen Retiro and the restrictions of which the palace servants were victims and which, in their own words, 'they fought till the blood flowed'.[11]

The aristocracy which surrounded the king contributed as much to his ruin as it did to his splendour. Only in rare cases did high noblemen live on their own estates. They left them in the hands of managers, preferring to live at court, on the watch for the grace and favour which could be bestowed on them by the sovereign or by one of his favourites who manipulated the government in his name.

The main preoccupation of every courtier was to establish his status and, if possible, to eclipse all others by his sumptuous way of life – and this despite repeated efforts by the government to restrain the extravagance of the high nobility. In 1611, during the reign of Philip III, a decree put a limit on the use of 'furniture, vases, chafing-dishes, gilded and silver-plated carriages', as well as on the use of silver and gold in arrases, canopies, and tapestries, 'and other objects of pure display which consume even the greatest of fortunes'. The injunction, however, was made in vain, since, at the start of his reign, Philip IV was obliged to replace it by 'articles of reformation' promulgated in 1623. One of these proclaimed an important change in the costumes of people of standing, strictly prohibiting the 'Spanish ruff' (*lechuguilla*), which was made of white linen, fluted and starched, mounted on a frame of pasteboard and wire, on which the human head seemed to be served up on a platter. Not only did the purchase and upkeep of these accessories cost a great deal but, according to a contemporary source: 'Young people who are both intelligent and strong are occupied in ironing and fluting these extravagant baubles and would be far better employed in doing some useful work for the state or in cultivating the land.' This prohibition accompanied the injunction against the use of clothes embroidered with gold and silver thread, and the use of silk in men's apparel: and the king set an example by substituting black for the vivid colours of the former fashion.

But if, by comparison with the style of French gentlemen, Spanish clothes appeared to be more sober, there were many ways to set off their simplicity: the close-fitting doublet was supported by a whalebone frame, or by quilting inside, to give the wearer a more imposing bearing; the open tunic which covered it was embellished with false sleeves which flared out from the shoulders; beneath the breeches, which were fastened at the knee, false calf-muscles (*pantorillas*) added shapeliness to the leg. A man's silhouette – among people of quality – was completed by a felt hat with a large brim and multi-coloured plumes, and, withal, a huge sombre cape – camouflage for amorous adventures, since it permitted the wearer's face to be hidden behind his folded sleeve.

Since the days of Philip II the fashion of short hair had given place to the wearing of it long, or instead, a wig; the use of perfumes and even make-up was commonplace among men of high distinction, 'with the result,' says Lope de Vega, 'that you no longer know whether you are talking to men or to their sisters'.

The importance of the 'household' in the widest sense of the word, comprising not only the humble servants but also the 'clientele' of a *grand seigneur*, lay in the most brilliant possible display of social rank. During a joust held in the Plaza Mayor, at the end of the reign of Philip III, the Duke of Osuna, for instance, who had scandalously profiteered from his vice-royalty of Naples, appeared with a hundred footmen dressed in blue and gold, and fifty captains and other officers wearing luxurious uniforms set with precious stones.

The 'articles' of 1623 also set a limit to the number of 'major-domos, seneschals, pages, lackeys, servants, and outriders that the great lords always had in their train, thus keeping many hands from agriculture and other work'. Spanish grandees had the right to have only eighteen people in their establishment and ministers and king's councillors only eight. As for 'the ladies', a decree of 1634 forbade them, under threat of exile, to have more than four squires or gentlemen to escort them.

One doubts the effect of these measures since there is much evidence of grandees still being accompanied by numerous squires and pages, and Navarette, in his *Preservation of Monarchies* (1626), speaks of 'squadrons' of attendants waiting on certain ladies of quality. When the poorest of *hidalgos* – such as the half-starved knight of *Lazarillo de Tormes* – could not pass muster without a valet and a sword at his side, sole proofs of his standing, how could a *grand seigneur* be content with two or three squires? The king himself gave a poor example by suspending the sumptuary laws on grand occasions or simply to give an extra sparkle to certain court festivities. On the arrival of the Prince of Wales, the Duke of Medina Sidonia, master of immense domains in Andalusia, gave Philip IV a present of two dozen horses, their harness ornamented with pearls and encrusted with gold, and accompanied by two dozen slaves, clothed in livery striped with blue and gold trimmings. Horses and slaves entered the town in a convoy, preceded by the Duke's grand seneschal and trumpeters, all in splendid costume, 'a spectacle which drew such crowds to the squares and streets that it was impossible for anyone to move'.[12] Even during the lean years at the end of the reign the general misery of Spain did not stop these profligate displays of luxury. In 1657, for example, the Marquis of Helicia gave a party for Marie-Anne of Austria. Quite apart from concerts and plays, there was a grand banquet for a thousand people. It cost him 16,000 ducats, but he was recompensed by receiving a 'grandeeship' (a status of special privilege).

It was also expensive for a courtier to 'wait upon his lady', or, to put it in plainer language, to keep a mistress. For, even if the *galanteo en palacio* was supposed to be nothing more than platonic homage, if it was prolonged it often led to adventures of a less spiritual nature. At the beginning of the seventeenth century a Portuguese, Pinheiro, describing the life of the court (then at

Valladolid), emphasizes the immorality of the courtiers, among whom there was no lack of complaisant husbands. This evil worsened in the reign of Philip IV, and an anonymous Memorandum in 1658 denounced 143 married women to the King and accused them of 'loose living'. It is even more surprising that the King, who in this respect set a deplorable example, pretended at times to tighten the moral code of his entourage.

But, like the glittering costumes or the innumerable servants, extra-marital affairs appeared to be the natural complement of the elegant life, and its toleration is affirmed by much evidence. Brunel wrote:

'I find one thing singular and not at all in accord, as I see it, with a Catholic kingdom. This is the tolerance shown to men whose relationships with their mistresses are so obvious that they are an open secret. These mistresses are known as *amancebadas*. Even though married, they are permitted to behave in this manner and often their bastards are raised with their legitimate children. . . .'[13]

Countess d'Aulnoy confirms this; she explains that the apparent meekness of the legitimate spouse in the face of these liaisons is that she regards her rival as a person so inferior that it would be beneath her dignity to be offended.

In effect, if the *galanteo* sometimes led to clandestine adventures, the noble lords as a rule did not recruit their avowed mistresses from the court, but more often chose a famous actress or a high-flying courtesan. But all such liaisons produced rivalries which sometimes ended bloodily. A Jesuit priest writes to a colleague:

'Recently the Count Oropesa and the Duke of Albuquerque were driving along the Prado in a carriage. Another, with women inside, drew up alongside. It was about ten o'clock at night. One of the women called out to the Duke. Both men came out of their carriage and started to talk to the women. They were attacked by three men. One of them hurled himself on Albuquerque and the others on Oropesa. Albuquerque knocked his man down but Oropesa received a sword-thrust which pierced his cheek and shoulder. . . . The next day, the Marquis of Almenara was stabbed during the night in a brawl. He is in danger of losing his arm.'[14]

Passion engendered by the wish to appear passionately in love often led to ruin; for it would involve a loss of face not to satisfy even the most extravagant of a lady's caprices. 'When one speaks of the great expenses incurred by the Spaniards and asks why they bankrupt themselves', Antoine de Brunel remarks,

'. . . all those who have lived or still live in Madrid have no doubt it is the women who wreck most of the homes. There is not a man who does not keep a mistress or does not spend money for the favours of some whore or other. In the whole of Europe, there are none livelier or with more effrontery and expertise in their damnable profession. As soon as a man falls into their clutches he is well and truly plucked. They demand dresses which cost thirty pistoles, and other costly clothes, jewels, carriages, and furniture. It is an ill-spent generosity in this country to waste so much money on the fair sex.'[15]

Certain noblemen, backed by enormous wealth, were able to maintain their high estate at court, despite all the expenditure and 'accessories' entailed. Nevertheless, even the nobility felt the pinch of the general impoverishment of the kingdom. Most courtiers turned to fawning on the king in the hope of being subsidized for their life of luxury. As a result, any courtier's devotion to public duties was soon to disappear. 'To the Marquis of Leganès, *as an encouragement to take up his post* [nothing less than the government of the Milanese], an income has been granted of 6,000 ducats in perpetuity, an indemnity of 12,000 ducats, and a monthly salary of 2,000 ducats: yet, with all that, *he goes off with bad grace.*'[16]

When Philip IV, in 1644, put himself at the head of his troops to reconquer Catalonia, then occupied by the French, he had to cajole and threaten the nobility to accompany him. A broadsheet of the time, *The Spirit of France and the Maxims of Louis XIV*, draws this ironic conclusion: 'The Grandees of Spain are a great help to the king of France, working unwittingly for his cause, because they prey on the substance of their master and remove from their country the possibility of maintaining an army.' Brilliant, useless, immoral, and ruinous, the court, according to a contemporary Spanish historian, had become 'a sad national calamity'.

II

However, Madrid, benefiting from the presence of the court, demonstrated both in its outward appearance and in its social life the tight unity between the monarch and his entourage. In half a century, its population had been at least quintupled and exceeded enormously the figure of 100,000 inhabitants estimated during the reign of Philip IV. This demographic increase and the new buildings required caused the destruction of the ancient wall which enclosed the medieval city: most of the fortified gates which closed the town on the east disappeared: others survived with the remnants of their ramparts more or less in ruins in the new urban conglomeration. This was more widespread because most of the houses were single-story buildings, as a result of the 'maliciousness' of the Madrilenians to avoid a charge on property ordained by Philip II when his court and government offices were installed in the city. In fact, the King had decreed that the owners of large houses, especially those with two stories, should hold their property in part at his disposition, to enable him to lodge not only his administrative personnel but also the members of his court. Even though the owners had been allowed since 1621 to buy out these new charges, Madrid had already seen a proliferation of 'malice houses' (*casas de malicia*), all of them single-story residences; during the seventeenth century such houses represented three-quarters of all new building.

Important edifices often looked mediocre from outside. In common with the humblest homes, they were generally made of cob or brick, and only a façade of stone indicated the house of a rich bourgeois or nobleman. The windows were small, often without glass (in lieu of which a piece of paper or greased parchment allowed only a meagre light to filter through), but nearly always fitted with iron grilles. The purpose of these was less for ornament than for security against amatory enterprise and the prowlers of the night. The prices of houses and leaseholds remained very high and was proof of the 'housing crisis' from which the capital continued to suffer.

The establishment of the court none the less produced certain improvements. The most remarkable was the construction by Philip III of the Plaza Mayor. Its breadth and majestic style were not only a matter of pride for the people of Madrid but also a source of admiration for foreigners. Its rectangular shape was bordered by five-storied houses – the tallest in Madrid – and their architecture was a happy blend of stone and brick. The first story stood on porticos which sheltered shops and the stalls of street vendors. The other stories were flanked by wrought-iron balconies which also served as a grandstand from which the king, his courtiers, and the authorities could watch spectacles and festivities, such as *corridas*, jousting, and *autos-da-fe*, for which the square had been the natural setting since it was built.

Nearby, an edifice which was built between 1629 and 1643 was a surprise to all those who visited the capital, on account of the contrast between its architectural beauty and the purpose it served. Brunel describes it as 'long and wide, a massive structure, the windows of which have iron lattices which seem to be as much for ornament as for security: moreover, they are not cross-barred and are bigger than those of the religious houses; they are gilded and the iron is artfully wrought. Thus it is not strange I mistook it for the palace of some Spanish grandee when I first saw it'. In fact it was sometimes – though only temporarily – the residence of certain grandees, since it was the 'prison of the nobility'.[18]

The Calle Mayor was the main thoroughfare of the town; it stretched from the royal Alcazar to the square which still retained its ancient name, Puerta del Sol. Beyond, it passed between tall houses, like those of the Plaza Mayor, flanking its façade, and continued beyond the Puerta del Sol into the street of Olives (*Olivos*), a street of quite a different character. The area which it next traversed, situated as it was within the confines of the old town, had witnessed the building of many convents and churches, whose enormous gardens still retained the atmosphere of the countryside. Here also were the homes of rich aristocrats, built on the sides of this street right up to the Prado, which had been laid out in the sixteenth century as a public promenade and was adorned with numerous fountains.

The other main streets which fanned out from the Plaza Mayor or the Puerta del Sol to the confines of the city, were mostly wide, comparing favourably with those of other European capitals; but, as in Paris, the streets in the interior of the old city were narrow. Many foreigners make the same observation, but they are completely unanimous about the filth in the streets and squares, the stench of which was sometimes intolerable. Camille Borghèse (the future Pope Paul V), who visited Madrid in 1594, explains the reason for this: 'Among other defects, the houses have no privies. Thus the inhabitants relieve themselves into chamber-pots which are emptied out of the window.'[19] It is true that this practice was regulated; the 'emptying' was permitted only during the night, when the streets were presumed to be deserted; it was also customary, before discharging the contents of pots from windows and balconies, to warn the occasional passer-by with the cry of '*Agua Va!*' ('Beware Water!') To judge from the contemporary satires, however, there were malodorous surprises for the *galantendores*, as they dallied and whispered tender nothings beneath the windows of their lady loves; and one gathers that such 'accidents' must have been fairly frequent. To counter these 'accidents' the sheriffs in charge of the city police imposed further restrictions. It was forbidden to throw 'water, refuse, and other things' from windows and balconies; only the street door could be used for this purpose: and the time for the disposal of rubbish was precisely stipulated – after ten o'clock at night in winter and eleven o'clock in summer. The penalty for infringements of these regulations was four years in exile, for the householder, and six years for servants, the latter, for good measure, to be whipped in public.[20]

But these by-laws in no way modified the actual disposal of domestic and other filth. 'Conservative estimates have been made,' says Brunel, 'about the muck thrown out, and it has been calculated that the streets are perfumed every day with more than 10,000 turds. . . .' In winter, the rain turned them into a nauseating sludge; in summer, the sun dried them to a dust. Hence the saying: 'That which one s. . . . in winter, one drinks in the summer.'[21]

None the less, nature provided her remedy. Camille Borghèse declared, in respect of the stinks of Madrid, that 'in this region fragrant things grow in great abundance, but for which life would be unbearable'. But the best antidote was the very air of Madrid which was, according to Bertaut, sparkling and penetrating. 'It is like quicklime, drying and consuming a corpse in a trice; and one smells no putrescence. In fact I have often seen dead dogs and cats in the street and they gave off no bad smell. This is because the air prevents corruption and, moreover, prevents it by a solution of elements which have an effect both fast and imperceptible.' This was generally admitted by the citizens of Madrid and, indeed, the theory was reaffirmed by physicians in the eighteenth century, that the air of the city was so potent, insidious, and penetrating that it would be noxious unless diluted by the fetid exhalations given off by the streets of Madrid.

No less notable than its peculiar climate was the abundance and the quality of the waters which supply its needs. As long ago as the Arab era a network of underground conduits had been constructed, channelling water from a distance of several leagues around the city. Government and municipal works greatly increased the flow from various sources to the public fountains, the number of which grew, both for the use of the people and for the embellishment of the town. Certain of these were specially renowned for the peculiar qualities of their water. Thus we find the Cardinal-Infanta, the brother of Philip IV, the commander of the Spanish troops in Flanders, having skins of water sent to him from the same spring which fed the Spanish court.

The supply of food and other provisions posed difficult problems. 'It is a marvel,' says the astonished Bertaut, 'how this city subsists. It is as big as the suburb of Saint-Germain in Paris, as big as Bordeaux, but, as it has no river and no barges, all has to be transported overland and not even in wagons as in France. Everything is carried on the backs of mules or donkeys; this is why goods are so dear.' On the roads leading to Madrid, within a distance of forty to fifty leagues, there were long caravans. These converged from the wheat-fields of Salamanca, from the vineyards of Valladolid, and from places much farther afield – even from the Cantabrian coast long lines of beasts with their pack-saddles incessantly wended their way to the capital. Interminable queues piled up; for although Madrid no longer had its fortified walls, the municipality had built brick postern-gates at the ends of the roads leading to the open country and at these gates city tolls and other taxes were levied. The municipality also had the arduous tasks of assuring a regular supply of provisions and of preventing an excessive rise in the price of necessities. The fear of famine was always present, and a specially vigilant eye was kept on the sale of wheat and the baking of bread.

The supply of meat was easier from the table-land and sierras near the capital. There, great flocks of sheep were raised. Mutton was, in fact, the main meat food. According to a contemporary, Mendez Silva, Madrid consumed annually 50,000 sheep, 12,000 oxen, 60,000 goats, 10,000 calves, and 13,000 pigs, figures which, if they are correct, bearing in mind the size of the urban population, were not less than the average of the whole Madrilenian conurbation. The observance of days of fasting presupposes, moreover, a large supply of fish. City toll records in 1584 enumerated the various kinds which were eaten. Among them were trout, carp, and other freshwater fish, as well as black cod, sole, bream, and sardines. All these had to be carried over long distances, and this raised the problem of preserving the fish, even though it was salted or dried. In 1599, the people of a certain part of Madrid complained to the municipal authorities that 'on Friday as the fish-carts go to market, the stench is such that one has to close the windows'.[22] As a consequence fasting was not only the observance of a holy precept but a veritable penance!

However, ice and snow were already being used for the town supplies. But they were used not so much to keep foodstuffs fresh as to cool drinks and sherbets, which were much in vogue. Great quantities of snow were taken during the winter from the Sierra, which is some forty miles away from Madrid, and deposited in 'snowpits', dug specially to preserve the snow for the summer. Finally the snow was dumped in *puestos* (centres of sale), located in various parts of the town. The importance of this trade is shown by the fact that the municipality held a monopoly over it and fixed the wholesale and retail prices.[23] The main anxiety of the authorities was caused not only by the irregularity of supplies but by the fear that certain people might 'corner' the market. This explains a paradoxical fact about a city which, as the capital, was thronged not only by strangers from other parts of Spain but from abroad as well. Those who ran *pensions*, the equivalent of hotels, were forbidden to keep a stock of provisions: travellers who lodged in them having the choice of buying food which could be prepared for them by the landlord or of feeding in *bodegones*, or taverns. There were many of these in Madrid and their tariff was fixed by the municipal authorities.[23]

For those in a hurry or with slender purses, there were *bodegones de puntapie*. These counters, or stalls, were to be found in various squares; at them the traveller could eat, standing up, 'cooked meals' of dubious quality, especially the meat pies (*empanadillas*). If one is to believe Quevedo in his *Bucsón*, the contents of these pies were minced from the bodies of men who had been condemned to death and previously displayed at the gates of the city! Hence Pablos of Segovia, when he ate a meat pie, always crossed himself and said the Ave Maria for the soul and body of the man upon whom he was feeding. But, even if Pablos did get his information from a reliable source – he was the nephew of the public

E

executioner – one must take his jest with a pinch of salt, and look upon it merely as evidence of the suspect and detestable reputation of *empanadillas*.

One of the significant characteristics of Madrid's economy was that it lived almost entirely on imported goods. In 1658, Núñez de Castrol published an extravagant eulogy of the town in his *Sólo Madrid es Corte*, proclaiming Madrid's manifest superiority over other cities, 'because only foreigners work on the goods used by the capital, and this very fact proves that all other nations labour for Madrid, the overlord of all other capitals since all of them work for her and she serves none'. In fact, Madrid had no exports and, apart from its trade in foodstuffs, its actual economy was dependent upon the arts and crafts of embroidery, gilding, tailoring, etc., which transformed imported materials into luxury goods for the benefit of the courtiers, the government officials, and that aristocratic and indolent society drawn to the court by the presence of the King.

In addition to the established tradesmen there were numbers of hawkers who sold trinkets, perfumes, toilet accessories, and trumpery articles smuggled in from abroad. Most of these pedlars were French and there were so many of them that one gets the impression of a veritable invasion. Bertaut, greatly exaggerating, estimates their numbers at 40,000. The government was worried by the drain on the currency which resulted from their activities. A law was passed in 1667, renewing various previous measures and recalling the prohibition against the sale of objects originating from other countries 'with which trade is forbidden'. As a result, pieces of eight, that is coins with a high silver content, virtually vanished from Spain.[24]

The influx of foreign merchants was only one example of Madrid's attraction for the great numbers who were drawn to her from every part of Spain, beguiled by her image. The government, worried by the problems of supplies and security which had arisen from the continuous growth of the city, tried to apply the brake. In particular, a time limit was put on the visits of those who came to prosecute their business before the courts and in government offices, but such limitations remained a dead letter. Worse still, the most undesirable elements did not belong to the group whose genuine affairs kept them for various periods in the city, but consisted of adventurers, *picaros*, and every kind of scoundrel, all parasites of the corporate body.

In his *Guide to Foreigners who visit the Capital*, published in 1620, Liñan y Verdugo, under the pretext of warning 'provincials' against the perils of the big city, took great pleasure in describing certain representative species of the Madrilenian animal and in relating some of their exploits. Soldiers were high on his list: soldiers, either deserters or on leave, plumes in their hats and swords at their sides,

'. . . who swagger along the Calle Mayor as if setting out on a campaign to the roll of drums and, although they have never set foot beyond the Cartagena, where they went to join a company, dub themselves *"Seigneur Soldier"*. They invite themselves to your house without having been asked, borrow money which they have no intention of paying back, and eat at the expense of those whom one day they will kill'

– for certain of them, on occasion, took on the job of killing people.

There were also those who preyed on people who were too trusting: first the bogus gentleman, who pretended to be a relative and installed himself in the house of some worthy bourgeois, remaining there until arrested for receiving stolen goods; then the adventuress, who under the guise of being a lady of distinction, complete with her pages and a mounted attendant, all of whom acted as touts, set out to lure rich foreigners and 'plucked' them to their last feather. There were also unofficial go-betweens, claiming great influence at court and in government offices, who prowled around the palace to ambush the newcomer and make him pay through the nose for their so-called 'services rendered'.

The newly-arrived provincial was the favourite victim of crooks and *picaros*. This is admirably illustrated in the story of the *mequetrefe* which was recounted by Liñan y Verdugo. A peasant from Zamora comes to Madrid carrying a bag which contains evidence for a law suit which he is bringing, and some money – all his worldly wealth. At one of the gates of the town, he is stopped by two men.

'Is this your first visit to Madrid?' the peasant is asked.

'Yes.'

'Have you registered your name with the *Mequetrefe*?'

'No,' says the peasant, never having heard, and for a very good reason, of the existence of this important 'official'.

'So you do not know that His Majesty imposes extremely severe penalties on those who come to Madrid without being registered and that you risk a fine of 12,000 *maravédis*, plus thirty days in prison?'

The wretched peasant, trembling, protests his good faith and begs the two men to get him out of his plight. The two have a discussion. One pretends to be sorry for the peasant; the other appears to be intractable.

'Don't you realize,' he says to his fellow, 'that if this gets out, you and I will be punished? That if you and I, on duty at this gate by order of the Lord Mequetrefe, do not take action against those who enter without registration, we fail in our duty? We then have no right, in all conscience, to draw the salaries paid to us to do our duty.'

After a long debate, the 'inflexible functionary' appears to relent and, after they have inspected the contents of the peasant's bag, which contains only eight ducats, the two jokers show their generosity. They take only six ducats, leaving two for the peasant to pay for a meal and the costs of his legal action.

If this story is not true, it ought to be, because it typifies the Madrilenian confidence trick, in which dishonesty is matched by cunning, which makes one laugh at the victims and, at the same time, pity them.[25]

At the bottom of the social scale was a rabble of beggars and common malefactors who cluttered the streets of the capital. 'The streets of Madrid,' according to Navarette, 'offer a singular spectacle. They are crowded with vagabonds and loafers who while away the time playing cards, waiting for the soup kitchens of the monasteries to open or to get ready to ransack a house.' In vain did the police double its patrols and justice make terrible examples – the quartered carcasses of criminals were exhibited in various parts of the city – but no good came of it. It is hard to believe Pellicier's *Avis* (1637), in which he states that the numbers of robbers and malefactors who prowl around Madrid are so great that no one is safe when night falls, whether he be on foot, mounted, or in a carriage. 'Recently, a Spanish grandee, a nobleman of the highest rank and a marshal of the court of His Majesty, was stripped.' Twenty years later, in January, Barrionuevo writes: 'It is said that since Christmas, more than 150 men and women have met violent deaths and there has not been a single arrest.'[26]

These gloomy reflections were in direct contrast with an exuberant social life and a climate which enabled the population, largely made up of idle people, whether courtiers or beggars, to spend the better part of their day in the open. A street, where men of all sorts and conditions rubbed shoulders, offered a diversion to the less fortunate, giving them a glimpse of the lives of others and bringing them closer to those who were separated from them because of their wealth and rank.

Among the rendezvous of the idlers and gapers were the *mentideros* – literally, 'lie parlours' – which are frequently referred to in chronicles of those times. In these places people met to hear the latest gossip of court and city, to discuss the newest literary works or the merits of this or that actor or actress, and, of course, to criticize the government. But there is a more specialized name for certain of the *mentideros*; they were nicknamed 'flagstones of the palace' and were to be found inside the Alcazar. Here particular attention was paid to political intelligence. Newsmongers lay in wait for royal couriers arriving from different parts of the Spanish empire or from foreign parts, and tried to find out from 'leakages' what was going on in the corridors of the palace and in the offices of the Council.

In Lion Street – where after Cervantes both Lope de Vega and Calderon lived – the *'mentidero* of the actors' drew together not only all kinds of theatrical folk, but also authors and poets. There, men tore the works of their rivals to pieces, and many epigrams were coined, some clever, others just bloody-minded, which were soon being repeated throughout the city. The most celebrated of all these meeting-places was, however, on the steps of the church of San Felipe el Real which was at the top of the Calle Mayor, near the post office (*casa de correos*). The habitués gathered together at the end of the morning to hear the latest news from each other. Amongst them were a number of military types who, from actual or alleged experience, commented with assurance on the news about the state of military and international affairs. Liñan y Verdugo remarks: 'They are informed about the intentions of the Grand Turk, revolutions in the Netherlands, the state of things in Italy, and the latest discoveries made in the Indies.' Velez de Guevara, author of *The Lame Devil*, adds his own touch of irony: 'Here is the *mentidero* of the soldiers. From here comes advance news of events which have not yet happened.' There was also talk

69

about more frivolous topics: the latest amours of the king, the recent gallant escapades of a noble lord with an actress, the evil spells to which the Duke of Olivares had recourse in order to be assured of a descendant . . . and the wild gossip, the suppositions based upon fact, soon spread throughout the city.

In effect, it was in the *mentideros* that public opinion was shaped, criticisms of and attacks upon abuses and upon the Establishment were launched, and often found expression in *pasquines* – lampoons, pamphlets, satirical verses – which flourished in the seventeenth century. One political theorist, Saavedra, advised the king always to bear these in mind. 'Because mischief inspires them, truth inscribes them and the king will find in them those things which his courtiers conceal from him.'[27]

Nobody who visited the palace could avoid the Calle Mayor. It fairly bustled with the traffic of carriages and cavaliers with their escorts of pages and equerries, so that it was sometimes difficult to make one's way along it. All the same it was the custom to 'do the street' (*hacer la rúa*), to saunter along its arcades, stopping every now and then to inspect the luxurious shops which displayed expensive materials, damascened and engraved weapons, embroidery, carpets, and jewellery. The Calle Mayor, like the Plaza Mayor adjoining it, the shops in which held equal reputations, had a redoubtable reputation as a 'pickpocket'. When young bloods saw a lady stopping her chaise or carriage in front of one of the shops 'they take a flight as if from an outbreak of the plague': for gallantry required that a man should not deny a fair lady – even sometimes a complete stranger, if she beckoned – a silver brooch, some gold braid, or an amber or tortoiseshell comb which had taken her fancy.

The Prado, further from the city centre, with its poplars and cool fountains, was frequented by high society on starry summer evenings and often late into the night. The ladies drove in their carriages and the gentlemen were mounted on their fine horses. It was understood that, if the women were not already escorted by a mounted attendant, any gentleman could engage them in conversation through the window of their carriage. Intrigues developed fast and were helped on by the darkness and by the fact that the women were incognito. They hid their faces with mantillas which they might lift deliberately on occasion. But this anonymity could lead to confusion and it tended to favour the enterprise of 'professional ladies', who, more and more, haunted the lanes and groves. A contemporary of Philip III remarked: 'It is useless to search for the home of the chaste Diana in the Prado, nor the temple of the virgin dedicated to Vesta. But one can certainly find Venus and blindfold love.' And, half a century later, Brunel wrote: 'Meanwhile these sinful women have acquired the freedom of the city, for great ladies and gentlewomen hardly get out at all, neither for a walk nor to a fashionable parade.'[28]

On the other side of the town, the banks of the Manzares provided rustic walks for those in search of fresh air. This river, the 'apprentice river' scorned by Quevedo, the river 'whose name is longer than its course' (Brunel), the river which 'they call *rio* ['I laugh'] because it laughs when people try to swim in it and there is no water' (Velez de Guevara), nevertheless did not always merit all the gibes flung at it by Spaniards and foreigners. Sometimes it had water and the women of Madrid bathed in it without a stitch on, a spectacle by which foreigners were shocked – or pretended to be.[29] The river was also a rendezvous for maids who went there to wash the laundry, but according to the *Guide for Foreigners*, worked their tongues harder than their hands, whispering the secrets of their families or recounting the little ructions in the noble or bourgeois homes in which they were employed. The banks of the Manzanares were frequented mainly by the common people who came there to picnic (*merendar*) in the somewhat meagre shade, to sit on the patchy grass, and, from time to time, to enjoy the fairs (*verbenas*) which were organized locally during religious festivals.

One of these festivals gathered together all the people, whatever their class, on the banks of the Manzanares: the festival of Saint-Jacques-le-Mineur or James-the-Green (May 1st), which was also called *El Sotillo*, the name of the place from which the procession started near the Toledo bridge. This great occasion was celebrated by one and all; the women showed off their newest fashions, the dandies their elegance and generosity, and the rest simply came to enjoy the spectacle. Antoine de Brunel, who took part in the *Sotillo* of 1655, left us a description which provides curious pointers to the habits of the Madrilenians:

'On 1st May, we saw the concourse outside the Toledo gate. This is one of the most celebrated gatherings, at which one sees a great

71

number of carriages and coaches, those belonging to grandees and dukes being pulled by four mules. The leading mules have long reins, and each carriage has a postillion. Other carriages have six mules, and one can but imagine the grandeur and might of *their* owners. The glamour of the festival is provided mainly by the fashions of the ladies, who have spared no effort to appear radiant. They wear their best finery, and they forget neither the rouge nor the make-up, which they put on to the best effect. They behave in differing ways in the carriages of their lovers. Some are only half visible and partly veiled, or have their curtains drawn; others have their curtains open to show off their dresses and beauty. Those who have suitors who cannot, or will not, provide carriages stand at the edge of the assembly and line the streets which lead to it.

'One may not speak to a lady if she is accompanied by a man; but to the others one can say anything, whether it be sweet, bold, or frank, without giving offence. Such is the freedom (or licence) of these ladies that they can ask indiscriminately whom they please to buy them limes, biscuits, sweetmeats, and the other dainties which are on sale at the parade. They send the women who sell these things to their swains, and it is considered impolite not to offer to pay. The men find out afterwards that they have to pay a silver crown for a few penniesworth of goodies.

'During this festival, moreover, one sees many beautiful horses showing off their fine saddles and with their forelocks and manes freshly braided with ribbons. Their riders are either the gentlemen who have lent their carriages to their ladies or men who have simply come to enjoy the festivities and have no carriages of their own. After they have done the rounds and passed along the rows of carriages and as night falls, they stop and take some refreshment in the carriages, which for the most part are stocked with provisions.

'One can also see virtuous women who have come with their husbands, as well as ladies of the streets who have come with their lovers; but being under the eyes of their masters both sorts comport themselves with such modesty that they hardly dare look up or wave their hands. The little shopkeeper is to be seen here and there in the neighbouring fields where, on the bank of the river or in some corner where the grass is green, he enjoys a frugal meal with dignity and much pleasure in the company of his wife and family or with some lady friend.'[30]

Although the king normally resided at Aranjuez at this time of the year, he did not hesitate to travel the six leagues which lay between him and Madrid to be present at the festival – or, more exactly, to honour it with his presence for a few moments – but with somewhat unusual ceremony. For, when the king passes by, everybody must, as a sign of respect, draw the curtains of his carriage, a custom which, remarks Brunel, destroys the pleasure which one could derive from his presence, especially if one was allowed to show oneself and the women were permitted to uncover their faces. It was, in fact, a curious custom – but how typical of the peculiar life of Madrid in those days. In a flash, it united the king with the people of the city in a rigorous respect for etiquette.

CHAPTER FOUR

SEVILLE, THE MIRROR OF THE INDIES OF CASTILLE

Seville, port for the Indies. Economic activity. Fleets and galleons. The centres of urban life – The population of Seville. Foreigners and slaves – Ambience of Seville and its contrasts: luxury, ostentation, corruption – Seville and Spanish opinions.

If Madrid is proud of being the 'court', of the fact that the vast domains of the Spanish monarchy are ruled over directly from the royal palace of Alcazar and if she is proud of the benefits conferred on her by the presence of the sovereign and his entourage, the prestige of Seville is, in the eyes of most people, equal to it. Seville also rules a world of its own – that world which Christopher Columbus and the *conquistadores* gave to Spain, with all the treasures which flow to the banks of the Guadalquivir, dazzling the visitor. A Spanish proverb says: 'Who has not seen Seville, has not seen a wonder' (*Quien no ha visto Sevilla no ha visto maravilla*).

Seville reached its full glory at the end of the sixteenth century and in the first twenty years of the following century. This is the period when the exchange between Spain and 'the Castillian Indies' reached its culminating point and the prosperity born of that traffic contrived to give to the Andalusian capital an original look in which new characteristics were blended with traditions inherited from the medieval past.

Reconquered from the Moors in the thirteenth century, the city retains many of the marks of Arab domination: the *Giralda*, the minaret of the ancient Grand Mosque – now the steeple of the cathedral – dominates the whole town and its silhouette is a landmark for the traveller. On the left bank of the Guadalquivir, where a corner of the ramparts joined the river, stood the 'Golden Tower', a little fortress with a crenellated summit where the Mussulman kings used to lock up their treasures. The royal palace of Alcazar, although much of it dates from the fourteenth century, was built in Spanish-Moorish style, with extravagant arches, fine stucco decorations, baths and vast courtyards, and gardens, which are refreshed by springs and fountains. Most of the buildings, low, bleached by the sun, with hardly an opening to the outer world, faced the central *patio*. Between the buildings there were narrow, tortuous streets through which it was often difficult for a vehicle to pass. On the other side of the river is Triana, which has much the same look, and is linked to the other bank by a pontoon bridge.

The powerful imprint of Christianity, however, is clearly manifest in the number and size of Seville's religious buildings; the grandiose cathedral constructed in the fifteenth century; the many monasteries and convents which cover enormous spaces; and finally the innumerable churches, chapels, and oratories dedicated to numerous saints revered by the pious people of Seville and, above all, to the Virgin Mary who is seen in various guises: Notre-Dame de Triana, Notre-Dame dela Macarena, and many others.

Other buildings, dating from the sixteenth century or rebuilt in that epoch, proclaim the peculiar function of Seville in the Spanish realm: that of being the sole depot for all trade and commerce with the West Indies. Such were the Custom-house and the Mint, to which was added at the end of the century the magnificent Merchants' Hall, a noble edifice of stone and brick close to the cathedral. The *Casa de Contratación* (Chamber of Commerce) had its offices in one wing of the Alcazar. Its inspectors had the duty of enforcing the regulations which had assured for Castille, since the time of the Catholic kings, the monopoly of all trade with the Americas. It was their duty not only to organize the merchant fleets which sailed from Spain to the New World, but also to train their captains and navigators. They formed a tribunal to which all legal problems were referred. Finally – and most important – the inspectors had to see to it that the king's rights were meticulously respected, especially the 'quint', that is to say the levy of a fifth of all the silver brought back from America.

The arrival and departure of the transatlantic fleets were the main events, and regulated the rhythm of life in Seville. Since no ship was allowed to make the crossing on her own, each fleet comprised several dozen vessels, some merchantmen, others armed galleons, the task of the latter being to protect the fleet against enemy ships – at that time, mostly English – and also against the corsairs and pirates which lay in wait to seize the cargoes of precious metals on their way to Spain.

Generally speaking these fleets sailed twice a year. In May the fleet from New Spain set out from Vera Cruz, the only port through which Mexico and part of Central America got their supplies. In September it was the turn of the fleet known as the 'Terra Firma', which, after calling at Cartagena off the Indies (now Colombia), ended its journey at Porto Bello, on the isthmus of Panama, where it unloaded the cargo. From there the merchandise was transported by cart or on mule-back to Panama on the south side of the isthmus. There is was loaded on to ships which traded in the South Seas (that is, the Pacific Ocean) and then returned to Callao, the port of Lima. In fact, the use of the routes through the Straits of Magellan and round Cape Horn were forbidden to all shipping and the same monopoly system, which was so beneficial to Seville, was applied to Spanish America, where only certain ports (Vera Cruz, Cartagena, and Porto Bello on the Atlantic, Callao and Acapulco – which was the key to the Philippines – on the Pacific) were authorized to trade, through the compulsory agency of the 'fleets', with Spain.

As the Spanish Indies had few industries (apart from the exploitation of minerals and certain raw materials) they were dependent on imports from the metropolis for a large range of products. But Spain could furnish only a small part of what was needed for the Americas. Andalusia sent them wine and oil and various products of local manufacture, such as soap, *azulejos* (coloured ceramic tiles, the speciality of Triana), and certain silken materials. Castille exported mainly cloth, and, from the mines at Almaden in the Sierra Morena, large quantities of mercury were transported to the banks of the Guadalquivir to be used in the Mexican mines for the extraction of silver by amalgam. The mounting demand from America in the second half of the sixteenth century, however, coincided with a decline in the production of Spanish textiles. Moreover, Spain produced a sadly insufficient quantity of a whole range of exports: tools, ironware, haberdashery, and luxury goods, all of which were eagerly sought after in the countries of the New World.

As a result, recourse had to be made to foreign markets; but, since Spain had reserved for herself the exclusive rights of commerce with her colonies, it was in Seville that one saw all the cargoes piled up, awaiting transport to the West Indies. From Rouen and St Malo ships arrived laden with cloth from Normandy and linens from Angers and Laval; Italy sent fine brocades and other luxury goods; other ships came from Hamburg and Lubeck, carrying timber and hempen cordage, which were indispensable to the building of ships, and also the salted cod and herring needed for their victualling. Statistics for the year 1597 give some idea of this intense maritime activity: between October 7th and November 19th, ninety-seven ships arrived in the Guadalquivir, half of them from Hamburg and the Hanseatic towns of the Baltic: the rest hailed from Scotland, from Scandinavia, and from Holland.[1]

Moreover, river traffic was not limited to the arrival and departure of the transatlantic fleets. Hundreds of barges sailed up and down the twenty leagues of river which separate Seville from the open sea and, from the heights of the Golden Tower and its ramparts, one could survey a permanent forest of masts and rigging opposite the city.

The Andalusian capital had insufficient warehouses for all the goods that come by land and sea. The cargoes piled up on the banks of the river, especially on the *Arénal* (the Strand), which stretched from the bastion enclosing the city to the left bank of the Guadalquivir and had the look of a multi-coloured and permanent market-place. Its air of vivid life struck all who visited Seville:

> These river banks sustain
> Italy, France, and all the realm of Spain,
> For they are the market-place
> For commerce and for gain.[2]

wrote Lope de Vega in his comedy, *The Arénal of Seville*, and there are numerous literary references to this 'supermarket of the world'.

The bustle on the river and its banks was even greater before the West Indian fleets started on their voyage, which normally took from three to six months. Shoals of small sailing-boats – tartans, shallops, and feluccas – went about their business with the big ships, loading them with goods for the markets of America and with victuals needed for a passage which was always of uncertain duration: dried meat, salt fish, biscuit, oil, wine, and not forgetting munitions for the cannons of the galleons.

Gradually, as the holds filled up, the captains, aided by the merchants or their agents, prepared the bills of lading (*registro*), which then had to be inspected by the *Casa de Contratación*. When the loading was finished officials of the *Contratación* went aboard to check the bills of lading against the cargo, and commissioners from the Inquisition arrived to see that there were no books banned by the Holy Office to be smuggled abroad.

Finally the date of departure arrived. Everyone in Seville massed on the banks of the river to see the sails fill and gently set the ships in motion, carrying with their cargoes hopes of big profits from a share of their sale.[3]

Now they had to wait for the fleet's return – a long wait since normally a year elapsed before they arrived back off the shores of Spain: a period of great anxiety, for entire fortunes had been put aboard. The loss of a single ship could mean the ruin not only of the owner of the cargo but also of his creditors and underwriters. What would happen if some of the fleet became victims of storms or pirates? The whole of Seville would suffer from such a catastrophic blow.

As the date for the return of the fleet approaches, therefore, feeling in the city reaches fever pitch. It reaches its climax when a fast sloop, sent ahead of the fleet, enters the Guadalquivir with news of its imminent arrival. But days, sometimes weeks, may pass between the arrival of this news and the appearance of the fleet off the coast. What anxiety there is! In the churches, processions pray for the ships to be saved from all perils and to make a safe landfall. Finally, the fleet is signalled. But there is still danger; English privateers may be lurking off-shore. Had they not, in 1596, sacked the port of Cadiz? Even when all seems at last safe, all their hopes can be dashed and the ships sunk. For there is, at the mouth of the river, a bar which is very difficult to cross. Even the skill of the 'shoal pilots', who are accustomed to negotiating it, does not always prevent shipwrecks, and a magistrate of Jerez remarks 'Happy is the year when three or four ships are not lost.'[4]

One can well understand the explosion of joy which would be set off by the arrival of the fleet under the walls of Seville. Thanksgiving and the sound of people rejoicing are punctuated by salvoes fired from the treasure-ships. Then, when the officers of the *Contratación* have completed their formal inspection of the cargoes, the ships start to unload. A horde of stevedores, and some layabouts who are attracted by the hope not only of earning a few reals but also of pinching a little booty, go on board to bring off the merchandise – leather and skins, cochineal, sugar, cocoa – from the ships to the quayside and the customs. What everyone wants to know, however, especially the King's officers, is how much gold and silver has been brought back by the galleons; for these precious metals are not consigned to the merchant-ships but to the ships of war. 'It is an admirable sight and one which you would not see at any other port,' says a contemporary writer, 'to watch carts drawn by four oxen transporting the immense quantities of gold and silver bullion from the Guadalquivir to the royal chamber of the *Contratación* for the Indies.'[5]

At times it seemed as though all the fabulous treasures of Peru had showered on the town:

'On 22nd March, 1595, the ships from the Indies berthed at the quays on the banks of the river of Seville. They began to discharge and deposit with the *Casa de Contratación* 332 cartloads of silver, gold, and pearls of great value; on 8th April, 103 cartloads of silver and gold were unloaded from a capital ship; and on 23rd May, 583 loads of silver, gold, and pearls were brought overland from Portugal from the flagship which had put into Lisbon because of a storm. This was a sight to see. For six days loads arriving from the flagship never ceased to file through the gates of Triana and that year one beheld the greatest treasure within living memory at the *Contratación* – the accumulated cargoes of three fleets. Since there was no room in the interior of the building, quantities of bar gold and chests full of precious metal had to remain outside in the courtyard. . . .'[6]

This was an exceptional case, but even during its usual business, the customs provided a spectacle hardly less astonishing of 'inexhaustible and prodigious abundance which arrives without ceasing from the vastness of America – mountains of silver, bars of gold, cochineal, timber, and other goods in immense quantity, for which this city and this building become the repository'.[7] Of course these immense treasures did not all remain in Seville. The same ships that brought cargoes for the Indies took on again the greater part of the goods which had been unloaded. Among those who were always impatient for the return of the Spanish fleets, were foreign merchants or those of foreign extraction. The Genoese who, at the end of the Middle Ages, played an important part in the maritime economy of Seville, retained a privileged status at the beginning of the seventeenth century; moreover, many of them were united by marriage to Spanish families. This assured naturalization and allowed them to be active in the West Indian trade. Foreigners, however, even those long established in Spain, were excluded from the *carrera*, that is from direct commerce with the

New World; but there were many ways around this prohibition which were more or less tolerated by the Spanish authorities.

There were, for example, big foreign commercial concerns which carried on their business in Seville through the intermediary of 'factors' or agents, who were Spanish and were able to buy and sell goods from America and elsewhere. Other foreign merchants, established in Seville itself, did business by using Spaniards who were mere figureheads, to procure all the official documents (bills of lading, invoices, etc.) which were essential for the loading of their goods on the fleets; and there were certain Frenchmen who passed themselves off as Walloons or Francs Comtois – who were subjects of the king of Spain – and were thus regarded as Spanish citizens.

But for all these merchants, no matter what their nationality, there remained a grave problem – that of getting hold of the silver, which represented the profits from the sale of their goods in the Spanish Indies, and was brought back in the galleons. They could not dispose of it as they pleased. Bars and ingots of metal had to be taken to the Royal Mint where they were made into coins, and a fixed rate for the minting was charged, thus reducing the actual profits of the merchant. But there was worse to come: the constant financial difficulties of the sovereign forced him quite purely and simply to lay violent hands on the fortunes of private individuals, reimbursing them either with copper or nickel coinage at a very poor rate of exchange or with government bonds (*juros*), the more of which were issued, the quicker they were devalued. This problem was aggravated still more by the prohibition against the export by foreign traders of silver coinage from the realm.

A very keen eye was even kept at the gates of Seville to prevent coins, struck by the Mint, from being smuggled out by ships bound for other European ports. Hence, by all sorts of stratagems, foreign businessmen and their representatives in Seville contrived to elude the complex rules of currency control. In collusion with Spanish skippers they managed to unship secretly all or part of their money and to transfer it to other ships. Brunel says,

'There are many who do not declare the amount of their gold and silver when it is shipped in the Indies, where the formalities are the same as they are in Seville, and thus deprive the king of his dues. These people prefer to come to terms with the ships' captains,

5. Auto da Fe in the Plaza Mayor de Madrid

6. Punishment of those condemned in the Inquisition

even though it may cost them a pretty penny, than to run the risk of getting nothing but fine words in return. Even before the Spanish fleet arrived off Cadiz, Dutch or English ships awaited it at this port or at St Lucar. As soon as it is sighted, the ships go alongside the fleet, taking from those captains who are in the plot the consignments which have been entrusted to them, and carrying the merchandise to England or Holland or elsewhere without putting into a Spanish port. The same merchants of Seville send all their ready money on these ships to those countries where they can freely dispose of it without fear of being collared.'[8]

Brunel's observation comes tardily (1655), for already a century ago a Spanish Dominican monk, Father Tomas del Mercado, had deplored the fact that, 'Despite all the laws and their rigorous penalties, foreigners despoil our country of gold and silver and swell their own fortunes thereby, in the process making use of a thousand tricks and dodges.'[9]

However, even if this wealth did not all pass through Seville, its circulation and the prices quoted on the market were enough to sustain a commercial activity and an exuberant social life which distinguished the city of the Guadalquivir from all others in the kingdom. If the Arénal, situated 'without the city walls' on the banks of the river, never ceased to hum with activity, the nerve centre of its affairs was in the heart of the old city. Here, up to the end of the sixteenth century, were grouped all those engaged in high commerce: the merchants, the courtiers, the shipowners, and the bankers. They would assemble on the steps (*gradas*) leading up to the Orangery, the remains of an ancient mosque which flanked the north side of the cathedral. There they would discuss the price of gold and silver and rates of interest; there they would compare the current prices of merchandise in the Americas; there they would weigh the news from the other great centres of European commerce, whose activities affected those of Seville. But the *gradas* 'each of which is worth all the gold in the world', to quote a Sevillian poet,[10] were too narrow for the crowds that thronged them. And the Orangery, which one entered through a door in the *mudéjar* style, surmounted by a bas-relief – what irony! – showing Jesus driving the traders out of the Temple, was invaded by the businessmen. In bad weather, they took refuge in the nave of the cathedral to pursue their transactions and their commercial

F

gossip. It was on account of the protests of the archbishop and his chapter that the Hall of the Merchants (*Lonja de mercaderes*) was built and opened for business in 1598. In order to cause as little upheaval as possible to the habits and customs of the businessmen, the building was sited near the cathedral, on the south side. Care was taken to surround it with *gradas*, which, despite the vast rooms provided in the new building, continued to be the rendezvous for the men of commerce.

In neighbouring streets there were shops bulging with merchandise; its variety evoked the envy of all the countries whose ships sailed up the Guadalquivir. In his *History* of the city published in 1587 the Sevillian Morgado said,

'It is marvellous to see the riches piling up in many of the streets of Seville, where there are shopkeepers from Flanders, Greece, Genoa, France, Italy, and England and from other northern countries, as well as from the Portuguese Indies; and also to see other great treasures of the *Alcaiceria*, consisting of gold, silver, pearls, crystals, precious stones, enamels, coral, brocades, costly materials, and every sort of silk and the finest cloth. This *Alcaiceria* is a quarter full of the shops of silversmiths, jewellers, wood-carvers, and silk and linen merchants. Its immense riches are in the care of a special alcalde and of a number of night-watchmen who lock up the area at night.'[12]

The street of the Francs (or French Street) specialized in selling the latest fashions. 'There one can find crystal, jewellery, cosmetics, perfumes, and everything else that women have invented for their adornment.' These items soon came to be on sale in Castrol Street and Sierpes Street which bordered the neighbourhood of the artisans: the joiners, the carpenters, the farriers, the gunsmiths, the embroiderers, etc.

The prosperity of the city was evident from the increase of its population, which doubled in the second half of the sixteenth century and reached a total of 150,000 inhabitants. It thus became Spain's main urban centre, for Madrid had less than 100,000 people. In its composition, the population of Seville differed notably from that of the capital and other Castillian cities. The minor nobility, the *hidalgos*, as rich in pride as they were poor in income, hardly existed in Andalusia. By contrast, there were very great families, often with palaces in Seville, deriving their income essentially from the immense domains which they possessed in the vast plains of the lower reaches of the Guadalquivir. Some who had lost money owing to the depreciation of ground rents tried to enter the business world and 'through cupidity or for lack of money, have lowered themselves if not to actual commerce, at least to become associated with merchants'.[13] But the characteristic class is that of the middle-class businessman, who was fired by the spirit of adventure, and to whom overseas trade offered ample scope to make a fortune. This class, however, could not avoid entirely the snobbish longing for ennoblement which affected all Spaniards. These merchants, wishing to climb up the social ladder, could buy titles or public appointments such as becoming 'one of the Twenty-four' (a municipal magistrate), which considerably enhanced their social status.

This explains why there was never a social and stable upper middle class such as was to be found in other comparable great centres of commerce and why foreigners have been allowed to play such a considerable role in the economic life of the city. Side by side with Genoese families, whose houses had often been established for a long time, there were Flemings and Portuguese – all subjects of the king of Spain; these last had a bad reputation. The French continued to play only a secondary role in big business until the middle of the seventeenth century; on the other hand, some of them, attracted by the high prices and high wages, had established themselves as shopkeepers and artisans, like Pierre Papin, a vendor of playing cards, whose memory is enshrined in a comedy by Cervantes, *The Happy Ruffian*:

> This Pierre Papin who sells playing cards,
> That hunchback Frenchman:
> The very same who keeps
> A little shop in Sierpes Street.

In this motley population, there is one striking element which astonished foreigners: slavery. Brunel is indignant about it:

'Trade with the Indies has again established slavery in this country. Thus, in Andalusia, one sees almost no servants who are not slaves. Mostly, they are Moors, or complete blackamoors. By the law of Christianity all those who embrace the faith should be enfranchised, but it is not observed in Spain.'

In fact, slavery had never ceased to exist since the Middle Ages, and it had always been agreed that infidels could be put into bondage. But it is also a fact that this servile class was much more numerous in Andalusia than in any other part of Spain, to such a degree, indeed, that Castillians, travelling through Seville, got the impression that the slaves made up half the population. 'The inhabitants of Seville look like pieces on a chessboard,' one of these travellers wrote, 'There are as many blacks as there are whites.'[14]

This is an obvious exaggeration. But it does express the surprise felt at seeing so many coloured people against the background of a city where all the walls were white. Moreover, it was at the beginning of the seventeenth century that slavery reached its peak: the Portuguese, united to Spain, had the monopoly of the negro slave-trade in Guinea, Angola, and Mozambique. For the most part these slaves were destined to labour in Spanish America; but some of them lived in Europe, and Seville – with Lisbon – was the city which received most of them. There was a busy market on the steps leading up to the cathedral, and scarcely a well-to-do family without one or more slaves. For some, the purchase of a bondsman was a sort of investment; one bought a slave to hire him out, or to make him work as a labourer or as an 'independent' artisan (those trades which were organized into guilds refused to employ them). When, in 1637, an urgent need for men to row the galleys led Philip IV to commandeer the slaves of individuals, the municipality of Seville rose up against a measure which hit at *Christian* slaves 'mostly born and bred in his realm, who work to support their employers, nearly all either poor people or widows, and also people of good standing who have no other means but that which is gained by their efforts – *a usage generally accepted in this region*'.[15] This municipal objection shows that, contrary to popular belief, the greater part of the slaves had been baptized. This is confirmed, moreover, by the existence of a number of pious confraternities founded especially for coloured people: in particular 'The Brotherhood of Little Negroes' (*Cofradia de los Negritos*), a name which is preserved to this day in Seville.

Seville did not owe its original character simply to the economic activity and the cosmopolitanism of its people. There was a very particular Sevillian mentality, to which people from other parts of Spain, who had settled in Seville for some time, were sensible.

Affluence raised the price of everything higher than anywhere else, and the sight of all those riches exposed to the public gaze with the return of each merchant fleet had the effect of creating a veritable 'psychological depreciation' of money. 'Silver,' says Mateo Alemán, 'was the ordinary coinage as copper used to be, and people spend it without a second thought.' This state of mind was heightened by the peculiar character of the trade with the Indies, which for the most part remained a gamble, 'a high adventure' which could bring shattering reverses or sudden fortunes. A cargo arriving from America, after a long interruption in the traffic, because of the war, could make fabulous profits amounting to as much as 100 per cent of the value of the merchandise. But a slump in trade or a loss of part of the fleet could mean failure and ruin for the merchants who had pledged their capital and for those who were associated with the enterprise. So arose a sudden desire to enjoy the pleasures and refinements which wealth could provide and a certain detachment in regard to money, which should not be hoarded but spent.

Thus the whole of the social life of Seville reflected a certain *insouciance* combined with a taste for ostentation. The new style of houses which had been built by the newly-rich middle class reveals an orientation towards a more brilliant and freer social life. Alonso Morgado, in his *History of Seville*, in 1587, notes that:

'The inhabitants now build their houses with an eye to the exterior. Formerly all the attention was focused on the construction of the interior of houses and no one bothered about the outside, as had been done in the days of the Moors. But today, people are concerned to make their houses more splendid outwardly, with plenty of windows giving on to the street, which set off and beautify the appearance of the many ladies, distinguished and noble, who look out from them.'[16]

Sartorial luxury was evidence of the same preoccupation.

'The inhabitants [Morgado says again] ordinarily wear clothes made of fine cloth or silk, gold-braided material, satin, or velvet. The ladies, for their finery, use a great deal of silk, muslin, embroidery, swanskin and soft flannel, and cloth of the finest weave: even the more modest are dressed in linens of every colour. The fashion of small hats suits them marvellously as do the bonnets trimmed with starched lace. . . . They pride themselves on walking very upright, taking small steps, which gives them a noble bearing famed throughout the kingdom, especially as they understand the art of making themselves even more glamorous by veiling their faces *and allowing only one eye to be seen. . . .*'

One would be tempted to attribute a Sevillian pride to Morgado for this flattering image of his compatriots, were it not that numerous reports confirm the renown which their elegance and grace of movement had won for them throughout Spain. Lope de Vega says: 'Seville was made for this: the beauty of its women, with their audacious mouths, in which pretty teeth sparkle.'[17]

Sevillian ostentation found gratification in the eyes of all during the great public festivals. These were not only the rejoicings organized for the happy return of the galleons but also the religious ceremonies, which, in Seville, assumed an unrivalled magnificence. 'The services for Holy Week are so sumptuous that they leave Rome, summit of the world and heart of the Church, far behind.'[18] Religious confraternities, which were more numerous here than elsewhere – each quarter of the city, each trade had its own – bedecked their statues of the Virgin, or of their patron saint, with precious ornaments of gold and jewels. Splendid processions, whose traditions are still preserved by the modern Seville, wound their way through the narrow streets between houses which were illuminated and hung with tapestries.

At length, Sevillian wealth and piety combined as a Maecenas to the benefit of the studios of the sculptors and painters who were established in the city. They received many commissions from the rich *bourgeoisie* and from monasteries and convents, as well as from the cathedral authorities who had immense funds at their disposal. It was in this Sevillian atmosphere that the genius of Velazquez took shape and Murillo flourished, while, despite the restlessness of the great city, Zurbaran painted the great series of works which evoke both the serenity and the asceticism of monastic life.

This brilliant picture had its other side. 'I do not know if it is the effect of the climate in this land,' wrote St Theresa, 'but I have heard that demons have extra hands here to tempt men with . . .', and, after having spent a year in the town to found a reformed Carmelite house, she adds: 'The injustices that are committed in this region are peculiar, as are its lack of veracity and its duplicity. I think I can say that Seville has indeed earned the reputation in which it rejoices.'

The southern climate and the blue sky no doubt had something to do with the peculiar atmosphere of the city, the *insouciance* of its citizens and their thirst for pleasure. But there were other and more certain reasons: the unending procession of goods and wealth on the Guadalquivir and in the streets and the seeming ease with which enormous fortunes were built up overnight – even those who had no part in the commercial activity of the city picked up a few crumbs or, one way or another, gained some advantages out of the city.

The example came from above, since a number of municipal magistrates were in league with speculators, if not with thieves. Speculation on goods helped to maintain very high prices even in years of plenty, despite the official tariffs, fixed by the *Cabildo* (municipal council). It is as true that this body put less zeal into enforcing their application as it is certain that a number of its members were associated with the *regatones* (monopolists) who 'benefit from the protection of magistrates and influential persons and escape the penalties. All this injures the poor because by the time the food reaches them it has been through the hands of three or four speculators who, relying on the favour of their protectors (by reason of the presents given to them) completely ignore the prices which have been fixed.' To these grievances, which were brought before King Philip IV in 1621 by the jurors (elected representatives of the people), were added others concerning the negligence of the Twenty-four (municipal councillors) who 'having the duty to watch over the common weal and its proper administration, let themselves be guided only by their own particular interests and forget the well-being of the public. This is why the city is in such a lamentable state; both on account of the cost of living and because of the impossibility of walking through the streets which are so neglected and so full of refuse that there is good reason to fear outbreaks of grave epidemics.'[19]

The filthiness of the streets, in such contrast to the embellishment of the city by new buildings, both public and private, was denounced in many documents. To quote from one in 1598: 'It is shameful to see the city half buried in filth and rubbish, so that all its squares and roads have become veritable dunghills.' In order to counter this evil the citizens had recourse to a somewhat unusual method – employed, moreover, in other Spanish towns, and particularly in Madrid – of painting or erecting crosses on walls or in nooks and crannies which were to be kept clean. But a synod assembled in Valladolid in 1607 objected to the practice, alleging 'that not only were the required results not obtained but also that practice offered opportunities for the greatest irreverences, because people did exactly the same as if the crosses were not there'.[20]

But more serious still were the results of the negligence or complicity of the authorities as far as justice and the police were concerned. It is not only the ordinary police officers who were sometimes the accomplices of the malefactors whom they were supposed to pursue and catch; the latter for what little they had could bribe magistrates of high rank. In vivid language, Porras de la Camara, one of the canons of the cathedral, said:

'Here they only punish those who haven't a long purse, and they only condemn to slavery in the galley those whose arms are not long; the only ones sentenced to death are the needy ones, those who have no means with which to bribe the clerks of the court, the attorneys, and the judges. Six years have passed during which no one has seen a single robber hanged in Seville. . . .'

One can understand how, under these conditions, *picaros* (ruffians) of all kinds, ranging from the beggar and the *esportillero*, who arranged the 'pickings' from the merchandise landed on the Arenál, right up to the redoubtable hired killer and the ruffian who lords it in the criminal world, operated in Seville as freely as fish swim in the sea. It is easy to understand, too, why swarms of all sorts of adventurers, many of whom were foreigners, were attracted by the reputation of this European El Dorado.

Among the rendezvous of the light-fingered gentry were some which had acquired a veritable fame: for example, the Court of the Elms (*corral de los olmos*) and the Court of the Orange Trees (*corral de los naranjos*), situated on each side of the cathedral but within the chains that marked the limits of ecclesiastical jurisdiction. Lay justice had no power to enter one or the other (especially the Court of the Elms in which there were several taverns) and they became sanctuaries for law-breakers; there they gambled and there they fought, and the women of the streets went in to keep company with these 'recluses'.

The abbatoirs of Seville had no more savoury a reputation.

'What shall I tell you,' says one of the two dogs which Cervantes makes to talk in *The Conversation of the Dogs,* 'of what I have seen in the abbatoirs and the grossly excessive things that happen in them? First of all, you must assume that all who work there, from the humblest to the greatest, are people with very accommodating consciences, devoid of souls, and fearing neither justice nor the king . . . they are carrion birds of prey. They live and feed their mates on whatever they steal. They pride themselves on being fine fellows and are all more or less desperadoes.'

Finally, we should not forget the prison which played such a part – materially and morally – in the life of the city that its chronicler, Morgado, does not fail to mention it as one of the most notable of the public buildings:

'One should make a point of seeing the royal prison at the entrance to Sierpes Street. It has a character all its own; it is easy for foreigners to find because of the endless flow of people at all hours of the day in and out of the main gate, as well as the inscriptions on the gate, which is emblazoned with both the arms of the king and the arms of Seville.'

All who sojourned there were not necessarily robbers – Cervantes spent two spells in it, in 1599 and 1602 – but nevertheless they formed the majority of the inmates. The number of prisoners kept increasing and at the beginning of the seventeenth century amounted to 2,000, from which we may conclude that, despite evidence to the contrary, the police were not entirely in the pockets of the law-breakers.

The attorney, Christopher de Chaves, writing during that period, gives a very curious description of the peculiar life in the prison, and especially of the initiation ceremonies for the newcomers in his *Account of What Happens in the Prison of Seville*:

'The old lags subjected them to a torture session, the point of which was to find out the "musicians", that is, those who were likely to "sing" on the wooden horse of torture and denounce their accomplices. These are sent to Coventry in the gaol, while the "braves" are admitted to the community to the sound of guitars and drums.'

Morgado, the attorney, described the incessant stream of those coming and going from the prison, the gates of which were not closed until ten o'clock at night, as being 'like a procession of ants, night and day, bringing provisions'.

This city so full of contrasts, where luxury and destitution, piety and crime lived side by side, was at the heart of the anxiety of all Spaniards, for all great public and private enterprises were suspended at the arrival of silver from the Castillian Indies. It was not only on the banks of the Guadalquivir that people uneasily awaited the return of the fleets laden with precious metals. There was equal anxiety in Madrid, where both the court and the city were on the look-out for the couriers from Andalusia with the latest bulletins. 'We wait from hour to hour, by God's grace, for the safe arrival of the galleons,' King Philip IV wrote to Sister Maris of Agréda, his confidante and counsellor. 'You know the great importance this has for us. *I hope that God, in his mercy, will bring them safely home. Nevertheless, I would fain ask you, through your prayers, to help us obtain this favour from the Divine Majesty.*' And, after the happy return of a fleet, a Madrilenian citizen notes in his diary:

'It was high time because, without this guarantee, the financiers refused to transact any further business. . . . The galleons brought five million ducats for the king and about the same sum for private investors. . . . Since one believes that the king will not take anything away from individuals, we begin to breathe.'[21]

CHAPTER FIVE

URBAN AND RURAL LIFE

I. Decline of the towns and its causes – Economic activity. Corporations and guilds. The bourgeoisie – The urban scene. Town and country.

II. The feudal régime and slavery. Imposts and the tax quotas – Agriculture. Common lands and the rearing of cattle and the alternating of pasture – The life of a peasant: The village: Festivities and recreations. Life in the theatre during the Golden Century.

I

In 1618, the University of Toledo addressed to King Philip IV a petition which gave the gloomiest picture of the decline of the ancient imperial city and of other Castillian towns which, not long before, were thriving centres of the textile industry:

'The two classes of people who used to make their living by weaving, now have no work and, from lack of practice, will soon forget the functions and skills which brought their trade to a peak of perfection in Spain. . . . For formerly our commerce and industry were the best in the world, since not only did we make the goods of which Spain had need but we also produced merchandise for the whole of Europe and the Indies. Today it is these foreigners who bring their merchandise, especially their cloths, to Spain, and in exchange take away a full measure of hard cash. All the products which they bring, if they had been made in our realm, as used to be the case, would have brought enormous revenue to the royal treasury. . . . We also note that today, with a population only half of what it used to be, there are twice as many monks, clerics, and students, for they can find no other way of earning the bare necessities of life.'[1]

This complaint obviously contains notable exaggerations. That the decline followed prosperity 'within a few years' – as the university asserts – is doubtful, especially since the Cortes of Castille, from 1573 onwards, had denounced foreign competition as the cause of the ruin of Spanish manufacture and the impoverishment of her people. Nor can one attribute the complaints solely to a nostalgia for the 'good old days', whether they were addressed by representatives of the towns to the Cortes or expressed in the writings of numerous economists and *arbitristas* (planners), who put forward their remedies for the sickness which gnawed away at the monarchy – the decline of industry and of the towns which had thrived on it.

All were not equally affected. It is precisely around 1620 that Madrid experienced her most rapid demographic advance and that the commercial activity in Seville reached its peak. These two great Spanish capitals, one political, the other economic, benefited from very special conditions – as we have seen – their importance being achieved partly at the expense of other towns in the kingdom. Barcelona, still extremely active at the end of the sixteenth century, went through a stagnant period; in the Catalan capital, as in Saragossa and Valencia, foreigners – especially the French – were taking an ever-increasing and important part in small businesses and among the artisanry.

But unquestionably Castille, traditional centre of the manufacture of woollen goods, was hardest hit. The demographic statistics which can be established for this epoch, however imprecise in detail, prove beyond doubt that there was a steep decline in the towns which formerly – and sometimes quite recently – had played such a vital role in the economic life of the country. Between 1594 and 1646 Toledo lost half its population and around 1650 had only fifteen textile factories as against some hundreds that were working in the days of its splendour; and Segovia was but a shadow of its former self. Burgos, which specialized in raw wool for export, dropped from 2,600 'hearths' (approximately 13,000 inhabitants) to 600. Medina del Campo, a great centre for trade fairs and a great place for barter and exchange at the beginning of the reign of Philip II, saw its prosperity ruined by the general waning of the Spanish economy. Of its 3,000 'hearths' in 1570, only 650 remained in 1646. It had become a straggling semi-rural village whose inhabitants lived mainly on the revenue from the land and from the vineyards which had been cultivated in the neighbourhood.[2]

Competition from foreign products, so vigorously denounced by the Toledans, was without doubt one of the basic causes of this decline; but it found conditions nowhere more favourable than the economic and psychological conditions peculiar to Spain; the abundance of wealth coming from the Indies, which enabled the country to double its purchase of imported goods; the growing preoccupation with 'purity of blood'; and the passionate desire to ascend the social ladder, leading to contempt for manual labour and neglect of 'mechanical occupations'. The enterprising spirit which had spurred on a part of the Spanish *bourgeoisie* to take part in a great surge of expansion in the preceding age, changed to a mood of prudence and recession. The middle classes no longer took part in big business and industry, but invested their capital gains in government bonds (*juros*) and in rents from landed property (*censos*).

After the collapse of the ancient urban industries and in the absence of active middle-class businessmen, the mainstay of the economy shifted to the artisans and to retail trade in a very limited market. Contemporary records reveal a surprisingly high proportion of artisans and shopkeepers in the total of the general population,[3] but the multiplication of this class, as well as their corporations and guilds (*gremios*), between the era of Charles V and the middle of the seventeenth century, was far less an index of a rise in urban prosperity than a sign of stagnation. In fact, the increase in the number of guilds corresponds not with the creation of new undertakings but with the disappearance of 'free enterprises'. What now happens is that these became part of the corporate framework, with all the restrictive practices imposed by it, and the duplication of different corporations – generally rivals – which dealt with professional work in which there was no clear line of demarcation: jewellers and goldsmiths, gilders and gold-beaters, the cutters of doublets (*jubeteros*), and of breeches (*calceteros*). This development was accompanied by a number of statutes which sought more and more to define strictly the domain of each 'trade' – the need was more pressing the nearer the trades were to each other – and also to fix for each of them conditions of work and regulations governing the methods of manufacture. One of the essential aims of these statutes was to limit the effects of competition by apportioning the raw materials among the masters and by fixing the numbers of apprentices and workmen to be employed by each, so that no man could raise himself above another: characteristics of a state of mind more concerned with

93

maintaining moderate stability than with opening up the field for great enterprises.

The conservatism of the corporations in economic matters was matched by the way they played their social role through confraternities (*confradias* or *hermandades*) which grouped together the masters, the workmen, and the apprentices in the same trade. The confraternity was not only concerned to give as much lustre as possible to the worship of its patron saint and to maintain his shrine; it played a further role as a mutual insurance society, assuring to its members in the case of illness or incapacity a lump sum of money or daily payments according to scales meticulously fixed by law. For example, the regulations of the confraternity of St Joseph of Madrid (whose members were master carpenters and their workmen) state:

'We ordain that if one of our brothers is suffering from a tertian or a quartan ague, he shall receive 50 reals; and if he remains sick and is unable to work, he shall receive a second payment after thirty days; but if his malady continues, he cannot make a further claim. ... If he dies, his heirs have the right to claim whatever money was due to him for his convalescence at the rate of 10 reals a day, less whatever he received during his illness.'[4]

Naturally, all his *confrères* were expected to attend the funeral service, and the statutes often laid down the number of candles to be lit in the church, as well as the number of the masses to be said, at the expense of the confraternity, for the soul of the departed.

Despite this particular spirit, more likely to depress than to enliven economic life, the corporations and fraternities were among the most active elements in civic life. They had their place in all the popular celebrations, whether these were religious festivals or secular rejoicings. One can also say that they constituted the most authentic representation of the local people, since, after the disappearance of the 'democratic' institutions on which the administration of the medieval cities was founded, local authority was nearly everywhere borne by the *poderosos* (the mighty ones).

These were composed of the local aristocracy who lived on the rents from properties which they owned on the outskirts of the city, and of the richest of the burgesses. If some of them had remained faithful to professions which were considered to be sufficiently 'genteel' – such as the goldsmiths and silversmiths, and sometimes the vendors of silks and spices – most of the newly rich wanted to escape from their original social class and to mingle with the nobility, which they contrived either by means of the legal purchase of an *hidalguía* or by their mode of life. The composition of the population of Burgos, as established by statistics in 1591 when returns were made for the tax on the *millions*, clearly reveal this economic and social trend. For example, for the 3,319 *vecinos* (that is, heads of families, on the one hand, representing several people and, on the other – especially church dignitaries – constituting individual units) who appeared on the register, the figures were as follows: 1,722 described themselves as *hidalgos*, 728 as clergymen, and 295 as secular priests. There remained, therefore, only 572 *pecherols* (taxpayers) to make up the active and productive element – about 17 per cent of the total.[5]

The mediocrity of urban activity, together with the violent contrasts in social conditions, was immediately evident in the appearance of the towns, where life had slowed down in surroundings often too grand for them, which the previous century had transformed and embellished. The epoch of the Renaissance, which coincided with the influx of precious metals from the Indies, was marked almost everywhere by a feverish round of new building. To the great religious buildings inherited from the Middle Ages were added new churches, hospitals, town halls (*ayuntamientos*), and rich residences for noblemen and burgesses; and an effort towards town-planning was made in most of the important cities.

In the north and centre of Spain, the Plaza Mayor, a rectangle framed by porticoed houses and flanked on one side by the law courts, remained the centre of urban life. The roads which branched out from it were also frequently bordered by porticos and arcades, under which sheltered small workshops and shops, generally grouped according to their specialist trades and giving their names to the streets. Thus there were streets called *Plateria* (Goldsmith Street), *Sederia* (Silk Street), *Lenceria* (Linen Street), and so on. In Andalusia and the Levant district, where the shops were not usually sheltered by portico or arcade, it was the custom during the torrid days of summer to hang awnings (*toldos*) from one house to the next above the busiest streets to shade passers-by from the fierce heat of the sun.

Around this city centre, dominated by the great houses of the

95

aristocracy, stretched out a confused conglomeration of plebeian houses, where the greater part of the population lived. These were squat houses, nearly always of one story, and made of mud or bricks; for stone was a luxury reserved for rich houses and even there was sometimes used only for the 'noble' façade. Roads wound their way between these hovels, often made only of packed earth. Such roads were dusty in summer and were sometimes transformed by rain into quagmires in which men and beasts floundered and carts cut deep ruts. For here country met town: not only because the gardens and even the fields, mostly belonging to religious orders, covered such vast areas, but also because many of the inhabitants of these humble cottages were agricultural day-labourers who earned their living on the great estates near the town. City-dwellers by the location of their homes, they belonged in reality to the rural world because of their work.

II

The traveller, leaving the bare plateaux of Castille or the stony mountains of Aragon, sees with wonder the olive groves of Andalusia or the *huertas* of Valencia. One associates these landscapes with a nature which is more welcoming and a way of life which is easier and happier for the inhabitants. But contemporary accounts give a different impression. Everywhere, even in the privileged lands, the life of the peasant was hard and often wretched, and official records – royal decrees and complaints to the Cortes – which deplored the 'poverty and calamities' of rural existence, were examined in a whole series of works which denounced this state of affairs and attempted to find remedies for them.[6]

Whereas in France, a steady evolution had transformed medieval 'tenures' into true ownership, there were very few peasants in Spain who had freehold property – perhaps only a fifth of the total number. These were mostly to be found in the humid regions of the north (the Asturias, Galicia), but the patches of ground which they owned were hardly big enough to provide subsistence for one family. In Castille, peasant holdings, still considerable in the Middle Ages, had been progressively diminished by the economic and social pressures of the 'men of power', who had been largely incorporated in great ecclesiastic or secular domains and exploited

7. Spanish Theatre, 1660. Corral de la Pacheca

8. Court Joker of Philip IV

by farmers and *metayers,* often to a precarious condition. In Andalusia the vast 'states' belonging to a few aristocratic families were cultivated by 'brassiers' (agricultural labourers) who lived in towns and cities and who, hired seasonally by the estate managers, went and camped for a few weeks in the fields, to return to town with only a miserable pittance.

Whatever legal rights were attached to the land which he cultivated, it was the peasant who bore nearly all the weight of the political and social edifice. More than half of the Spanish land consisted of the '*tierras de señorio*' (manors) in contrast to the '*tierras de realengo*' which were subject to the direct authority of the king. Hence the Castillian saying 'Bird, build not thy nest on manorial land!' attests that the living conditions for the peasant in the *señorios* were generally very hard. In fact, the extent of these feudal powers and the severity of their enforcement varied greatly from one region to another.

In no part was this feudal authority more widespread and oppressive than in Aragon, where, even in the seventeenth century, jurists admitted that the region is 'free of all trammels and its power unlimited in all matters concerning the life of the vassal' (that is, the subject), on condition that 'he be not mutilated or burial denied to him. . . .' Without doubt it had become exceptional for this power of life and death to be used in reality. But the fuss caused when the seigneur took possession of Leiva – so great that it was described in a document in the middle of the century – symbolizes the survival of the principle of absolute authority over people and their belongings.

'As a sign of real possession, he strolled through the square and the public streets, pulling up various shrubs, opening and closing the doors of warehouses; he then walked through his pastures where he plucked out plants and bushes and behaved in such manner as to leave no doubt that he had truly taken the land into his physical possession. At the same time, as a sign that he had taken over the administration of criminal justice, he caused a gibbet to be erected in the market square and ordered a gauntlet to be hung from it.'

Homage was then paid to him by the *concejo* (the rural council):

'His Lordship sat on a bench, and everyone, from the sheriff to the least of the councillors, gave him his allegiance, kneeling before

G

97

their illustrious lord and swearing to pay the usual tributes and taxes in return for the safeguarding of the customs and usages which they had heretofore enjoyed.'[7]

Even though the seigneur did not have *complete* sovereignty over his lands the peasant was always reduced to economic slavery by the domainal and manorial system of government, and had to pay dues which were often very heavy. Generally (like tithes paid to the clergy) these dues consisted of a proportion of their agricultural produce; sometimes this *champart* was replaced by the payment of a yearly sum of money or by presentations in kind – the handing over of a certain amount of wheat, wood, oil or wine, cattle, or poultry, the details of which had been fixed by ancient custom. In Galicia, where the condition of the peasant depended on monastic seigniories (*abadengos*) and was particularly hard, there was also the right of mortmain (*luctuosa*), which authorized the abbot to claim, when a tenant died, the best animal in his herd; in default of an animal, a chest, a table, or any other piece of furniture which had four legs.[8]

Added to the manorial imposts, there were the royal taxes, always increasingly heavy, especially in the 'kingdom of Castille' between the middle of the sixteenth century and the end of the reign of Philip IV. The levies of 'services' – that is special taxes – were increased in number, in particular the *millions* (duties on sales which were added to the *alcabala*), which in principle hit all classes, except the clergy, and were particularly crushing for the peasant. The reason for this, says a contemporary, was that

'... prelates, grandees, and nobles, who collect almost all the grain which the labourers sow and harvest, pay nothing: the prelates by virtue of their exemption, and the other great ones because, to be blunt, there are few who do not find some means of tax evasions. As a result the real burden falls back on the labourers who cannot escape from their taxes even on a single grain of that which they sell.'[9]

If a wretched man could not pay the royal dues, the collectors of taxes proceeded to distrain on his goods:

'They enter the villages, and tell the authorities of their mission. The latter beg them to have pity on the inhabitants who are in dire straits. . . . The tax-collectors reply that it is not up to them to grant graces and favours and that it is their job to collect the exact amount of money due from the village and, above all, they say, they must recover the amount of their own wages. So there they are, going into the houses of the unhappy peasants and, after producing a grand array of reasons and calculations, they remove what little money the peasants may still have. From those who have none, they take their movables and, if those are lacking, they seize the miserable beds on which they sleep, taking all the time necessary to sell what they have picked up. Finally, they make an account and often enough there is no surplus to pay their salaries even though from all this the king receives only some very small change. This sort of pillage occurs continuously. As a result, most of the villagers are forced to take flight, leaving the lands waste; and the tax-gatherers have no more pity for all this misery than if they were entering an enemy country, They sell the abandoned houses if they can find purchasers; if not, they rip off the roof and sell the tiles and timber for a small sum. As a result of this whole-sale destruction, only about a third of the houses remain standing and a great number of people have died of hunger.'[10]

Doubtless we must take into account the indignant feelings which prompted this sort of diatribe and not take it all literally. It is certain, however, that the crushing burden of taxes contributed to the depopulation of certain regions, and even the fertile land of the kingdom of Granada, whose apparent opulence stirred the traveller to wonder, did not escape from the fate common to the provinces of the 'kingdom of Castille'. For example, a deputy writes to the Cortes in 1621:

'Many villages are deserted and have even disappeared. Churches have fallen down, houses have collapsed, and inheritances have been lost. The fields are abandoned, and the inhabitants wander along the roads with their wives and children, eating grass and roots to sustain themselves, seeking for a way out of all these evils. Others migrate to other provinces and kingdoms where they do not have to pay the *millions* tax.'[11]

When there were peasant smallholdings, they were often encumbered by ground rents (*censos*) to the enrichment of the citizens in the neighbouring towns. The contract consisted of the loan of a sum of money against the payment of an annual rent on a

99

property, the value of which at least equalled the capital involved, and was equivalent to a mortgage. The transaction enabled the peasant to acquire the capital which he needed to improve his cultivation, but it also gave the rich bourgeois control over the loan and the interest and a safe investment. If, because of a poor harvest or for some other reason, the peasant found himself unable to pay the annual rent, his creditor could seize the land. Theologians railed in vain against this practice. One of them remarked: 'As everyone can see that by lending a hundred ducats, they receive 200 ducats in return each year and that, after seven years they receive 2,000 into the bargain. . . .' Moreover, mortgages multiplied at the end of the sixteenth century and during the seventeenth century, and if this form of tenure did not always end in the dispossession of the tenant, it at least increased the peasant's burden.

In order to face so many obligations, the peasants had only limited resources which provided for them a soil often unproductive and poorly cultivated. If we leave aside the *huertas* of the Levant area, and certain parts of Andalusia which were planted with olives and vines, cereals were the staple crop. But they gave only mediocre yields (on average fivefold; sometimes only threefold) because of the aridness of the climate and the poor quality of the implements. Ordinary ploughs were mostly unknown; it was the swing-plough which was commonly used; for it was generally better adapted to soil in which humus forms only a thin layer or none at all. Except in the northern provinces, where oxen were yoked to the ploughs, the draft animals usually used were the donkey and the mule and one sometimes saw a poverty-stricken peasant, with only one animal to his name, trying to work a swing-plough with its aid.

The extent of the fallow land was considerable. This was not solely due to a system of crop rotation – common to all the grain areas of Europe – which allowed the soil to rest for one out of two or two out of three years. Cultivable land occupied only a very small perimeter around the villages, between which lay vast areas of heath land (*monto bajo*) or wasteland (*monte alto*). But these wasteland regions were not totally unproductive. They constituted 'commons' which played an essential role in rural life, offering poor but vast areas where cattle could graze, and permitting even the poorest peasant to keep a few beasts – mostly sheep and goats

– which their smallholdings could not feed. Moreover, customary rights governed the manner of using these *baldios* ('empty' lands). But the peasant communities were constantly having to defend their rights against attempts by the big neighbouring landowners to enclose these lands and – especially on the plains of Castille – against the encroachments of the powerful sheep-owners' corporation, the *Mesta*, who were constantly moving their flocks.

The flocks of the *Mesta* at the beginning of the seventeenth century comprised about two million sheep. Each spring, the sheep left their winter pastures (*invernaderos*) on the plains of Andalusia and Estremadura to wend their way to the summer pastures (*agostaderos*) on the sierras and high plateaux of Castille, from which they would return in the autumn. Guided by the shepherds and by tough cross-bred dogs, who were trained to pen the sheep and keep them together (and also to protect them against wolves), the flocks slowly advanced, raising up great clouds of dust. From their midst there would emerge the pack-animals – donkeys and mules – carrying in nets the cooking-pots, the food for the shepherds and the dogs, salt for the sheep, and also the young lambs born during the migration and still unable to bear the hardship of the journey. If, in crossing cultivated regions, the flocks were supposed to follow certain tracks (*cañadas*), their passing was nevertheless a calamity for the peasants of the neighbouring regions; for the flocks grazed at will on the heaths and the commons of the villagers, who naturally wanted to retain their own rights to these lands. In fact, the *Mesta* had gained the recognition of the kings of Castille – anxious to increase the woollen industry and its exports – and had received all sorts of privileges which were against the interests of the peasants. The peasants were forbidden to cultivate the commons or to fence their fields and, worse still, they were obliged to allow the sheep of the *mesteños* to graze on their fallow land to the detriment of their own livestock. These privileges led to continual conflicts which usually ended in favour of the *Mesta*, which had its own sheriffs, who were endowed with large judicial powers and could summon offenders to its own tribunals.

Thus, on every side, the peasants were hemmed in by masters and enemies. Brother Benito de Peñalosa wrote in 1629:

'The peasantry is the poorest, most crushed and trampled on of all classes; it seems that all others are in league to destroy and ruin it. It has come to the point when the very word "peasant" sounds so bad that it has become a synonym for "slave", "villein", "boor", "malefactor", and even worse.'[12]

However, a real picture of the peasants' lot is not to be found in the generous protestations of theologians or economists, but in the eloquent document which contains the findings of an enquiry ordered by Philip II into the condition of the towns and villages of Castille. The questionnaire which formed the basis of this enquiry covered every aspect of rural life; the extent of the *pueblo*, the judicial situation (*señorio* or *realengo*); husbandry and the various resources of the population; the shrines and relics preserved in the villages; local festivals. The answers given by the peasants themselves and faithfully transcribed indicate that only in exceptional cases did they own the land that they farmed. Nearly all were tenants of the local notables, of the great monasteries, or of landlords living in the neighbouring towns, to whom all sorts of payments were due. In Belvis, a little town in the province of Toledo, of 1,500 *fanégas* (about 2,200 bushels) of the wheat harvested each year, 150 were paid in tithes and 400 to the owner of the land. Since a farmer had to keep at least 200 *fanéga*s for seed, only half of the harvest remained for the peasant's own use in a normal year. When the grain was sold, allowance had to be made for the royal tax on its sale, 'but it often happens that the peasants do not harvest enough grain to pay all their expenses, and then they are lost'.[13]

Constantly, when the commissioners of the enquiry asked the peasants about the 'standard of living', they got the same response: 'Everybody here is poor'; 'Most people are hard-up, some have barely enough to keep themselves going'; 'Generally speaking two-thirds of the people are poor and the rest live in modest circumstances'; 'The village has 230 inhabitants: of these, a score are moderately well off, but no one could call them rich; and all the others are poverty-stricken.'[14] One must also bear in mind that, between the date of this enquiry (started in 1575) and the reign of Philip IV, the condition of the peasant worsened.

The very aspect of a village and its houses reflected the bare competency of peasant life. It was only in the mountain regions that houses were built even partly of stone. In the Castillian plains the cottages, made of mud, blended with the colour of the earth.

Sometimes one saw a portal of brick or stone surmounted by an escutcheon: this was the home of some *hidalgo* or other, often just as poor as his neighbours, but marked by the coat of arms as a man of quality. In the south and east of Spain, walls, carefully distempered each springtime, gave the villages a happier look. But inside, these houses were equally bleak; many had only one room and it was exceptional if they had more than two. The furniture comprised a roughly made table and some wooden benches. The beds often consisted only of a simple plank, or one simply slept on the floor. In a corner of the main room was the hearth, where occasionally a brushwood fire was lit – nearly everywhere wood was rare and expensive. In any case, food needed little preparation: for the poor peasant, rye bread, cheese, and onions – in Andalusia, olives – made up the staple diet.

Can it be said that the countrymen of Spain were uniformly plunged in misery? There were, even in the heart of the countryside, notable differences which arose from varying local conditions and personal situations. In Catalonia, where the farmers had old and solid beams over their heads, there were prosperous peasant estates – the centre of which was the *masia* (farmhouse), solidly built in stone, in which some architectural details – an ornate front door, colonnetted windows – hinted that the owner was a nobleman. Even in less favoured regions, such as La Mancha, one could also find labourers who enjoyed a high standard of living; the character Gamache le Riche, whom Cervantes in a famous episode of *Don Quixote* opposed to Basil Pauvre, was not a figment of imagination. He represented a real type, a *cosechero* – a rich landed farmer – who employed a number of farm labourers and moreover made a handsome profit from the plots of land which he leased to peasants. But it seems that this sort of countryman was becoming increasingly rare; the writer Navarette deplores this trend in his treatise on the *Preservation of the Monarchies*:

'As they see that the major part of all the impositions, charges, dues, salt-taxes, are imposed on the landowners without rebates on their rents, it is an easy decision to free themselves of all the trammels of running a farm and to retire and enjoy their savings with tranquillity in a town.'[15]

Thus only the poorest section of the people remained in the villages.

One would therefore be tempted to reject entirely the false picture of the countryman's life as depicted in such a large part of the literature of the Golden Age, particularly in the *comedias*, which show the peasant leading a simple and comfortable life, often enlivened by rustic entertainments. Clearly one must take account of the idealization of country life which had such a long vogue in the 'pastorales'. But it is also clear that, even for the poorest, the daily grind was relieved by fêtes and public merry-making which was enjoyed by all the villagers: religious festivals, a celebration for the local patron saint, *romerías*, which were akin both to the *fête champêtre* and the pilgrimage – a solemn procession to a neighbouring shrine to pray for divine protection or to give thanks to God.

The *Reports*, published by the order of Philip II, which generally give such a dismal picture of country life, are sometimes relieved by such events, which lingered long in the minds of the people. When questioned about the relics preserved in their church, the people of Alameda (near Madrid) replied:

'They keep in it a very sacred image of Christ, nailed to a great cross, which altogether weighs seventeen pounds and was brought back from the Indies by one of the men of the village. We went to Madrid to seek it in a very solemn procession, with many priests, crosses, and banners, and accompanied by a multitude of folk from this and neighbouring villages. And it should be noted that, at the beginning of the month of May 1573, on account of a great drought throughout the whole region, the villagers, having carried this Crucifix in solemn procession, made their way to the Monastery of Atocha in Madrid, where they all offered up a pious prayer. Our Lord granted this prayer, and on the very day that the procession reached our church there was a great flood of rain and our grain was saved, and the yield of wheat gained great profit for us.'[16]

The end of a good harvest was an occasion for rejoicing in song and dance, and often there were rival festivities between the inhabitants of neighbouring villages. In many parts of Aragon and the Levant area, people organized each year a 'combat between Moors and Christians', and nearly everybody joined in. Sometimes a puppet-master – and there were still many in Spain – would erect his little booth in the market square or on a threshing-floor, making people laugh at some farce or thrilling them – like Maître Pierre whose characters were torn to shreds by *Don Quixote* – with the 'animation' of the heroic legends which the *romancero* had made so popular. If a village was near a main road, it might have the chance to see a performance by a troupe of strolling players, who would amuse the audience with a 'comedy of saints' or a religious play.

Thus, however idyllic the lighthearted scenes about rustic life in the comedies of Lope de Vega may be, they do reflect certain real aspects of life in the country. But the theatre of the Golden Age did more than portray the peasant. It vindicated him, according to Brother Benito de Peñalosa, in a fashion generally approved by other classes. Whether one is considering *Fuente Ovenjuna* by Lope de Vega, *El Alcalde de Zalamea* by Calderon, or one of the many other *comedias* the action of which is in a village setting, the authors invest the peasant with the highest virtues in order to heighten the contrast between his native nobility and the villainy of other social groups.

CHAPTER SIX

THE CHURCH AND RELIGIOUS LIFE

*The Church of Spain. The Clergy and Ecclesiastical possessions –
Monastic life: mysticism and worldliness: Religious practice: charity
and fervour – The cult of the Virgin and the saints – Deviations of
religious sentiments: ritualism and its excesses. Illuminism and sorcery
– The Spanish Inquisition.*

The Catholic faith permeated the Spanish soul so profoundly that
there was no single aspect of individual or collective life which
was not bound up in it. This omnipresence of religious feeling
explained the role of the clergy in Spanish society, the importance
which clothed all the manifestation that exalted God's glory,
and, lastly, the part played by the Inquisition, the rampart of
orthodoxy against heresy and all deviations of religious thought
and practice.

The second half of the sixteenth century and the beginning of
the next were marked by an increase in the social power of the
Church which resulted from the increase in the number of clerics
and the acquisition by the clergy of real estate which assured a
considerable revenue. Among the factors which impelled many
Spaniards towards the priesthood or the cloister, one must take
account of a religious fervour linked with Catholic reformation
which expressed itself in the level both of thought and of action.
The foundation of new holy Orders, among them the Jesuits,
and the reform of ancient ones, such as the Carmelites and the
Augustinians, attracted a spiritual *élite* to monastic life. But other
reasons intervened to explain, in all classes, the bias towards
ecclesiastical vocation. For the younger sons of noble families
(*segundones*), excluded from the paternal inheritance by the law of
majorat, the church offered an honourable career with the prospects
of a rapid advancement generally assured to those of high birth.
To those of humbler birth, holy orders offered the only means of
escape from their original condition and even of reaching high
office either in the Church or the state. In this hope, many a peasant

made heavy sacrifices so that at least one of his sons could get a degree at a university which would qualify him for a prebend or a benefice. Finally, contempt for manual labour also played its part in increasing the number of those who entered monasteries, not so much to discover the eternal truths as to find a haven free from worldly worry. In 1624, the Bishop of Badajoz wrote: 'There are some who say that religion has now become a way of earning a living and that many people take to religion as they would to any other trade.'[1]

According to the complaints presented to the king by the *Cortes* in 1625, there were 9,000 monasteries (many of which, in fact, housed only a small number of those in holy orders); the number of convents could hardly have been less. If we add to the monks and nuns the lay clerics, we arrive at an estimate of at least 200,000 souls as the number of clergy in a total population of eight millions. It was not only the *Cortes*, representing the urban *bourgeoisie*, who protested against this great intake of clerics and clerks, which caused a diminution of business activity. Even the clergy complained and demanded that a stop be put to it. In his book *Preservation of the Monarchies (1626)*, Father Navarrete argues that one must 'ask the Pope not to open the door to the foundation of new religious orders and to hold fast against the creation of too many monasteries'. He adds: 'With a multiplicity of orders and convents, it would be fatal to put heavier burdens on the shoulders of the working-classes.'

Even graver than the increase in the number of those attached to the Church was the continual increase in earthly possessions which went with it. To the landed heritage passed down from the Middle Ages, which represented a large part of Spain, were added bequests to monasteries, the dowries of young and wealthy girls taking the veil, the chaplaincies and pious institutions endowed with land by certain families whose aim was to reap a monetary reward, generally speaking, for their children and descendants, and, finally, purchases made by the religious communities themselves. A writer of the seventeenth century notes: 'When a peasant is obliged to sell a part of his heritage, he will find no purchaser other than one of the communities.'[2]

How much did the clergy draw from their domains, in addition to the income from tithes? It has been estimated that the sum was one third of the revenue from all land throughout Spain. Apart from the number of monks, the splendour of the Spanish churches was one of the things which most struck the foreigner. When he was living at Valladolid (then the capital of the realm), Barthélemy Joly, almoner to the King of France, noted that the churches were not as well built as those in France but 'surpass them in the beauty of their gilded paintings, superb shrines, statuary and ornaments'. He admired the crosses, the chalices, the big jewelled altar curtains with which the piety of the devout had enriched the church, and concluded with a reflection that was tinged with envy: 'Add to this the nation's obsession for the ostentatious and outward appearance, its anxiety for a reputation of having given this or that, and, because of a concern that no one shall deprive it of its belongings, its great affection in matters of the Church.' This affection, as travellers would note, was well illustrated by the obvious well-being of the clergy 'who live a comfortable life everywhere', and even more so by the consideration generally shown to them. 'Monks find their real element in this country. They are always addressed as *Padre*, honoured, respected, welcomed, and well esteemed by all.'[3]

In the description of Valladolid given by the Portuguese Pinheiro during that period, we read: 'The monasteries are big enough to be towns in themselves and I am surprised that Valladolid can support so many convents and churches. The one Franciscan monastery, with its 200 monks, occupies half the city.' Even more astonishing was Toledo whose archbishop, the primate of Spain, had lordship over more than 700 localities and its chapters accumulated enormous revenues. 'The town is fairly big', writes the Pole, Jacques Sobieski, during a visit in 1611.

'It quite certainly contains more monasteries, monks, and nuns than any other part of Spain and probably throughout all Christiandom. The churches and monasteries alone seem to comprise the whole town . . . The cathedral is not only majestic and beautiful but its treasures, even disregarding the golden reliquaries, the precious stones, and the jewels, are in my opinion, unique in all the world.'[4]

The wealth of the Spanish Church was counterbalanced by a certain slackening of principles due mainly to the way in which members of the high clergy were selected. The sovereign nominated men to high ecclesiastical office, and, whereas Philip II had taken great pains over the choice of his prelates, his successors were less scrupulous. The most typical example was that of the Infanta Fernand, son of Philip II, who, at the age of ten, received his cardinal's hat and the dignity of Archbishop of Toledo, which made him Primate of Spain. Being by vocation a soldier, the 'Infanta-Cardinal' never appeared in his primatial city but distinguished himself on the battlefields of the Thirty Years War. An exceptional case, no doubt; but many of the bishops, preferred because of their noble birth, led a life in their episcopal palaces which was more princely than religious, surrounded by their equerries, their pages, and sometimes their jesters. On the other hand, the real spirit of the Church dwelt in some of them, such as Antonio of Estrada, Bishop of Palencia, who died penniless in 1628, having given away all his earthly goods in alms.

At the bottom of the ecclesiastical hierarchy, although there were exemplary priests, the influx into the priesthood of people who had no vocation accounted for the mediocre moral quality of many of them. The cases of parish priests living with concubines – the *devil's mules* as they were then called – and having children by them, are frequently cited. One is surprised by the relative indulgence which the Inquisition showed in this regard.

It was among the regular clergy that the greatest contrasts between the highest spiritual values and the relaxation of discipline and moral standards was to be found. The spirit of the Reformation in the sixteenth century was kept alive not only among the down-to-earth Jesuits, whose influence was increasing, but also in certain contemplative orders, such as the reformed Augustinians, to which St John of the Cross belonged, or the reformed Carmelites, who remained faithful to the tradition of Theresa of Avila, that spirituality which was earthly and heavenly at one and the same time.

But the convents – and the same was true of France of those days – were often refuges to which women of quality could retire or pass away their widowhood. But often they were also asylums for the young daughters of the nobility, who, without regard to their vocation or their wishes, were put into convents by their families. This provoked a Dominican friar to address a *Memorial* to Philip II in 1574, protesting against the sale of church property which was intended to be a means of balancing the budget. Nuns

'who constitute a large part of the Spanish nobility will be particularly hard hit'. He emphasized the fact that,

'. . . the great lords and most illustrious people cannot marry off
more than one of their four or five daughters because of the
excessive dowries demanded. There is no other course but to send
the younger sisters to convents. The founders of the convents *with
this in view* are obliged so to endow and enrich them that poverty
will not lead them into evil or to a life of discontent and despair.
*In order that their monies shall be assured and collected, they
have been given land and serfs.*'[5]

Under these conditions, it is natural that these nuns considered
themselves to be still part of the outside world – which only
necessity made them leave – and that they should want as far as
possible to retain its pleasures.

The two convents of the commanderesses (*comendadoras*) of
Calatrava and St James, founded by two knightly orders of similar
names, would not, like them, receive any but those of noble birth
and were notorious for the easy, and even showy, way of life of the
nuns. Speaking of the *comendadoras* of St James, Madame
d'Aulnoy wrote, at the turn of the century: 'The establishment of
these ladies is magnificent; anyone who wishes to visit them can do
so without hindrance. The furnishings are the same as they would
be in the outside world. They enjoy large allowances *and each has
three or four women to wait on her.*'

Clearly, in these sophisticated convents, life was far removed
from contemplation and penitence. The parlours were frequented
by numerous visitors of both sexes. There were fêtes, amateur
dramatics and poetico-theological 'jousts' (modelled on the literary
tournaments which were then very popular in the whole of Spain).
These often included 'daring' points for discussion, such as: 'Which
is better in love; desire or fulfilment . . . ?'

Such a deviation found, if not justification, at least an explanation in a style of mystical literature which imitated the *Song of
Songs*: divine love was expressed by comparisons, metaphors, and
terms borrowed from the idioms of a very worldly love. This also
explains an even more singular practice: the *galanteo de monjas*,
that is, the art of paying court to the nuns. This would appear to
be incredible if there were not so much written evidence about it.
To be a *galan de monjas* was to declare oneself to be the esquire of

a Dulcinea who is locked up in a convent. He would convey to her by his demeanour and fond looks the passion she inspired in him; he would make every endeavour to see her from a distance behind the grille of the choir of the conventual church or through the bars of her cell. If he was a poet he would dedicate verses to her; he would find some sister at the entrance of the convent to smuggle in the message and would hope eventually to find some pretext to visit his lady. Then he might meet her in the parlour of the convent and discuss with her various proposals of amorous casuistry. Far from being shocked, many nuns enjoyed this game, and the fact of having a 'gallant' was considered almost as natural as it was for a young girl in those days to have a recognized fiancé.[6]

The gusto of the satirists had a free rein in dealing with the monastic *galanteo*. Among the different 'ploys' which Quevedo commended to Pablos of Segovia for use during his career as an adventurer was that of a *galan de monjas*:

'When I quitted the vile life of being an actor, I became a "gallant of the grilles", if I may so express myself. The reason for this was that I had discovered a nun, whom I found more beautiful than Venus, at whose request I composed several songs. She took a liking to me when she saw me playing the part of John the Baptist on the day of Corpus Christi. I resolved to write her the following letter: "Madame, I have left my present company, because all the company save yours is a dreadful loneliness, etc." '

The nun replies in similar terms and fixes an 'appointment' with him at vespers, so that he can peep at her through the grille. 'You would find it hard to believe the number of vespers I listened to. Through craning my neck to see her, I am two ells taller than when I embarked on this romantic intrigue.' Then, after kicking his heels for days against the walls of the convent, along with several other *inamorati*, 'reckoning up how much it costs to live in hell – a place reached so agreeably and in so many different ways', he decides to abandon this career which has no future. . . .

Others, however, were not content with these visual satisfactions, and the sacrilegious Don Juan, who burst open the convent gates, prevailed only on the stage, where they showed Tirso de Molina. The 'news items' (*noticias*) of that epoch frequently mentioned the raping of nuns, and the perpetrators were sometimes monks themselves. The complaints about these and other excesses persuaded the government of Philip IV to adopt a decree prohibiting all intercourse between the sexes of all in religious orders. But this was never published, one of the reasons alleged for this being that 'conditions must not be imposed on the clergy which oppress them more than other men'.[7]

There was an even more regrettable permissiveness in many of the monasteries; to quote Father Juan de Cabrera, 'they are full of lazy and sensual people, incorrigible vagabonds always ready to disturb religious peace and concord'. Many monks, who had broken away from the cloister, lived by their wits, mixing with the dregs of society and becoming common criminals. In 1665 a priest called Barrionuevo records:

'In Cuéllar, a Franciscan monk kidnapped a very pretty nun of twenty from the convent of St Claire; and in Seville another brother – both a Carmelite and a good preacher – having had difficulty with his prelate who had him put in prison, escaped and took refuge in the Sierra Morena. He is now actually in command of a large band of fine fellows, who beg for alms through the mouthpieces of their blunderbusses.'[8]

We must not then be surprised if the parish priest and the monk have pride of place in the satirical literature of the period; and the fact that the Inquisition allowed the publication of works in which they were so roughly used shows that the accusations levelled against them were not ill-founded. But we must always be on our guard against accepting these attacks as if they were true, word for word. Apart from the most scandalous cases, which attract our attention, they are set in the anti-clerical tradition of the Middle Ages. They are characteristic of an age in which a sound faith should not be damaged by the unworthiness of certain of its earthly interpreters, all of whom are subject to human frailty.

Sincerity and fervour were the characteristics of the Spanish faith even though some of their manifestations seemed to belie these stirling qualities. This 'living' faith was most apparent in the hallowing of the poor in the image of Christ, and in certain charitable practices which went far beyond alms-giving: 'To treat a poor man without courtesy is to affront the King of kings, for the man who asks is a man sent from Heaven to ask you, in the name of God, to do a good deed. To refuse him alms, is a squalid trick,[19] wrote one author of the time. There was scarcely one last will and testament, made by those who were well off, which did not provide large sums of money for those of the poor who would accompany the deceased to his place of rest and help open for him the gates of Heaven; in the impoverished Spain of the seventeenth century hospitals and hospices for the destitute were still numerous. Finally, the *sopa boba* ('convent broth') saved great crowds of the poverty-stricken from dying of hunger in the streets. Every day, the gates of the monasteries were opened at noon at the sound of the Angelus to permit the passage of monks or lay brothers carrying a huge cauldron of soup and a basket of bread to be shared by the wretches clustered around the entrance: for professional beggars, men out of work, disabled soldiers, and half-starved students this was the one daily meal they could rely on.

Strict adherence to the dogmas and commands of the Church was evident in the assiduous attention given to religious practices: attendance, often daily, at Mass, frequent attendance at sacramental services, telling the rosary, observance of days of abstinence, and also the fervour with which the devout followed divine worship and listened to every word of the preacher. The preachers often tended to give their sermons a virulent character, sometimes as if they were on the stage, changing from invective to tenderness and tears in order to sway the congregation. Barthélemy Joly writes,

'In their sermons the priests are far too vehement. . . . There were two things that troubled me about these sermons in Spain: the extreme vehemence, not to say turbulence of the preacher, and the continual sighing of the women, which was so loud and vehement that it completely distracted one's attention.'[10]

Worship of the Virgin was an essential part of the Spanish faith: a cult which was diversified by a multitude of 'incarnations' and representations of the Mother of God, each linked with local traditions. Some of these benefited, however, from a veneration which attracted to their shrines pilgrims from all over Spain: the Virgin of Pilar to Saragossa; the Virgin of Guadeloupe in a monastery lost in the Sierra of Estramadura; the Virgin of Montserrat, whom they came to adore at a festival in September at the cost of a difficult climb among the rocks and precipices of the Catalonian mountains.

To the dogmas of the Catholic Church Spain had already added

H

on its own account in the sixteenth century that of the Immaculate Conception, which its theologians had tried to get the Council of Trent to adopt. In the justification of this dogma the state and all classes of society were united; on many occasions the Cortes demanded that it should be proclaimed by the Church. The order of Calatrava insisted that its knights should profess the mystery of the Conception of Our Lady; and even the brigands in Seville were prepared to draw their swords in defence of this article of faith, if needs be.

The splendours of the Church in Spain were enriched in the first part of the century by new saints, among whom were St Theresa, St Ignatius Loyola, the St Francis Xavier, whose triple canonization took place in 1622 and was an occasion for splendid celebrations. But the desire of a body of the clergy to have St Theresa recognized as the patron saint of Spain was attacked by many of the faithful and by certain religious orders who feared that the traditional patron, St James of Compostella, might be offended by this new 'competition' and withdraw his protection from a nation which he had led to victory over the Moors. It was, however, convenient for foreigners (from whom the bulk of the pilgrims were recruited), who by the old 'French road' which had been used since the twelfth century made their way to Galicia to venerate the tomb of the Apostle, to rest in the hospices which had been built in former times. 'The King's Hospice' in Burgos received every year between eight and ten thousand pilgrims, 'French, Gascons, and men from other nations', who by rule were sheltered for two or three days. As the governor of this hospice remarked: 'There is no means of knowing whither these people are going, nor whence they have come, nor whether they are genuine pilgrims.' It was impossible to distinguish between those whose piety led them to St James of Compostella and those whose pilgrimage was merely a sort of profitable vagrancy.[11]

Various brotherhoods and sisterhoods played a vital role in the worship of the Virgin and the saints. Their numbers had continued to increase since the end of the Middle Ages, and had reached perhaps 20,000 by the middle of the seventeenth century. Some were affiliated to the guilds of merchants and artisans; others drew their membership from the liberal professions – doctors and lawyers; yet others had a regional basis, reuniting in the great cities the faithful who originated from the same province. Those from

Navarre were under the patronage of St Firmin; those from Galicia, under St James. There were even certain confraternities whose members were all foreigners resident in Spain. In 1615 the French in Madrid founded the confraternity of St Louis, to maintain the hospice founded at the instigation of the royal saint. In fact, most confraternities had a charitable aim. But they were all anxious to obtain as much renown as possible for their patron saint, by the maintenance and embellishment of his chapel and shrine. There was a fierce rivalry between the wealthier ones when it came to processions during big religious festivals. The statue of the saint was dressed as gorgeously as possible and was followed by all the members of that confraternity, wearing the *habito*, or hood, in the colours of the order.

One of the characteristics of the religious life was an ever-increasing fondness for outward display. The epoch of Philip II and of St Teresa, during which convents and monasteries of strict observance were founded in the remotest parts of Castille and Estramadura, marked the apogee of mystical and ascetic meditation, which showed itself in a religiosity turned towards the inner life. In the next fifty years, the outward and visible expression of religious sentiments became increasingly important. In the churches, continuously enriched by the piety of the faithful, the ceremonies of worship became more sumptuous: the great celebrations – canonizations and the transference of relics – gave place to spectacular displays lasting for several days, like that organized by the Franciscans of Madrid in 1627 in honour of the martyrs of their order:

'There was a procession from the church of St Francis to that of St Giles and their effigies were carried in great pomp, dressed in cloth of gold and silver, with the insignia of their martyrs. Next came the glorious father St Francis wearing a rich vestment; then followed more than 400 Franciscans, shod or barefoot, Capuchins, and more than 500 tertiaries of the order, bearing lighted torches. The standard was carried by the Duke of Medina de las Torres accompanied by all the Grandees of Spain and the great Seigneurs of the highest rank. The procession passed by the palace and the king and queen watched its progress. The church of St Giles was beautifully bedecked. Eight sermons were delivered by the best preachers of the court.'[12]

The spectacular character of the religious ceremonies frequently gave to the public manifestations of the faith the appearance of a popular fête where the sacred and the profane met. The procession during Corpus Christi were the most typical example, but Holy Week itself, despite its sorrowful commemoration which could not be entirely ignored, and its demonstrations of extreme fervour which had a place even amid the worldliness, gave an impression of libertinism. Throughout the week the bells were silent, the use of carriages and other equipages was forbidden and, in token of contrition and humility, the gentry had to go on foot, unarmed and unescorted by squire or page. The traditional visit to the churches, open night and day, sometimes gave the ladies, normally under constant watch, the opportunity for romantic meetings, and offered the men the chance of easy conquests and brief adventures.[13] The upshot was that in Madrid the royal government was forced to issue instructions to the magistrates responsible for the policing of the city to 'pay special attention to veneration, and the decency and respect due in the sanctuaries, forbidding the opposite sexes to have verbal intercourse or to indulge in unseemly behaviour'.[14]

The processions which followed each other daily from Palm Sunday to Easter were extraordinary spectacles. They would start with a phalanx of public officials. Then came, carried on the shoulders of ordinary folk, the *pasos* (carved groups in colour) depicting the stations of the cross. Some of these – at least in great cities like Valladolid, Seville, and Valencia – were masterpieces which came from the studios of the greatest painters and sculptors; and the striking realism of the faces and postures – a cadaverous and bloody Christ, a Virgin drenched by her tears – were in contrast to the brilliant ornaments with which the carvings were draped. Behind each *paso* came the attendant confraternity, with its standards, its banners, and its crosses shrouded in black *crêpe*. Each man carried a lighted candle, the flickering light of which set off the long lines of the nightly processions, from Wednesday to Good Friday.

Even more moving was the march past of the penitents, their heads hidden by pointed hoods, loosely dressed in robes which revealed their backs and shoulders, carrying heavy wooden crosses, which weighed them down and chafed them until they bled. Barthélemy Joly, usually prejudiced against the religious practices of Spain, could not conceal his emotion when he went to Valladolid and saw the 'doleful procession of the penitents wending their way through the city. . . . They flagellate themselves horribly and pass in the night so sadly that one would be hard-hearted indeed not to be deeply moved.' In contrast to this 'company of lost souls', adds a French traveller,

'. . . you see other people of quality, preceded by pages carrying torches, in Valladolid and pretty well all over Spain. Even those of very high rank spare themselves no more than other penitents, and they are carried home covered in blood and half dead. Others carry bigger and heavier crosses; *it will be a blessing if the devil in his subtlety can be kept out of this vain show. What makes me think hard is how their pages and footmen can identify them when their masters are dressed up in monk's rags.*'[15]

The final sentence is even more significant, since Barthélemy Joly completely accepts the sincerity of the penitents who, despite their anonymity, wished it to be known that they were people of high rank. This ostentatious character given to the crudest penances has, moreover, been underlined by several Spanish writers of that time. 'I have no doubt,' wrote Francisco Santos, 'that many of them lash themselves for the love of God; but I think that it is mostly to please their own vanity.' To quote the Countess d'Alnoy, there were in fact many who whipped themselves out of love for their ladies. In front of their mistresses' houses 'they flog themselves with marvellous patience. . . . When one of them meets a handsome woman, he strikes himself in a way that makes his blood bespatter her. This is a very great courtesy and the lady, aware of it, thanks him for it.' One would be dubious about this if Lope de Vega, Quevedo, and others had not poured scorn on the 'amorous penitents' (*disciplinates de amor*).

If the importance given to the external manifestations of faith by no means excluded sincerity, it ran the risk of substituting the form for the spirit. *A propos* the gorgeous vestments with which the faithful bedecked the holy statues, St John of the Cross rose up against 'this abominable vogue of tricking out holy images with the luxury and fashions of the profane world', which reduces true devotion 'to the mere art of dressing up dolls, certain of which are only idols for personal satisfaction'.[16] But far from withering, this trend tended, on the contrary, to grow, becoming fused with a type of devotion in which gesture and ritual, instead of appearing as sign and symbol of a higher reality, now assumed a propitiatory nature: in a constraining sort of way *vis-à-vis* the Divinity whom they 'placed under an obligation' to those who had discharged the duties. What struck Cervantes' two characters, Rinconete and Cortadillo, when they came in contact with the underworld of Seville, was 'the assurance that all these people have that, although they are accused of robbery and murder and all sorts of offences against God, they will still go straight to heaven, *provided they do not default in their devotions*'.

Ritual, even seen in the most formalist light, at least keeps the faithful in contact with the Church and its ministers, who must remain its sole guides on the path of faith.

But even more dangerous – especially in the eyes of the Inquisition – was the opposite excess, that is, the quest for direct communion with God, without the help of any earthly intercession. Such an attitude appeared as the consequence and as the counterpart of the mystical thought of people like St John of the Cross and St Theresa. The latter, in *Las Moradas*, described in astonishingly concrete language and with an extraordinary wealth of imagery, the stages through which the spirit must pass in order to be united with God, in ecstasy. But she put her sisters on their guard against an excess of 'visions' in the quest for God. These must be controlled, as St Theresa had kept them under control by humility and complete submission to the precepts of the Church:

'I have known more than one sister, of the highest virtue, who has passed seven or eight days in a state which they thought to be ecstasy. The faintest spiritual exercise completely possesses them in such a fashion that they allow themselves to be paralysed, obsessed by the idea that they must not resist Our Lord. . . . From this, little by little, they die or become idiots, or go mad unless a remedy can be found for them.'

St John of the Cross also denounced those who mistook for divine inspiration what was not more than the figments of their imagination.

'I can well speak here of certain women who have simulated false stigmata, wounds, crowns of thorns, and images of Christ on their breasts, since in our epoch one has seen all these things. . . . People who are sensible and versed in the spiritual life will take no account of these chimeras; but simple folk think that such things are the mark of sainthood. And because some woman or other has swooned four times, these people extol her saintliness, and henceforth she is assured of her food and keep. . . .'[17]

But in this sphere there was veritable emulation, and a Jesuit priest wrote to one of his colleagues: 'One sees such a plethora of these "stigmatized" people that one can no longer consider them as the servants of God unless they exhibit all the Five Wounds. . . .'[18]

Mystical illusion can lead only to a sort of absolute quietism in which the spirit, thinking to fuse in some way with the Divinity, has no need for further recourse to the outward observance of the faith. But mysticism can also lead to graver deviations from morality. If the human will loses itself in God, it ceases to have any responsibility and even the possibility of sinning disappears. Under cover of the reaction against the value of 'works' linked with the diffusion of reformist thinking, there appeared a certain state of mind among some groups of illuminati (*alumbrados*). Some of them sought only to reach a state of pure contemplation, whereas others pretended to seek in sensual love a sort of initiation to divine love. Despite vigorous repression conducted by the Inquisition in the reign of Philip II, new cells of 'illuminism' were formed, especially in Seville in the first half of the following century. The very language of mystical literature with its 'erotic' vocabulary and undertones, gave a formidable weapon to certain confessors who were possessed by the demon of the flesh, a weapon which on account of their ambivalence, they employed to delude their penitents. The number of proceedings arising from these 'solicitations' – a technical term used by the Inquisition to define this crime – indicates the relative frequency of this abuse. Cloistered nuns, exposed to the mystical illusion, against which St Theresa had given them such stern warning, were easy prey to their spiritual directors, the illuminati – or rascals – as was shown by the affair of the convent of St Placide, which between 1628 and 1633 was the subject of the pious and scandalous tittle-tattle of Madrid.[19]

Whether or not the pure nuns of St Placide were 'seduced' by the Benedictine friar who was charged with the care of their souls,

119

it is certain that this man found in the convent a powerful accomplice, as we discover from the records of the Inquisition. The Devil took possession of the souls of the abbess and most of the sisters under her authority, despite all the mortifications that they imposed upon themselves in order to escape from temptation. This case is evidence of a connexion which sometimes exists between 'illuminism' and that other form of deviation in religious thought which we call demonology. It would be quite wrong, however, to think of belief in the devil and the practice of sorcery which springs from it as being particularly characteristic of Spanish religiosity. The seventeenth century, especially in its first fifty years, was the great age of witchcraft and there was no part of Europe, even in the time of Descartes, which was not obsessed by the Devil.

This obsession seems to have been strongest in countries where the faith was most alive, and in this respect Spain was fruitful territory for the Devil. How could one doubt the existence and power of Satan when the very Church had fixed on what might be called an 'orthodox' conception of the Devil and had laid down the rules to be followed in fighting him? A whole literature of demonology – the work of the theologians – flourished in the seventeenth century and it gives us a lot of information about the various incarnations of the Angel of Darkness. For the Devil is at the same time both a singular and a multiple being, and there exists in the underworld a veritable specialization. At the summit is Satan assisted by Lucifer, Beelzebub, and Barabbas; then Asmodaeus, the prince of lust, Leviathan, the demon of pride, Belial, the patron of gypsies, fortune-tellers, and witches, and Auristel, who rules over gamblers and blasphemers. Among the lesser demons is Renfas, 'the devil with a limp', the amiable pander of all the vices in which man seeks his pleasures.

One cannot deny to the Evil One great power over men. Thus, Canon Garcia Navarro in his *Tribunal of Superstitions* (published in 1631), informs us that: 'Satan is well versed in medicine and philosophy, familiar with the properties of all plants and herbs from which he distils a quintessence, which, *by invisible means*, he applies to the affected parts.' Hence the miraculous cures attributed to him by witches which, in fact, resulted only from the *natural* properties of the plants. The Devil often used his power of invisibility to disturb people in their sleep.

'He sometimes manifests himself in a tremendous noise, *especially in religious houses,* he bangs on doors and windows; shakes inner and outer walls; smashes cooking-pots, plates, and utensils. . . . Sometimes, he even goes to people's beds, lifts the sheets, and abandons himself to indecent acts, and in many other ways scares them and prevents them from sleeping peacefully.'[21]

Much more serious than these simple devilish pranks were the cases in which the Devil or one of his friends took possession of a human being, body and soul. Madness, hysteria, and all mental diseases were explained by this 'alienation' of an individual possessed by the Devil. There were symptoms by which one could surely diagnose possession by the Devil: the ability to speak a tongue which one has never learnt, revealing events which took place in distant countries, blaspheming in front of holy objects, refusing to pray or to make the sign of the cross.

The sole remedy was exorcism, which cast out the evil spirit. As a medical cure, exorcism was practised only in accordance with the precise instructions of the Church, which had been codified to prevent abuses and frauds.[22] Exorcism could be practised only by a qualified priest, able to address the Devil in Latin – since the latter only understands the language of the Church. It was also very important to know the exact name of the devil to be cast out – Satan, Lucifer, Beelzebub, etc. – in order to be a jump ahead of him, and it could be very efficacious to burn a piece of paper on which his name was written. Equally well one could make the person possessed kneel down and kiss the cross; enraged by this act of humility, which is contrary to his nature, the Devil comes out of him. But the surest way was to make manifest to the Devil the mysteries of the Church, especially the Incarnation, the idea of which was intolerable to him. Finally, there were more material, though doubtless no less efficacious remedies. Brother Luis de la Conception recalls that, having to exorcise a lady of high rank, he ordered the women present to slap her face. Her demon was so outraged that he left her, never to return.

Besides those who fell victim to Satan, there were those who sought to benefit from his power. There were different degrees of sorcery, ranging from the wizard who could heal wounds by pronouncing magic words, and the witch who concocted love potions and cast spells, to those wicked men who, says Father Garcia

Navarro, 'have signed a pact with the Devil, and try to talk to him, in the hope that he will reveal certain secrets to them and help them to attain certain ends of their own'. Numbered amongst these wicked men there were sometimes people of high rank: the Count of Olivares, the favourite of Philip IV, was generally thought to have a devil in the hollow of his walking-stick, and popular opinion accused him, undoubtedly with some justification, of having sought the help of sorcerers to retain the favour of the king.[23]

Proceedings against witches would seem to afford 'objective' confirmation of the existence of deals between Satan and human beings. The accused, under oath, described the same experiences and with the same detailed precision: fantastic rides through the air to the place where the Black Sabbath is held; the bestial coupling of witches with demons in the form of he-goats or dogs; sacrilegious ceremonies during which the initiated renounced their Catholic faith and trampled on the cross of Christ. But the same details were already to be found in the indictments against witches in the last centuries of the Middle Ages, and the identical phrases are found again coming from the mouths of sorcerers and witches under the threat of the stake in the seventeenth century in France, in England, and in Germany. One explanation is that the prosecution conducted its enquiries in such a way and under the threat of torture, that the confessions of the accused – through madness, auto-suggestion, or the hope of avoiding the supreme punishment – described the Devil and his works in the traditional form given to it by the imagination of Western Christianity.

Certain voices were, however, raised to question the validity of these forced confessions. In 1610, the humanist, Pedro de Valencia, dedicated to the Grand Inquisitor a *Discourse on Witches and Things concerning Magic*. In this he demonstrated the incredibility of the avowed confessions and argued that little confidence could be placed in evidence which was given under torture. There is a singular contrast between the moderate punishments meted out by the Inquisition – exile, prison, the pillory – a moderation which seemed to reflect reasonable doubts among the ecclesiastical judges, and the stringency of the secular judges, who, sharing the popular hatred of witches and sorcerers accused of causing the death of children and cattle, of spreading epidemics, and of ruining the crops, were without pity to those who were indicted in their courts. There was a very real witch-hunt in Catalonia at the start of the seventeenth century, which, in ten years, claimed more than three hundred victims.[24]

The Spanish Inquisition! After four centuries, the name still evokes images of gloomy prisons, fearful tortures, and the flames from the blazing wood-piles at the *autos-da-fe*. One can understand why a considerable part of Spanish historiography is devoted to the rectification of judgements far too summarily made against this institution, and argues that the punishments meted out by the Holy Office were not different from those normally inflicted by other tribunals, that the *auto-da-fe* was an exceptional ceremony, and that not all those found guilty suffered the supreme penalty.[25] These facts cannot be contested; but it is equally true that the Inquisition occupied a very important place in Spanish life during the sixteenth and seventeenth centuries, not only because of the jurisdiction which it exercised, but also because of the impression it made on people's minds and the mixture of terror and veneration which was conjured up by its very name, and which made its presence, even though invisible, constantly felt.

The Supreme Council of the Inquisition, at whose head was the Grand Inquisitor, appointed by the king, was a department of the monarchic government, as were the other Councils (dealing with Castille, Finance, and the Indies) which functioned in the palace. But the Inquisition derived a peculiar independence by virtue of its function as an ecclesiastical court. Its authority was exercised by fifteen 'tribunals', or local courts of enquiry, which were composed of judges, 'consulters', and 'qualificaters', whose job was to classify in theological terms ('erroneous belief', 'tending to heresy', 'heretical', etc.) the cases referred to them in order to frame suitable indictments. Apart from this function, the Inquisition had at its disposal 'familiars', a sort of honorary and often fanatical police. Their number was considerable in the seventeenth century – without doubt more than 20,000, for there were many who wanted to benefit from the perquisites of working for the Inquisition (the most important of which was immunity from the jurisdiction of other courts). Moreover, they coveted the prestige which such work gave them, and which was of great importance in the 'proof of purity of blood' so rigorously demanded by the Holy Office. Many great lords and illustrious writers – such as Lope de Vega – considered it an honour to belong to this militia.

123

The power of the Inquisition was at times directed against ideas and individuals. In every important town, generally during a period of fasting, the proclamation of the *Edict of Faith* was made, preceded by a solemn procession and followed by a sermon in a church or in some public place. The edict invited the faithful to denounce

'. . . all who hold opinions which are heretical, suspect, erroneous, reckless, scandalous, or blasphemous against our Lord and the Holy Catholic Faith . . . and especially those who are still attached to or speak favourably of the Law of Moses, the sect of Mahomet, and that of Luther, and also all those who have read or possess books written by heretical authors or others who are listed in the *Index of Prohibited Books,* published by the Holy Office'.

After a few days, there would be a similar ceremony to pronounce the anathema on those who had not obeyed the previous admonition. 'May all the maledictions of Heaven and all the plagues of Egypt come: let them be cursed in the towns and the fields: let the curse of Sodom and Gomorrah fall upon their heads.' The effect of these threats, thundered out by the preachers, was considerable; it was not unusual to see people denouncing their nearest relatives to the Holy Tribunal, and sometimes even denouncing themselves.

It was, then, these denunciations, in most cases, which set the machinery of the Inquisition in motion, but the Inquisitors could also proceed on their own account. Protestantism having been extirpated in the reign of Philip II, and the Moriscos expelled in 1610, the 'marranes' of Portuguese origin, who were suspected of 'Judaizing', became in the first half of the seventeenth century the principal suspects in matters of faith. But the biggest contingent among those accused was comprised of the 'Illuminati', sorcerers, monks accused of 'solicitation', pseudo-mystical nuns, and simulators of religious ecstasy, to whom were added those who had been denounced for their blasphemous talk or reading banned books.

From the moment when the accused was locked up in the 'secret prisons' of the Inquisition, he more or less ceased to exist as far as the world was concerned, for all the Inquisitorial procedures were absolutely secret. Neither the names of the informers nor those of the witnesses were given during the trial, and even the verdicts were not made public as soon as they had been reached, the Holy Office preferring to wait until there was a sufficient number of condemned men before proclaiming the sentences at an 'act of faith'.

An *auto-da-fe* was in fact a solemn ceremony usually associated with the celebration of some great event. An *auto* was held to mark the ascension to the throne of Philip IV in 1621, and another in the year following the churching of Queen Isabella of Bourbon. The character of these festivities, to which the entire population was invited, would seem odd and almost sacrilegious, if one failed to understand that they were designed to celebrate the triumph of the true faith in the most vivid fashion and to strike terror in the hearts of her enemies. Furthermore, the principal *autos-da-fe* were fully described in reports which were circulated to the public for the edification of the faithful. One also finds numerous descriptions written by foreign travellers who were particularly struck by the strangeness of these spectacles.

In the morning, as the bells tolled and masses were said in the churches for the souls of those who were about to die, the condemned men were led out of their prisons to take their place in the procession on its way to the place of the ceremony. Drummers and trumpeters headed the procession preceded by the Inquisition's standard-bearer; then came the cross, the sword, and the olive branch, symbols of justice and mercy. Behind them marched an army of 'familiars' in their cohorts, bearing other banners, crosses, and lighted candles, and accompanied by the priests of various congregations. Next came the sad group of condemned men. Each of them was accompanied by two 'familiars'; a yellow candle was held in his clasped hands, and he would be wearing the sanbenito, a yellow tunic emblazoned with the cross of St Andrew, and sometimes decorated with a sign which indicated the nature of the punishment he was about to suffer. A pointed fool's cap – *la coroza* – completed a tragi-comical picture. Barthélemy Joly writes:

'After this horrifying troupe, taking part in its own funeral procession, came the lay and ecclesiastic authorities: the municipal magistrates and judges, officers of the king, "ministers" of the Holy Office, and finally the Inquisitor (in Madrid, the Grand Inquisitor), who was accompanied by the bishop of the town, representing the person of the Pope, all intoning the Creed in a low voice so that to anyone seeing the spectacle it might seem as though the great judgement of God was taking place'.[26]

All along its course, the masses watched out of windows or stood in front of shops which were closed, staring in silence at the impressive spectacle but sometimes breaking out into insults as the accused passed by.

At the place appointed for the *auto*, a huge platform had been erected, usually in the shape of a U. In the centre stood an altar and near it, the standard and the green cross of the Inquisition and a pulpit for the predicant. Part of the regular and secular clergy took their places there. On the right, behind the Inquisitor and the bishop who were seated on a dais, the functionaries of the Inquisition and of the local authorities (in Madrid, members of the various councils) disposed themselves. Facing them, on the other side of this tribune, was the space reserved for the condemned who were ranged on tiers which were reached by a ladder or staircase. Around them were gathered the 'familiars' and monks who were there to comfort them. On the highest tier were placed those who were condemned to death; below them sat those who were to be sent to prison or to the galleys, lowest of all were those who would suffer milder punishment. Around the scaffold clustered the crowds who had come to see the spectacle.

The ceremony began with the oath to defend the Catholic faith and the Holy Office, which was taken first by the authorities – in Madrid, by the king and the royal family – and repeated by all those present. A preacher went to the rostrum and exhorted the guilty to repent and the audience to draw a lesson from the fearful example that was to be made. After the sermon, usually very long, came the reading, much longer still, of the given verdicts. A number of secretaries of the Inquisition worked in relays to name the convicts one by one, to describe the crimes of which they were accused, and to read the depositions and statements made to the Tribunal. This reading went on for hours, and certain *autos* at which there were a large number of the condemned lasted from dawn to the setting of the sun.

Finally came the pronouncement of the sentences, those whom the Holy Office acknowledged as having repented were 'reconciled' with the Church, and punished with very varied degrees of severity, ranging from the wearing of the sanbenito for a certain period to imprisonment for life. The rest were 'released' to the secular courts, which was equivalent to a sentence of death. But this sentence was not carried out at the same place as the ceremony: the *relajados* (those 'released'), their hands tied on a green cross, were led off to the stakes which had been erected on the outskirts of town. If at this supreme moment they confessed their faults and repented, they were granted the 'favour' of being strangled before their bodies were consigned to the flames. Crowds came to watch the last scene of the drama, and some even brought faggots to heap on the fire.

But it must be emphasized that the *auto-da-fe* was an infrequent ceremony. There were about thirty during the forty-four years of the reign of Philip IV (1621–1665), the largest number of them (eight) being staged in Seville. But because of their spectacular character and the shattering impact which they made on the minds of people, these ceremonies gave to the whole of Spanish life in this epoch a particular psychological tonality. The very fact that he had appeared before the Inquisition left an indelible stain on the man denounced, even if he were proved innocent. All the more reason then that a man who had been convicted and given a light sentence – for example, the wearing of the sanbenito – was forever dishonoured and so were all his descendants. Alvarez de Colmenar says:

'To hear a familiar utter the words "In the name of the Holy Inquisition" is to be instantly abandoned by father, mother, relatives, and friends. For no one would dare to take up his defence, or still less to intercede for a man about whom these words had been spoken, for fear of becoming himself suspect in matters of the faith.'[27]

But this menace which thus weighed heavily on all, since everybody was at the mercy of slanderous denunciations, did not diminish the respect or the attachment of the Spanish people to the institution which defended the purity of the faith and appeared to safeguard the very spirit of Spain.

CHAPTER SEVEN

PUBLIC LIFE, FESTIVALS, AND POPULAR ENTERTAINMENTS

I. Festivals, religious and secular – dances and masquerades. Carnivals. The procession of Corpus Christi – 'Juegos de Cañas' and bull-fights.

II. The theatre. The playhouses and the public – The performance of plays: 'comedias' and 'autos sacramentales' – The troupes of strolling players – The actor's life. Addiction to the theatre.

I

'The most serious and prudent nations, like Spain, are the most foolish when they come to entertain themselves,' averred Antoine de Brunel, and a contemporary Spanish historian echoed the opinion of the French traveller when he wrote:

'Few, seeing Spain in the seventeenth century, especially Madrid, observing its brilliant exuberance, and seeing the people almost continuously merry-making, would realize that the country was afflicted by grievous public and private ills, but would think rather that it was swimming in a tide of abundance, and living in an era of prosperity, joy, and happiness.'[1]

Obviously we must not make generalizations from a way of life essentially relevant to the capital, where the presence of the court, as we have seen, provided a myriad pretexts for festivities at which the people, at least as spectators, could participate in the diversions of the great. But the larger provincial cities – Barcelona, Valencia, Seville – did not lag far behind; and even in places of small importance, down to the little semi-rural towns, the authorities seemed to tax their ingenuity to satisfy the popular craving for any sort of rejoicing.

Everything was an excuse for a fête, and in some years 'holidays', including Sundays, outnumbered working days. To the occasions provided by events of national importance: births and marriages of princes, visits of the king to one of the towns or cities in his realm, were added the great days of the religious calendar – those which were celebrated throughout Christendom, and those which were specially connected with the Spanish Church: the transference of relics, the consecration of a new shrine, or the canonization of Spanish saints. The infrequency of certain events was compensated for by their long duration: for the triple canonization of St Ignatius Loyola, St Theresa, and St Francis Xavier, Madrid remained *en fête* during the whole month of June 1622, and the festivity had scarcely finished when another began, in honour of St Peter of Alcantara, organized by the king, the city, and the monastery of the barefooted Franciscan friars, of which he was the patron saint.

It would be useless, moreover, to try to draw a line between religious and secular festivals, for both in their origin and in their manifestation, they had many things in common. The triple canonization in 1622 was not only an occasion for *Te Deums* and magnificent pageantry; there were also poetry contests, the presentation of plays, jousting on horseback, and bull-fights. The latter, with dancing and masquerades, were the pleasures most enjoyed by the public, and the most important festivals frequently featured them, thus responding to the various tastes of every social class.

The dance was, one might say, a national passion. Cervantes wrote in one of his plays 'He is not a Spaniard who does not dance as he emerges from his mother's womb.'[2] People danced everywhere, and everyone danced. At court and in aristocratic society, the pavan, the *branle*, and the allemande were danced to the sound of instruments; measured and formal, by the grandees and their ladies. In certain processions, professional men and women dancers performed various kinds of allegorical ballet on movable stages. Sometimes the dance crossed the threshold of the churches, and before the High Altar the *danse des six* was performed – perhaps an evocation of David's dancing in front of the Ark of the Covenant – a tradition which has survived in the cathedral of Seville to the present day.

But the dances of the gentry were very different from those of the common people, which were lively and sometimes frenzied, and danced to the throbbing of guitars, to tambourines, and to the

snapping and clicking of fingers. Their lasciviousness was underlined by the songs which went with them. A moralist asked:

'What decency remains in a woman who in these diabolical
exercises abandons all seemliness and restraint, who in her antics
reveals her breast, her feet, and those other parts which both nature
and art require to remain concealed? And what are we to say of
those provocative glances, the way of turning her head and tossing
her hair, of the twirling dancing, and the grimaces which are typical
of the saraband, the *polvillo*, and other dances?'³

Velez de Guevara maintained that these are diabolical inventions
and the Devil with the Limp is very proud of fostering such aids
to Perdition as the saraband and the *chaconne*.

But the maledictions of the theological were useless against the
attraction of the popular dances. From the taverns, fairgrounds,
and haunts of ill-repute, these dances invaded the theatre, even
rivalling the traditional dances: 'One begins to forget,' Lope de
Vega laments, 'the lovely instruments of the band as well as the
old dances when one is presented with the gesticulations and
lascivious movements of the *chaconne*, which offend against the
virtue, the chastity, and the quiet decency of women.' The celebrated Jesuit, Mariana, who devoted a whole chapter to the dance
in his treatise on public spectacles, declared that 'in a certain
city [doubtless Seville] the *chaconne* has been performed in the
religious processions of Corpus Christi and even by the nuns in
convents'.⁴

The craze for the masquerade was common to all classes, and,
in the reign of Philip IV, princely fêtes gave way to cavalcades in
which the king and the lords of his court rode through the streets
of the capital at night, their gorgeous silver and gold fancy-dress
sparkling in the light of torches. The festival of Corpus Christi –
the most popular of all religious festivals – attracted the people
principally because of the masquerades which accompanied it in
nearly all Spanish towns. The solemn procession in which walked
parish priests, members of religious orders, and the public
authorities – in Madrid the king and members of all the councils –
escorting the coffer containing the Host, were preceded by groups
dressed in motley 'dancing, leaping, and capering as if this were a
Shrovetide revel,' writes Brunel. Behind them came the *Gigantes*
and *Cabezudos*, papier-mâché figures in the shape of giants and

dwarfs, with enormous heads, which, animated by those concealed inside them, made grotesque gestures as they clumsily danced. Then came the tarasque, which Brunel described as

'. . . a serpent on wheels, of enormous grandeur, covered in scales, with a fearful belly, a long tail, horrifying eyes, and a gaping maw from which protruded three tongues and rows of pointed teeth. This bugaboo of little children glides through the streets, and those who are concealed beneath its pasteboard shell work it so adroitly by special contrivances that it knocks the hats off those who stare at it open-mouthed. These country bumpkins, terrified and apprehensive when they are trapped by the serpent, provide a good laugh for the townfolk.'[5]

During carnival periods disguises and masques had great vogue. Burlesque processions of people in fancy-dress, very often dressed up as animals, wended their way through the streets, singing, dancing, and playing traditional jokes, many in very bad taste: ropes tied across the streets to trip people up at night, and the bombardment of those passing by with various, often stinking, projectiles. In the capital, the young dandies had evolved a more sophisticated technique. Instead of hurling rotten eggs, they filled eggshells with perfumed water and lobbed them at the ladies who passed by in their carriages. Barthélemy Joly avers that in Valencia 'the Shrovetide revels are just as boisterous as in Rome'. The projectiles used are oranges 'which are cheaper than chestnuts in France'.

Simultaneous masquerades and jousts and the 'battles of the Moors against the Christians' were all frequently seen in Aragon and in the Spanish Levant (Valencia) where their tradition is still vividly alive to this very day. The re-enaction of the struggle between the people and the Moorish invaders often embraced everyone in a village or a small town. Long before the day of the combat these good people would have made the scenery, produced the costumes which would distinguish the adversaries, and rehearsed the different episodes of the battle. Estebanillo Gonzalez, passing through a hamlet in Aragon, writes:

'We found two companies of farm-labourers, one dressed as Moors with crossbows, the other as Christians, with fire-arms. They had built in the middle of the place a castle of wood, of medium height and size, where the Moors were to be. The next day, just as the procession appeared, the company of Christians would launch a general assault, and, after triumphing over the Moors, would lead them captive and in chains along all the streets, firing their arquebuses as a sign of victory.'[6]

In contrast to these rustic 'combats' were those in which great nobles displayed their skill, their courage, and their splendour to the crowds and to their own ladies. The custom of the tournaments *à la Française*, which had flourished during the last centuries of the Middle Ages, still persisted in Spain up to the time of Charles V. Then gradually they gave place to javelin jousting (*juego de canas*), which in many ways retained the chivalrous *mise en scène* of the ancient tourney, a form of mock combat, copied, it would seem, from Moorish 'chivalry'. The lists were sometimes specially constructed to this end, and surrounded by wooden stands embellished with costly tapestries. Very often the tournament was held in a public square (in Madrid, the Plaza Mayor), whose balconies served as boxes for spectators of high rank.

The ceremony begins with the introduction of the combatants. Formed up into troops, sometimes dressed in either the Moorish or the Turkish fashion and carrying on the left arm a shield of wood and leather painted in their own colours or those of their ladies, they enter the enclosure mounted on show horses magnificently caparisoned. To the sound of drums and trumpets, they ride around the arena, making sham combat with their swords, and imitating the figures on a carousel. Then their equerries, wearing their livery, lead on their chargers and give their masters the javelins which they will use in the combat. All then retire to the ends of the arena and form themselves into quadrilles, or squadrons, of three or four. At a signal given by the judge of the tourney, one of the quadrilles will launch an attack. The horsemen of the quadrille cross the arena at full gallop, hurling their javelins at their opponents who make great efforts to parry them with their shields, keeping control of their horses in order to avoid head-on collisions. As soon as one quadrille has left the arena, one from another side takes its place, and this goes on without interruption until all the riders on each side have taken part in the combat. A general charge, in which all the squadrons join, ends the tournament, which, because of the agility and horsemanship demanded of the participants, as well as for their splendid

132

costumes, constitutes at one and the same time an aristocratic and 'sporting' occasion for those who take part and a highly coloured spectacle for the public.

Like the *juego de cañas*, bull-fighting was associated with the most solemn ceremonies and it was not unusual to see one succeed the other on the same day. The passion for the bull-fight was widespread and was shared by all social classes. The Papacy, which had forbidden the clergy to attend bull-fights in 1572, at least on holy days, was obliged, some years later, to reverse its decision at the express wish of the king of Spain and because little notice had been taken of the prohibition. The fact is that the *corrida* – to which the Spanish code of the *Partidas*, drawn up in the thirteenth century. devoted several articles – had become the 'national sport'. The king, the local authorities, the guilds, and the aristocracy all organized bull-fights; they figured in all the great festivals, both sacred and secular. As we have seen there were *corridas* to honour the canonization of St Theresa; others, in the university towns, were held to celebrate the success which the students had had at their examinations.

The *corrida* was not normally, however, as it has since become, a 'sport' practised by professionals often of very humble birth, and if commoners did take part they were allowed only in the 'baser' parts of the spectacle. For the *toros* remained essentially an aristocratic game in which gentlemen could demonstrate not only their skill, as in the *juego de cañas*, but also their bravery.

There were no bull-rings (*plazas de toros*) specially built for the purpose (the first was built in the eighteenth century), and the spectacle was generally staged in the main square of a town, the entrances of which were blocked up, and stands were erected for the public. In Madrid, the Plaza Mayor offered an exceptionally fine setting and never did it appear more dazzling than on the occasion of a *corrida*. Brunel writes,

'It is graced by the high society of Madrid ranged on balconies, which are hung with many-coloured drapes. Each guild had a balcony to itself, surrounded by velvet and damask, in colours of their choosing and bearing the escutcheon of their own armorial bearings. The king's balcony is decorated in gold and is covered by a canopy. His queen and her children are by his side. To the right there is another spacious balcony for the ladies of the court.'

133

The general public was crowded on to scaffoldings erected between the pillars of the arcades which surround the square. 'And though these fêtes are usually fairly commonplace, and in Madrid there are three or four each year, there is not a man in the town who would not pawn his furniture rather than miss one because he lacked the entrance fee.'[7]

As in the *juegos de cañas*, each spectacle began with the presentation of the champions, that is to say the nobility, who, clad in short capes, swords, and daggers at their sides and hats with plumes of many colours on their heads, saluted the King or the local dignitaries. These were usually attended by their equerries and lackeys, dressed in their livery, their numbers indicating the importance of their master. After a 'lap of honour', the *alguazils*, who had the task of supporting the police at the spectacle, would give a signal for the release of the bulls and retreat to the edges of the arena to clear the field for the toreadors, the horsemen, on their specially-trained mounts, to go in to attack the bulls.[8] This involved planting a *réjon*, a wooden spear with a steel point, in the side of the bull, in such a way that the shaft broke leaving the wooden part in the hand of the horseman. The *réjon* is short (eight hands, or a little less than three feet in length). This meant that the toreador had to brush against the charging bull, avoid collision, and, at the same time, bend over to strike, demanding perfect control of his horse and exceptional skill. The winner was the one who collected the largest number of broken *réjones*.

If a toreador was 'affronted' by a bull, either because a dart had not been properly planted or the bull had jostled his horse and perhaps knocked him out of the saddle, the toreador was honour bound to kill the bull with a thrust of the sword. This he could do either mounted or on foot, but nobody was allowed to go to his aid. This obligation to wipe out an 'affront' was significant of the knightly character of the *corrida*. It was the equivalent of the desire of gallant gentlemen to display their prowess to their ladies; for, says Madame d'Aulnoy, in describing these cavaliers and the coloured scarves that they wore on shoulder or arm, 'they only ride out to please their ladies and to prove that there is no peril to which they would not expose themselves in order to amuse them'.

Except in the special cases when the toreador had to vindicate his honour, the noble part of the *corrida* was achieved without the necessity of killing the bull. As soon as the beast was seen to be exhausted, trumpets announced the final round of the fight. The toreadors quitted the arena, leaving to others the task of finishing off the animal. It was a task which fell to the peons, whose role up till then had been merely to tire the bull by 'worrying' it with their capes and banderillas. They would first hamstring the creature with blows from their cutlasses, or by using a blade in the shape of a half-moon, and soon what began as a combat became butchery. Brunel says,

'As soon as it begins to totter or to stand on only three legs, the wreched bull is hacked to pieces by cuts from short swords called *cuchilladas*. This is where the common people reveal their lust for blood; for one can see that they do not consider themselves good mother's sons unless they plunge their knives into the blood of the bull.'[9]

Right to the end, however, there would scarcely be a moment when the bull was not capable of terrible charges, and there were few *corridas* which did not claim some victims from among over-intrepid horsemen, the professional peons, or the amateurs who leapt into the ring to be in at the death. But these accidents were not out of the way if one takes into consideration the fact that in those days there were often twenty bulls in a single *corrida*, very many more than in a modern bull-fight. 'The bulls behaved well. They killed five or six men and wounded many others,' says someone in the *Narratives* of Luis de Cabrera concerning a *corrida* which took place in the Plaza Mayor.

If in Madrid and the big cities the horsemanship was the main attraction of the fiesta of the bull-ring, it is certain that in the *corridas* organized by the authorities in smaller towns and even villages it was the 'plebeian' aspect which predominated in collaboration with local 'amateurs' and professional matadors (bull-killers) hired for the occasion. These confronted the bull on foot, and it was they, not the brilliant horsemen who fought with the *réjon* or the sword, who were the prototypes for the later developments of the art of tauromachy.

II

The theatre played a vital role in the intellectual life in the Golden Age. But its importance, as far as we are concerned, does not arise from its place as one of the literary arts but because the Spanish *comedia* offers valuable evidence about society in those days and especially about the ideals and aspirations of the Spanish people. But the theatre needs special consideration among the public pleasures which were so important in social life because of its passionate appeal to people of all classes.

From an architectural point of view, the theatres were extremely primitive, and the word used for them, *corral* (a court), is very apt.[10] It was only in the big cities – Granada, Seville, and later Valencia – that there were buildings specially constructed for the presentation of plays. But generally speaking it was thought enough to set up a wooden structure in a main square or between a row of houses which provided the lateral walls. Such was the case in Madrid in the two *corrales*, the *Prince* and the *Cross*, the interior of which was much the same as that of most theatres of the day. They were shaped in a long rectangle, at one end of which was the stage and, at the other, the balcony reserved for women only. This was called the *cazuela* (the 'hen-house' or the 'basket'). The rooms of the house which had a view over the court were used as private boxes. Below them was another wooden balcony (the *aposento*) reserved for the gentry. The pit, on the other hand, was furnished with only a few benches near the stage; the other part was a sort of promenade where the spectators remained standing throughout the show. Only the *cazuela* and the lateral balconies were protected by a wooden roof. For the pit, the only protection from the sun was provided by a canvas slung between the buildings, and if there was a sudden downpour of rain, the show had to stop.

But these discomforts did nothing to cool the fever for the theatre which gripped the Spaniards. In Madrid, where there were daily performances, the actors usually played to a packed house. Since only the most expensive seats (the boxes and balconies) could be booked in advance, crowds pressed around the doors for a long time before the performance. This commenced, according to the time of year, between two and four o'clock, but the doors were opened at noon. The attendants had great trouble in controlling the tumultuous crowds long enough to collect the price of admission. There were many among them who would try to get in without paying, claiming that they were officials, or that they were of high social rank, or that they were men of letters (recognized playwrights had the privilege of attending the plays of their colleagues without charge). Yet others merely demanded free seats because they were friends of some actor or actress. A free seat became, in a sort of way, a status symbol, and in 1621 the government were forced to adopt a police regulation, one article of which provided that 'all alguazils and government employees must pay for their admission in order to remedy the present state of affairs, for not only are they not paying but they are bringing in two or three guests gratis'. Another article authorized ushers to wear buff leather doublets (as worn by soldiers), as personal protection 'in consideration of the risk they run in making people pay for admission'. Finally it was ruled that police officers (*alguaciles*) must be present to offer protection where needed.[11]

The uproar did not stop at the door; since there were no tickets and no numbered seats, there were frequent quarrels about the seating, and these sometimes ended in tragedy. 'Yesterday,' reads an entry in the *Notices* of Pellicier, dated December 29, 1643, 'Don Pablo de Espinosa, during a dispute over a seat in the theatre, killed a man named Diégo Abarca. The assassin himself was so seriously wounded that his condition is now critical.' When everybody had more or less settled down, they whiled away the time (often two or three hours before the play started) by drinking and eating, each theatre having itinerant vendors who passed to and fro with trays of food. There was also ample opportunity for them to direct saucy jests at the women boxed up in the *cazuela*, who gave as good as they received and threw down nuts, shells, and other projectiles on to the heads of the people in the pit.

Among these people the 'musketeers' formed a particularly redoubtable section. They were not soldiers but the sort of people who claimed to be great connoisseurs of the theatre and whose applause or whistling often decided the fate of a new play. 'One finds at the theatre,' according to Bertaut, 'all sorts of shop-assistants and workmen who play truant and arrive there with cape, sword, and dagger, calling themselves "Caballero" – even the humble cobbler – and it is these people who decide if a play is good or not. . . .' Forgetting the dictum of Pliny – *Ne supra crepidam sutor* – the cobblers were not content to be judges of buskin; they also played an essential part, at least in Madrid, in this *claque* to such an extent that dramatists were sometimes forced to assure themselves in advance of their support for the 'première' of their play. 'I heard,' said Bertaut, 'that a playwright sought out one of these musketeers and offered him a hundred reals to react favourably to his work; but this fellow replied haughtily that he would first see whether it was good or not, and the piece was booed off the stage.'[12]

After a musical prelude, the performance began with a *loa* (eulogy), a sort of prologue designed to present the general effect of the programme and to gain the goodwill of the audience and, above all, of the formidable 'musketeers'. Sometimes, the 'author' (at that time the word meant the director of the company) recited the *loa*, but generally the people preferred the most popular actor, be it for his voice, his talent, or his wit, to receive their applause.

The performance was always a *comedia*, that is a dramatic work, of a tragic or tragi-comic nature, or a comedy in the modern sense. It would be divided into three acts or 'periods', between which were interpolated 'interludes', light, satirical, or burlesque items which contrasted with the theme of the main play, whose action they interrupted. To the idealized characters of the play and the often superhuman sentiments which animated them, these lively interludes opposed types borrowed from everyday life – *hidalgos*, beggars, soldiers, duennas, with all their foibles, their vices, and their passions. The interlude was usually pure farce; sometimes it included singing and dancing and often ended, like the sketches in a puppet show, with the beating-up of the disagreeable characters. 'It will end in a cudgelling like an interlude,' says a Spanish proverb. The public had a lively taste for these sketches and, without doubt, many of the spectators found the interludes the most attractive part of the whole performance.

It is even stranger that these interludes were also associated with the enactment of the *autos sacramentales* in the streets and public places during the festival of Corpus Christi. Beginning no doubt with the liturgical plays formerly presented in churches, these *autos* had, in the sixteenth century, taken their own particular form, at the same time as their religious significance had been specified in relation to the development of the counter-Reformation.[13] Faced with a Protestantism which denied the presence of Christ in the Host, it now became important to glorify the mystery of the Eucharist and its power of Redemption. Thus Corpus Christi became at the same time both the most solemn and the most jubilant of all Christian festivals. In the morning there was the procession of the Blessed Sacrament, with its train of people in fancy-dress or disguised as giants or tarasques (a mythological amphibious monster); in the afternoon, the *autos* commenced. Their preparation, which was generally left to the municipal authorities (in Madrid there was a special committee presided over by a member of the Council of Castille), often lasted for weeks if not months. First, it was necessary to negotiate a contract with the producer or with the authors commissioned to write the work; then to engage a theatrical company, which was a comparatively easy matter, because during Corpus Christi all other theatrical performances were forbidden. But, above all, all the necessary material had to be prepared, especially the costumes for the actors, the scenery, and the wagons for their transport. Nothing was too good or too costly to give to the *autos* a dignity worthy of their spiritual function. A contract made between the municipality of Madrid and the impresario of a company of actors specified that the costumes should be made of 'velvet, taffeta, damask, satin, gold or silver cloth, and the frills and trimmings of silk and gold'.[14] The making and painting of the sets was entrusted only to the most skilled craftsmen and the most renowned artists. Sometimes – as was the case in Seville in 1575 – the municipal authorities organized competitions for the best floats, decorations, and dances, and gave prizes to those whose work was selected.[15]

One or two carts were at first enough to transport the scenery, often primitive, and the travelling stage; but, in the first half of the seventeenth century, as the art of the producer and director was perfected, their numbers had to be increased. At least five wagons were required to set up some of the *autos* by Calderon. In addition, flat wagons were joined together to serve as a continuous platform, often more than twenty yards in length, on which were erected more and more elaborate sets. These were often several tiers, representing the heavens, the earth, and the underworld; and contrivances, often improvised, made it possible to have certain quick changes – the appearance of celestial spirits, scenes from the underworld, tempests, etc. We find such stage directions referring to these in some of the works of Calderon and other dramatists: 'One hears an appalling sound of chains and a din as if a house was collapsing.' – 'A great rock cracks open and Indolin appears, a fiery sword in his hand' – 'Bugles and drums sound: the Demon and Idolatry appear with a large number of soldiers in the most dazzling uniforms imaginable'.[16]

In Madrid, the king saw a première of each *auto* intended for Corpus Christi, each theatrical company having to submit one or two. Accompanied by a merry crowd of giants and dancers, the wagons, which were drawn by oxen, with gilded horns, their necks garlanded with flowers, their backs covered by rich mantles, take their places in front of the royal Alcazar, where the stage was set facing the dais reserved for the king and his courtiers. When this performance was over, the wagons moved on to the residence of the president of the Council of Castille, who ranked as the second personage in the kingdom; thence they paraded before the houses of the presidents of other Councils and of certain *grand seigneurs*. But the jealousies and disputes which arose over the order of precedence for these special honours led Philip IV to reduce the number of private performances to two: one for the king and his court and the other for the President of Castille. Thereafter, performances were given in different parts of the town for the benefit of the general public, who remained standing as they watched the spectacle.

In other cities the première was given before the corregidor, the personal representative of the king, and the municipal authorities, and there were certain municipalities – Toledo, Valencia, and especially Seville – which rivalled the capital in the brilliance not only of their *autos* but also of all other aspects of the Corpus Christi festival. As much care was paid to the preparation of the masquerade which accompanied the procession as to the sacred dramas themselves. Madrid, for instance, spent the considerable sum of 12,000 reals in 1628 to provide a dressing-room for the 'giants': in Seville the cathedral chapter put up 8,000 reals for the organization of 'a dance for peasants and gallants; a ball (*sarao*), with new gala costumes, and another popular dance, with a score of persons'.[17]

The mixture of sacred and profane which characterized all the Corpus Christi celebrations (which included *autos*, which were never more than one act in length but which were always followed by gay interludes) invariably amazed and sometimes scandalized foreigners. Brunel explains it as the necessity 'to give a flavour to what the gravity of the piece made boring'. But this explanation from a Protestant to whom these ceremonies were mere 'mummery', does not take into account the original meaning of the festival in its contrasting aspects. The celebration and adoration of the Eucharist, the main purpose of the processions and the *autos,* was accompanied by a release of joy for the Redemption accorded to man through the Host; and the same people who enjoyed and applauded the spectacle of the tarasques and cardboard giants – symbols of the sin and the demons conquered by the Cross – were then called upon to learn from the presentation of sacred drama, which, in the form of allegory, evoked the fundamental dogmas of the Catholic religion.

It is nevertheless difficult to believe that, with the exception of scholars and the *literati,* the public would be capable of really understanding the sometimes difficult theological discussions which were put into the actors' mouths. At the best, people would only seize on some phrase or other which reminded them of the great doctrinal notions which the faithful had in common. The constant use of symbol and allegory is not very helpful to understanding. But there is no doubt that actors who personified God, Satan, Faith, Heresy, and so on made the common man aware of a conflict in which his soul was engaged and in which, through the grace of the Eucharist and the Cross, it could be triumphant. That was why the public fervently attended these performances, which Calderon himself – the most prolific author of *autos sacramentales* – described as 'sermons put into verse, problems of sacred theology in dramatic form which reason can neither explain nor understand, *but which today are the cause of both joy and applause'.*[18]

But it is certain that the spectacle and diversions which made up the festival of Corpus Christi did make people ponder on the truths of their faith. If the municipality of Madrid spent large sums on the costumes of the giants, it acknowledged that it was 'because their dancing is the most striking sight and one which gives the greatest pleasure to the public'. The same reasons explained why the tarasque dragons tended to become the most important 'personages' of the procession and to 'compete' with the Blessed Sacrament; and if certain dances performed by the actors or professional dancers during the procession or after the *autos* retained an allegorical air, there were others (those, for example, arranged by the chapter of the cathedral in Seville) which had nothing in common with the eucharistic mysteries. And so pious voices were raised against these excesses and, from time to time, efforts were made by the king to curb them. But it was not till 1699 that a royal decree forbade dancing in the Corpus Christi processions. It seems that it was not generally enforced because not only the man in the street, but a large part of the clergy, out of respect for tradition, remained attached to their tarasques and giants, which, even in the eighteenth century, were the main attraction of the Corpus Christi celebrations in Seville.

This passion for the theatre was not confined to the big cities which were able to support one or more theatrical companies. Certain humbler places had their own *corral*, in which amateurs organized theatrical performances, sometimes engaging a professional actor to direct and stage the production. But it was the strolling players (*comicos de la legua*) in particular who gave the small towns the chance to see 'sacred plays' and the *autos sacramentales* which were the most important part of their repertoire.[19] The picturesque, adventurous, and often wretched life of these itinerant players is vividly described by Augustin de Rojas in his *Amusing Journey*, which inspired Scarron to write his *Comic Romance*. The players bumping up and down in their wagons into which were crammed indiscriminately costumes, sets, and other properties, went from one town to another, and not neglecting to halt in a village if there was the chance of an engagement. So as to gain time between performances, the players did not even bother to remove their stage make-up and costumes. That was how Don Quixote came across 'a cart, packed with the most extraordinary characters that one could possibly imagine'. The one driving the mules and acting as coachman was a 'vile demon' and, in an open cart, was 'Death himself with a human face', having at his side an angel with huge painted wings and an emperor wearing a crown which appeared to be made of gold. At his feet sat 'the God called Cupid, without a blindfold, but with his bow, his quiver, and his arrows. . . .' To the gallant knight this presented a great adventure. But when he essayed to detain this Charon's bark, the demon-coachman explained to him:

'Milord, we are players from the troupe of Angulo el Malo. This morning we performed, it being Corpus Christi week, in a village on the other side of this hill, the *auto The Court of Death*, and we have to repeat the performance this afternoon in that other village which you can see from here; and, the distance being short, and to avoid having to undress and dress up again, we wear our stage clothes.'[20]

Popular interest in the theatre is seen in quite a different light when we consider the place it held in the moral preoccupations of Spaniards and the lively controversies which it sparked off. Critics of the theatre were not so much concerned with its mixture of the serious and the grotesque, as they were with the dissolute lives of certain actors and actresses who were then seen to play the role of saints and the Virgin in the *autos* and in other sacred plays; but worse still was the immoral school which produced the comedies of intrigue which were written solely to excite human passions. For these reasons, the Church was hard on actors and would not allow them to receive the sacraments; a paradoxical attitude, since it was these same actors who had the honour of edifying the faithful by their performances in the *autos sacramentales* and because, in addition, the profits arising from these theatrical enterprises were, for the most part, devoted to pious and charitable causes. In fact, it was generally the religious confraternities and the hospices who were the proprietors or the concessionaries for the *corrales* in the big towns and who let them to the managers of the stage companies. Furthermore, in 1646, following the political and military disasters which overwhelmed Spain, Philip IV forbade all public performances, including the *autos*, 'in order not to offend God and give aid to our enemies'. The confraternities and the hospices, deprived of their revenues, rose up in arms against this measure which was, however, not repealed until five years later.

The 'battle of the theatre', which gave rise to numerous writings,[21] did not cease throughout the whole century to provoke arguments and discussions between the friends and the foes of the theatre. 'What do you think of the plays?' asks somebody in *The Traveller's Guide*. His interlocutor replies: 'It's a question that is best left unanswered because the points of view, not only of people at the court, but also of the most learned, are so conflicting that, if you are against the theatre, you are odious, and, if you are in its favour, you obviously lack judgement.' And the author of this book, while acknowledging that Spain has produced some 'honest and exemplary plays', regrets that they have become the daily bread of Spaniards. In his opinion, there should be feasts and fasts: but as the custom demands its daily play and the Spanish people

143

are so bound by tradition that the custom had attained the force of laws, 'it will not be possible to put an end to this abuse'.[22]

The addiction of Spain to the theatre can surely be explained as merely the desire to be amused, but there is also something more profound. In the more significant of the pieces offered to the public, the Spaniard found, expressed with the abandon which is part of his own character, a sense of honour, an unbridled passion both for the things of heaven and for worldly things, in short, the mixture of idealism and realism which was the very foundation of the national temperament.

9. Velasquez. A self-portrait

10. 'Las Meninas', by Velasquez

CHAPTER EIGHT

DOMESTIC LIFE. WOMAN AND THE HOME

Woman's Estate and its contradictions – The house. Domestic life. Food and cooking – Female education. 'Blue stockings'. Clothes and feminine fashions. 'Outings'. The 'Tapado' and the carriages.

'Where are the simplicity, the discretion, and the virtue of women? Where have the days gone when they did not shamelessly flaunt themselves as they do now? What has become of the respectable seclusion in which young girls were kept until the day of their betrothal, so that, until then, even their closest relatives scarcely knew of their existence? Now, on the contrary, there is nothing but "fun"; frequent clandestine outings; no more modesty and no more respect for elders; hardly has a girl emerged from infancy than she mixes with married women, and even the smallest girls interrupt the conversation. . . .'[1]

Are we then to believe that, between the sixteenth and seventeenth centuries, there was a profound change in the condition and behaviour of women? Can we challenge the testimony of the 'theatre of honour' which showed women and girls so virtuous and irreproachable that even an involuntary fault, or the merest breath of scandal, merited death? This is most improbable since, from the start of the sixteenth century, more than one traveller was astounded by the saucy behaviour of Spanish women. 'They enjoy great freedom,' wrote an Italian priest in 1595: 'They walk about the streets, by day and by night, as men do. One can easily talk to them and they are quick to answer back. But they have so much liberty that they often exceed the bounds of modesty and the limits of respectability. They accost anyone in the street, no matter what their class, and ask them for snacks, dinners, fruit, sweets, seats at the theatre, and all that sort of thing.'[2]

We must bear in mind, moreover, that the theatre, apart from the 'plays of honour' consisted mainly of plays of intrigue, the plots of which frequently had recourse to passionate love, and the stratagems by which women, or young girls, sought to escape from the vigilance of which they were the object. Such plays abound in scenes of abduction and rape, scenes which are found also in the *novelas* (romantic novels) of Cervantes and his contemporaries. As for satirical literature it found an inexhaustible theme not only in the infidelity of wives but also in the complacency of husbands, which was, to quote Quevedo, 'part and parcel of daily life, especially in Madrid'. For instance, one can read this authentic piece of information in Madrilenian news sheet (*noticias*), dated April 18, 1637:

'On Good Friday, Michel Perez de las Navas, royal notary, having waited for the day and the moment when his wife had been to confession and to take Holy Communion, appointed himself her executioner, and, begging her pardon, strangled her in her own home, merely because of flimsy suspicions of her adultery.'[3]

Such an incident might well have come straight from a Calderonian drama.

Without doubt one can explain such inconsistencies by reference to the varying sources and witnesses. The satirists, like the moralists – but for different reasons – tended to blacken the facts, just as the 'theatre of honour' tended to idealize them. As for foreign travellers, who were almost unanimous in their denunciation of the bold and often provocative behaviour of Spanish women, their evidence carries little weight and is relevant only to those who frequented the public squares and promenades. They knew nothing about the women who stayed at home and became models of the 'perfect wife', as portrayed by Fray Luis de Léon.[4]

But whatever value is attached to their explanation, it does not seem to account entirely for the two conflicting feminine 'images' given by literary and other sources. The contradiction expressed there also holds good, in large part, for the contradiction inherent in the very way of life of the Spanish woman.

There is no question that Spain's Arab heritage was reflected again in the kind of confinement which, especially in the towns and in 'polite society', was imposed upon women. They seldom left their homes, and then only to perform their religious duties; someone described them as 'half nun, half odalisk'. On the other hand, their temperament made them particularly susceptible to the attentions of men, not that gallant proposals, even the most importunate, necessarily implied an intention on the ladies' part to fail in their duty. Madame d'Aulnoy, whose observations on feminine psychology merit more confidence than the accuracy of her facts, puts into the mouth of the Marchioness of Alcañizas, 'one of the greatest and most virtuous ladies of the court' these words about something which was not entirely implausible:

' "I declare that if a gentleman had been *tête-à-tête* with me for half an hour without asking all he wanted of me, I should have been so vexed that I would have stabbed him to the heart if I could." "Would you have accorded to him all the favours he asked?"

' "That is neither here nor there," replies the Marchioness. "I have reason to think I would have given him nothing at all; but at least I should have no reason to reproach him. Had he left me completely unruffled, I should have taken it as a sign of his indifference to me." '

'And,' concludes Madame d'Aulnoy, 'there are few ladies who would not have the same feelings in a similar situation.'[5]

Such an attitude explains why women who led a normal and cloistered life at home were tempted to break loose, when opportunity arose, and occasionally to behave like 'ladies of a very different sort'. The provocative boldness of which they were then capable seemed like the counterpart of the ordinary austerity of their daily lives, but they justified themselves on the ground of the increasing indifference of their husbands (and sometimes of their would-be lovers). It was this which so impressed the two French travellers who painted the truest picture of the Spain of Philip IV: 'Husbands who want their wives to behave are such tyrants that they treat their wives almost as slaves, fearing that reasonable freedom would emancipate them from all the rules of modesty, which are scarcely understood and badly observed by the fair sex,' wrote Brunel, and the counsellor Bertaut, for his part, noted that: 'The men lock up their women and cannot understand how the ladies in France have this liberty of movement that they have heard of without causing all sorts of trouble.'[6]

But we must be cautious in estimating the relative importance of these two aspects of a woman's life – conflicting, though sometimes complementary – because of the abundance of evidence about both. There is ample evidence about women at the two

147

extremes of the social ladder, the great ladies on the one hand, and the courtesans and prostitutes on the other, but there is little to be found about the domestic and family life of the middle classes. Although we have some picture of it, the precise details are nearly always of events which disturb the daily round.

It is difficult to catch a glimpse of the life of a girl up to her marriage. One guesses that she was under the strict and jealous watch of her parents, scarcely ever going out, except, always chaperoned, to the church of her parish, dreaming of a *caballero* whom she had met there, and finding sometimes in the feminine environment a loophole for an exchange of *billets doux*. But would her feelings be taken into account when marriage is afoot? It is fairly certain that in most cases marriages were arranged by the parents, and that the girl escaped from the tutelage of her parents only to fall under that of her husband. If, by chance, the proposed marriage was not determined by simple reasons of 'convenience', or if the girl fell in love with the man chosen as her future husband, she could have her taste of all the refinements of Spanish courtesy. Assiduous in paying her compliments, escorting her on all her outings, never allowing any man but himself near her, her fiancé was subject to her every wish, rendering him the most submissive of lovers, unable to refuse to humour her lightest caprice. Happy times, to which marriage usually put an end, for the wife ceased to be the idol that she was, and became the mother of children and the guardian of the domestic hearth.

In sketching an 'interior' of the Spanish middle classes one can glean certain indications from the works of the *costumbristas* (the painters of fashion); in addition, wills and inventories which have been preserved in great numbers give a fair idea of the framework of this family life.

Even in the big towns, with few exceptions, a family would occupy a whole house – whether modest or luxurious. In Andalusia and in part of the Spanish Levant the buildings had preserved the 'Arab' plan (actually its origin was Roman). They were square, with a central *patio* embellished with flowers and vines, and sometimes freshened by a fountain. All the rooms on the ground floor opened on to the *patio*, and if there was another story it would have a continuous balcony to which all the upper rooms had access. In other parts of Spain most houses had an entrance-hall or *zaguán*, a low room with an earth or paved floor which had no light except that from the doorway. It was there that people of modest means spent the better part of the day, for the alcoves which opened on to the *zaguán* were completely dark and served only for sleeping. In the richer bourgeois houses this vestibule was tiled and furnished with pieces of fine furniture. In one corner a staircase led to a floor containing living- and reception-rooms, which were not often used during the cold weather; for it was the general custom throughout most of Spain to spend the hottest months in the ground-floor rooms, which were kept cool by frequent sprinklings of water on the flagstones. The walls of the *zaguán*, like those of the other rooms, were usually whitewashed, with the lower part covered with rush or esparto matting 'to prevent,' says Madame d'Aulnoy, 'the chill of the walls from incommoding those who lean against them'.

The first floor consisted of an antechamber at the top of the stairs where the servants received the guests; then came the suite of *estrados* (drawing-rooms), placed one after the other, the number of which was related more to the number in the family than to its social status. Religious pictures, mirrors, and tapestries adorned the walls; the floors were flagged or tiled and covered with carpets to lessen the cold in the winter months. The houses of very rich people had a state salon (*estrado de cumplimiento*) for ceremonial receptions. Usually it occupied the middle of the apartment and its windows opened on to a balcony of forged iron, the angles of which were decorated with balls of copper. It was in this room that the splendours of the master of the house were displayed: pictures (nearly all with religious themes); heavy, carved, wooden chests; delicate chests of drawers (*bargueños*), sometimes inlaid with mother-of-pearl and ivory; sideboards and what-nots crammed with plates and dishes of silver or silver-gilt. Very often this salon was divided into two by a wooden screen. On one side there might be a dais (*tarina*), covered with velvet, taffeta, or silk, and strewn with cushions on which sat – or rather squatted in Moorish fashion – the mistress of the house, her daughters, and their guests. The space on the other side of the screen was reserved for the men, who sat on chairs or stools. Heating was provided by large metal braziers mounted on wooden stands in which were burnt olive stones, which gave off very little odour; the lighting came from oil lamps or candelabra of copper or silver.

149

The taste for ostentation, which was one of the features of the age, and feminine rivalry in matters of sumptuousness, led people of modest means to compete with the wealthiest in the decoration of their salons. A contemporary writes:

'The most ordinary housewife is not content with a single salon furnished with Turkish carpets and cushions of velvet. She must have three, each more elegant than the other; the braziers and the what-nots must be of silver; the carpets, canopies, and pictures will not do unless they are imported from Flanders, from the Indies, or from Italy ... He who sees his neighbour displaying such a treasure, not considering himself inferior but often superior to him, wishes to do the same, regardless of his income and runs himself into debt and ruins himself: all this because it is the thing to do, no matter the means employed.'[7]

In contrast with what 'meets the eye', the other parts of the house or apartment, which were reserved for the family's private life, were often extremely uncomfortable. Despite the fact that glass windows were becoming increasingly popular in the seventeenth century, many rooms still saw the light of day only through windows whose panes were made of paper or oiled parchment. There were no 'privies'; and chamber-pots, nicknamed 'servants', were kept in a corner of the room or under the bed until nightfall, when their contents could be emptied into the streets, whence a nauseating stench drifted back into the house.[8]

There was the same sort of contrast between the importance of a household and the frugality of its life. We have seen that the number of servants employed was an indication of social status, and from the major-domo to the grooms, and including duennas, equerries, pages, and lackeys of all kinds, the staff of an establishment might easily amount to several dozen. Clearly all these people could not be housed in the main apartment, especially as the duties of certain of them were limited to escorting the master or lady of the house in the street. The rich, therefore, often rented one or more of the neighbouring houses in which to install their staff. Less numerous in the centre and north of Spain than in Andalusia, slaves were often in evidence, and there was nothing more distinguished for a woman of the world than to have one or two slaves dressed '*à la Turque*', following behind her in a somewhat showy manner.

The permanent maintenance of a large staff, however, was beyond the budget of most families. For the mistress of a middle-class household, who wanted to engage a valet or a maidservant, there existed in different towns, and especially in Madrid, offices which specialized in placing servants, and if one is to believe Francisco Santos, author of *Day and Night in Madrid*, the abundance of 'jobs wanted' advertisements did not prevent the applicants from showing themselves hard to please in the choice of their future masters. 'What!' indignantly exclaimed a monk who ran an employment agency at the church of Buen Suceso, 'I have found you a soft job in a decent house; there are only a man and his wife; they offer sixteen reals a month and good food; and what's more, there's no need for you to go out of the house for it is *Monsieur* himself who does all the errands and the shopping.' 'Blow that!' replies the other. 'If the master is too mean to trust his servant, that's no house for me. . . .'[9]

The case of the 'Monsieur' who did his own shopping must have been fairly rare, and the reluctance to work in such a household is all the more understandable because shopping provided the servants with all sorts of excuses for going out. The law, in fact, prohibited private citizens (and even innkeepers, as we have seen) to hoard food, so that it was necessary each day to do the round of all the tradesmen, even for the most trifling purchases. Family rations were, in consequence, generally restricted, even in those houses with a large staff: the latter, with the exception of those needed in the kitchen and to serve at table, did not feed in the house, but ate in their own 'quarters' or at the stalls to be found in the streets of the bigger towns. Furthermore, Spain was extremely temperate in its feeding habits, and the ordinary frugality of the meals was a fact remarked upon by foreigners. This applied of course to the family meal, for on solemn occasions, or when it was necessary to honour a distinguished guest, lavishness of the menu knew no limit. When, in 1605, the Lord High Admiral of England came to Spain, the banquet which was set before him consisted of 1,200 dishes of meat and fish, without counting the desserts, the whole in such abundance that passers-by were allowed to crowd in to help themselves as they pleased.

Without doubt, this was a princely occasion, but at the other end of the social scale the culinary preparations for the wedding of Gamache, as described by Cervantes, show that on grand

151

occasions, a liberal feast was *de rigueur*. As for what these Panta-gruelian repasts consisted of, one can get some idea from the pro-visions delivered by the royal commissariat to the Duke of Mayenne, who came in 1612, with a large entourage to ask for the hand of the Infanta, Anne of Austria, for King Louis XIII: for each feast day, eight ducks, twenty-six capons, seventy chickens, one hundred brace of pigeons, 450 quails, one hundred hares, twenty-four sheep, two quarters of beef, twelve ox tongues, twelve hams, and three pigs, to which were added 300 *arrobes* (300 to 400 litres) of wine; for each day of abstinence, equivalent quantities of eggs and fish.[10]

Meat, as one sees, had an essential place in the diet of the upper class. It was usually served up in a stew or marinated, with an abundant assortment of spices and condiments (e.g. pimento, garlic, and saffron) which were not always appreciated by travellers from other countries accustomed to a less highly-seasoned cuisine. Certain dishes were particularly renowned, such as the *olla podrida* (a stew with a pork base), and 'blancmange', the recipe for which Francisco Martinez, chef to Philip III, has preserved for us in his *Culinary Art*. It consisted of a sort of hash, with a base of thin slices of chicken, very gently simmered in a sauce made of milk, sugar, and rice flour. As for desserts, of which the Spaniards were very fond, these consisted of fruit (grapes, pomegranates, oranges), con-fectionery (fruit pies, egg yolks preserved in sugar), and various kinds of almond cake.

But the ordinary family table was far removed from these gastronomic excesses. 'Elegant people as well as those of lower class,' notes a German traveller in 1633, 'eat their main meal at noon; in the evening they take nothing hot.'[11] Among the rich, dinner consisted of one or two different kinds of meat (or fish and eggs in Lent). The more modest contented themselves with a slice of kid or lamb, while the poor got their nourishment from vege-tables (e.g. artichokes and beans), cheese, onions, and olives.

Spanish temperance in drinking was all the more remarkable because the provinces of Spain produced excellent wines, spoiled it is true, for foreign palates because of the taste of pitch and resin given to them by their pig-skin containers. 'They are surprisingly abstemious as regards wine,' remarks the Countess d'Aulnoy. 'The women never drink it, and the men use so little that half a *setier* (about a quarter of a litre) is enough for a day. One could not outrage them more than to accuse them of being drunk.' On the other hand, there was a great demand for iced drinks – orange juice, strawberry water, and orgeat – which, thanks to the establishment of 'snow-pits', it was now possible to prepare in the summer months. But the Spanish drink *par excellence* was chocolate, which, originating from America, had become extremely popular among all classes because of its very reasonable price. People drank it not only at breakfast, but on every occasion throughout the day, swilling it down (for it was very thick) with a glass of water.

In the majority of houses, both bourgeois and aristocratic, there was no dining-room. Dishes were served on little tables in the ordinary living-room. In Castille, and especially in Andalusia, where the Arab stamp remained most strong, only the men sat on chairs when they ate; the women and children squatted by the side of the table, supported by cushions. Lunch was quickly dispatched and, after the siesta, which was obligatory even in winter, the head of the family usually left the house to concern himself with business or pleasure, for the greater part of a man's social life, as in most Mediterranean countries, was spent outside the family circle.

The women stayed at home, looking after the children, or occupying themselves with little jobs of sewing or embroidering or, more rarely, reading some pious book or some romantic work. Visits by lady friends sometimes relieved the monotony of this existence. Squatting on the dais and the carpet, the women talked of trifling matters, of the latest fashions, and of amorous intrigues, always sipping the inevitable chocolate or chewing bits of *bucaro*, a special kind of potter's clay with an aromatic flavour, which was imported from the Spanish Indies. Madame d'Aulnoy tells us that Spanish women were so fond of it that often their confessors merely imposed on them the penance of abstinence from it for a whole day.

Sometimes the sound of a guitar or other instrument was heard under the windows of the house. The practice of serenading was permitted on the part of a successful suitor for the hand of a young lady. But the serenader might perhaps be some 'spark' who desired to prove the ardour of his love for the woman of his dreams, and who, accompanied by musicians hired for the occasion, hoped to be rewarded for his attentions by a glance, a smile, or a loving word through the iron trellis which separated him from her. Such audacities were not without their risks because, even if the husband was not keeping an eye on his wife, her brother would not be less jealous of the good reputation of their sister, as was shown by the misadventure which befell the Duke of Sessa in 1619. We have it from the gossip writer of the time that the Duke was out for a breath of fresh air at midnight (it was in the month of July), in a side street in Madrid, accompanied by a mulatto page-boy, who was singing and playing the guitar. A voice from a nearby window asked the guitarist to play something or other, which he did by order of his master. As luck would have it the Duke of Maqueda, whose sister lived in the same place, happened to be passing. Infuriated, he went into the house to fetch a shield, and while his men were smashing the mulatto's guitar on his head, he fell upon Sessa and – without even recognizing him – launched an attack upon him and slashed open the whole of the right side of his face.[12]

Even though the education of young ladies was generally neglected, and many fathers, like Molière's Arnolphe, considered it to be the source of loose behaviour, there were some cultured women. Some of them prided themselves on their knowledge of literature and philosophy and sometimes gathered in little cultural groups in their homes, where they used all the refinements of language which the poetry of the time had made fashionable. Calderon, in his play *One Must not Trifle with Love*, presents a character, Beatrice, who reminds one of both *Les Précieuses ridicules* and Bélise in *Les Femmes savantes*. She would never soil her lips with vulgar words and uses affectations for everything: for instance, a mirror is 'an enchantment-crystal'. All this unleashed the fury of her father, Alfonso:

'I am going to put an end to this nonsense; enough of study, enough of poetry; in my home, no more of those books in Latin which I can't understand. A book of hours is quite enough for a woman. Let her learn how to embroider, to darn, to sew, and leave study to men. Now, pay attention to this: I will give you a crack on the head if I hear you call a spade anything else but a spade! . . .'[13]

As for Quevedo, he only laughs at the pretentions of his *Savante latiniparle*. For him, confirmed misogynist and connoisseur of women that he is, all it means is that these ladies, having been denied graces of the body, have tried to make up for them with those of the mind. 'Let us praise their pretty turn of phrase and their learning and give them a place in the library, but not in our hearts.'[14]

But, as is natural, the cares of the heart, and, in consequence, those of elegance and fashion were the real preoccupations of women, and for most of them the boudoir (*tocador*) was the most important room in the house. In his *Morning of the Day of the Festival* Zabaleta has amusingly described the preparations of an elegant lady who wants to go out appearing at her very best:

'She gets up and goes to her boudoir wearing a petticoat and bodice. She sits herself on a little cushion, in front of her dressing-table, and places on her right a little box which contains all her beauty-aids and about a thousand other accessories. While she paints herself in front, her maid powders her from behind.'

The use and abuse of cosmetics in the feminine toilet is a fact vouched for not only by contemporary writers and travellers but also by the portraits of Velazquez, who has preserved the evidence for us. It was not merely a question of a little make-up but a veritable box of paints applied to the face, to the shoulders, to the neck, and even to the ears. Ceruse (*solimán*) was the 'foundation-cream', on which was applied, without any discretion, pink and vermillion. 'They paint their cheeks with scarlet,' remarks Brunel, 'but so thickly that they appear to want to disguise themselves rather than to beautify.' Quevedo is more brutal in speaking of a lady who 'daubs the pallor of her complexion to look like the door of a tap-room. . . .' Their lips also were painted or covered with a thin layer of wax to make them gleam; and for the care of their hands they used a special almond paste and ointments made from bacon fat. They also used an abundance of perfumes – rosewater and ambergris – and, if one can believe Madame d'Aulnoy, if the lady had no scent-spray, her maid sucked in the water and projected it in little drops through her teeth all over the face and body of her mistress.[15]

One of the most bizarre elements of feminine attire was the wearing of spectacles, which became fashionable at the beginning of the seventeenth century. Quevedo in particular helped to launch this particular fashion, and the word 'quevedos' came to be used to describe them.

'Everybody wears glasses, regardless of sex or age, the young and the old, aged women and young girls, sages and fools, laymen and clerics alike. Different shapes are used, according to social standing. Aristocrats of the first water wear grand large ones and hook them over their ears. Nothing is thought more elegant than young women with their noses straddled by a pair of spectacles which conceal half their faces and serve no purpose at all. And they wear them all day long, even though they do nothing but gossip, and some ladies remove their glasses only when they go to bed.'[16]

This was not the only extravagance of feminine fashion, at least in the higher classes of society. It must be remembered that, up to the end of the Old Régime, feminine vogues – like men's clothes – indicated a social status. One only has to look at 'The Spinners' by Velazquez, to see women dressed in blouse and skirt, differing little from the feminine attire of today, to realize that the dress of the aristocratic ladies who sat for the court painters was the apanage of the idle minority for whom the concerns of the toilet were the main preoccupation (which 'professional models' copied because in their work they had to be dressed in the fashionable style of the day).

In society, the most characteristic of women's garments was the *guardinfante*, which, to quote Zabaleta, 'is the silliest extravagance which women who want to look elegant have ever fallen for'. A development of the farthingale, which was common in European feminine fashion at the end of the sixteenth century, the *guardinfante* was a framework of hoops made from whalebone and osier twigs and padded, the function of which was to 'belly out' the shape of the petticoat (or *basquine*) which hid it, and the gown which covered it, giving to the whole the shape of a bell. This outline was accentuated even more by a tight-fitting jacket, worn over a whalebone corset, which squeezed the breasts and restricted the waist – as it were cutting the body in two. To add to this deformation of the female silhouette, the sleeves are 'ballooned' at the shoulders and 'slashed' at the wrists to reveal vivid linings and ending in tight cuffs, which were often decorated by precious embroidery. Full-length gowns made of heavy materials – taffetas, watered silk or brocade – completely hid the feet, which it was immodest to reveal. They wore leather shoes, but it was customary to wear, over the shoes, clogs (*chapines*) with wooden soles and cork heels, which, by raising the body, gave Spanish women, generally rather small, a more imposing stature, and so helped a little to compensate for the grotesque silhouette of the *guardin-fante*.

This became more and more exaggerated during the reign of Philip IV, to the point where, according to a contemporary gossip, women could not get through the doors of churches;[17] a fact which provoked both the moralists and the satirical writers, and not without reason. In fact – and the nickname attached to this piece of feminine apparel is significant – the 'ball' allowed its wearer to conceal from the eyes of the world signs of a pregnancy which was not necessarily the fruit of legitimate passion; it thus also gave a certain security to feminine libertinism. So, in 1633, a royal decree forbade the wearing of the *guardinfante*, except by women 'who are licensed by the public authority to traffic in their bodies; they are at liberty to wear this costume'. Despite the first rigorous enforcement of this decree (the police on the beat, under a hail of coarse jokes from passers-by, stripped women who insisted on wearing the cumbersome *guardinfante*), and despite the risk of being mistaken for prostitutes, women of distinction reverted to the old fashion as soon as the first scare was over. The authorities were even more baffled when the second wife of Philip IV, Marie-Anne of Austria, set the example of wearing a larger and more voluminous *guardinfante* than had ever been seen before.[18] It was only in the following reign that this fashion gradually disappeared.

The articles of a 'pragmatic sanction' of 1639 were equally ineffective in checking the abuse of feminine *décolletage*. At the beginning of the century the tight bodice was high-necked and fitted closely over the throat. Gradually, however, the corsage shrank to reveal the shoulders, the upper part of the back, and, very often, that part of the body where neck and bosom meet. 'It is quite certain,' said Zabaleta, 'that women who dress *à la mode* clothe themselves in such a manner that would be more decent if they went about stark naked. . . .'

It is true that outside their homes these ladies wore a cloak, or more precisely a vast sleeveless cape which enveloped them from head to foot and covered the entire toilet. But, even when the *manta* was not made of tulle or transparent silk, which formed a 'mantle of mist, it was an instrument of coquetry and female seductiveness for the rare – and therefore all the more precious – outings which custom allowed them or which boldness won for them.

The most common opportunity was provided by the observance of religious duties at the parish church or in certain conventual chapels which had the reputation of being particularly 'refined'. For a lady of quality would not normally go alone into the streets; she would be accompanied by a duenna, or a squire, whose long beard guaranteed respectability and who escorted her, occasionally taking her hand, which she would keep wrapped in a fold of her cloak, so that he would not touch her bare skin. For those who were not rich enough to have an equerry permanently in their service one could hire an *écuyer de métaphore*, for whom there was, especially in Madrid, a permanent market in certain squares. These also provided pages to follow their mistress, carrying a velvet or silken cushion on which she would kneel to pray. But, if such an escort was a sign of the social standing of the lady he accompanied, he could not steer his mistress clear of all perils, and the duennas had at least in literature, and without doubt in real life also, the reputation, in return for little presents, of acting as honest brokers between the gallants and the ladies, married or not, whom they were wooing. We should not accept to the letter the strictures of the moralists who presented the churches as little more than places of assignation. Most women went to church with no other intention than to attend Mass and to listen to the sermon, but for more than one no doubt the divine office provided the opportunity for furtive meetings.

Women would also go on the arms of their husbands – sometimes of their lovers – to take part in the great public festivals, which the whole of the town's population attended. They could also go to the theatre, but there the rule of the segregation of the sexes was strictly adhered to, since there was a gallery specially reserved for the ladies.

Finally, even the most respectable women were sometimes tempted by the pleasure of escaping from their domestic seclusion to mix with the crowds of strollers and idlers in the streets and to amuse themselves with the attentions of the opposite sex, preserving their anonymity under the cloaks which completely covered them and which were pulled down over their faces, allowing only one eye to peep out. The wearing of the *tapado* (veil) was a typical deviation from a traditional custom. There is little doubt that the custom of veiling the face was part of Spain's Moorish heritage from the days when women were real recluses. But as early as the sixteenth century the veil became an instrument in the seductive art. The veil gave only a hint of the face beneath, but it could add a piquancy to a pretty look or lend imaginary charms to those women who were lacking in real ones and knew how to use it to excite the attentions of men who without this disguise would not give a second glance. In the reign of Philip II the Council of Castille inveighed against this abuse of the veil:

'The custom of women to go veiled [*tapadas*] has become so excessive that it is now prejudicial to the best interests of the State, for, because of this fashion a father no longer recognizes his daughter, nor a husband his wife, nor a brother his sister. Women use the veil as and when they please and it gives men the chance to accost the wives or daughters of gentlefolk, as if they were people of low and vile character.'[19]

On the other hand courtesans and prostitutes could easily pass themselves off, under the *tapado*, as 'ladies of quality'. Thus, by decree in 1590, Philip II forbade its use, without success, however, for his successors periodically tried to renew the prohibition, and, in 1639, Philip IV announced severe penalties for those contravening the regulations: a fine of 1,000 maravedis, double that for second offenders, plus the confiscation of the 'guilty' article.

For all that, a contemporary writer judged it necessary to temper the severity of this penalty by distinguishing between the different ways of covering the face, and write a very serious treatise entitled: *Veils, ancient and modern, on the faces of women; their seemliness and their danger.*[20] His argument is full of interest because, in describing the different methods of using the cloak, he clearly denounces the artifice of the *tapado*.

'To cover oneself [*cubrirse*] means to let the hood of the cloak fall over the face naturally and without affectation; to veil oneself [*taparse*] is to hide one's face *de medio ojo*, by folding and refolding the cloak so as to reveal only one of the eyes (which is always the left eye), the rest of the face seeming more hidden and disguised than if it were entirely covered up. To go about with a bared face is immaterial; to cover it is a good thing. But it is bad to veil only half one's face, for this is a lascivious thing, under the guise of propriety; it is a stratagem for women who wish to appear lady-like; it is a bait for grown men, a lure for youngsters; it is a fraud on beauty; *it is a double-agent who impels the enemy to the attack for the sheer pleasure of repelling it.'*

The author concludes that the *tapado de medio ojo* should be strictly proscribed, but that women should be allowed to be properly veiled, especially in churches. Such discrimination obviously lent itself to all manner of subtleties which justified all sorts of tricks. In effect, the *tapado* continued to be customary during the whole of the seventeenth century and even later; and, in many respects this practice can be considered as one of the significant elements in the condition of women, with all its contradictions.

The highest mark of distinction for a woman was, without gainsay, to have her own carriage and pair. Despite its high price, the carriage supplanted the litter and the sedan-chair more and more as the vehicle for people of quality for their journeys in town. The number of privately-owned carriages was already considerable at the beginning of the seventeenth century, when the court was held at Valladolid, but, during the reign of Phillip IV it increased to such an extent that at the time of the daily 'constitutional', movement of traffic in the main street of Madrid was very difficult, and there were 'bottle-necks' which immobilized the carriages on their way at the end of the day towards the promenade of the Prado.

The other great cities – Barcelona, Valencia, Seville – did not emulate the capital, where official measures were taken by the royal government to restrict the use of carriages to a minority of the very rich (for example, there was a prohibition on the use of carriages drawn by less than four mules, the cost and maintenance of which were very onerous). But nothing abated the 'carriage craze' (*fiebre cocheril*) which, fed by feminine vanity, caused havoc even among the middle classes. Zabaleta records the fact that: 'There is not a *hidalgo*, even the most penurious, who will allow his wife to go out in a carriage less elegant than that of his neighbour, forcing him into an expenditure which his entire inheritance was not large enough to cover.' Quevedo for his part was ironic about men reduced to misery because they are forced to fast in honour of 'St Carriage', and one could make a whole anthology of literary extracts, especially scenes from plays, which portray the hapless husband or the unfortunate gallant, tormented by the

11. A troupe of strolling players meets Don Quixote

THE
HISTORY OF
DON-QVICHOTE.
The first parte.

PRINTED FOR ED: BLOUNTE

12. 'The History of Don Quichote'

entreaties of their ladies who cannot decently venture abroad on foot.[21]

But if woman's vanity there received its due, it was not always the same with their virtue. The Portuguese, Pinheiro, in a picture which he has left us of life in Valladolid when that city played the role of capital, said: 'The ladies at the court spend the larger part of the life in their carriages, witnesses of their straying from the path of virtue, and it is their coachmen who act as their confessors: the sins of the one help them to forget those of the other. . . .' Malicious evidence perhaps but it seems to confirm a 'pragmatic sanction' of Philip III, which forebade the use of the carriages to men under the pretext that they were '. . . combining business with pleasure'. But the fact that a woman may be accompanied by her husband, her father, or her children shows well enough that, under the 'official' explanation, the real reason lay discreetly hidden – to prevent the leather blinds which covered the windows being used to transform the carriage into a 'love-nest'. The *cicisbeos* had, then, to content themselves with escorting the carriages, and exchanging conversation with their ladies sitting close to the window, its blinds open. A woman could not travel in a carriage with face unveiled and the *tapado* was strictly forbidden. These regulations, intended to improve the use of the carriages, soon became, like so many others, dead-letters, a fact confirmed by their repeal and re-enactments throughout the reign of Philip IV.

But confirmation by official documents of purely literary sources should not lead us to jump to general conclusions. The latter were often written in a satiric vein which distorts reality. The former were intended to curb excesses, not to approve the normal state of things. Futhermore, one should remember that their criticisms were levelled at only a small part of the female world, those who, living in big cities and especially in the atmosphere of the court, were more or less touched by the moral laxity – incontestable as it is – which affected the ruling classes. These things concern only a tiny minority, but their mode of life attracted attention and aroused envy.

In her little village in La Mancha, Theresa, the wife of Sancho Panza, sometimes had daydreams about life in the big city, symbolized by the joy she would see as 'she takes her leisure in a carriage, dazzling the eyes of a thousand envious people. . . .' But

L

all the same she continued to live the hard and simple life of a countrywoman or, indeed, of a suburban woman of modest means for whom the refinements of fashion, the luxury of a carriage, and all the displays of splendour of the grand life were nothing more than the trappings of a life completely foreign to her own existence.

CHAPTER NINE

UNIVERSITY LIFE AND
THE WORLD OF LETTERS

*I. University life. Salamanca, Alcala, and the 'sylvan' universities –
University organization. Education. Examinations and the conferment
of degrees – Student life. The 'major colleges' and grants for students.
The 'student hunger' – Recreations and entertainments. Bullying and
violence – The decay of the universities*

*II. The world of letters. The grandeur and bondage of a writer's life:
Lope de Vega – The passion for learning and the academies of poetry
Refinement of literary language.*

In the debate 'The Sword versus the Pen' which he puts into the
mouth of Don Quixote, Cervantes amuses himself by drawing a
parallel between the work and wretchedness which are the lot of
both the student and the sodier, to award to the latter the palm
for ability and endurance alike. Students and soldiers: the two
between them made the Golden Age, but while the superiority of
Spanish arms declined on the battlefields of Europe, Spain imposed
on her adversaries the hegemony of her culture. For the honour
of their country, the graduates of Salamanca and Alcala reinforced
the officers and men of the *tercios*.

I

Omnium scientiarum princeps Salmantica docet – 'Salamanca,
foremost in the teaching of all the sciences'. There is justifiable
pride in this motto because Salamanca was the first of the Spanish
universities and, to the end of the Middle Ages, maintained its
unique prestige and position against all rivals. But a sudden out-
burst, which was a reflection of the enthusiasm of the Renaissance,
produced the new foundations in the era of the Catholic Kings and
of Charles V. In the middle of the century a score of universities
came into being, for not only the big and ancient cities – Saragossa,
Valencia, Toledo, Seville – but even little towns – Oropesa, Baeza,

163

Osuna, and many others – demanded the right to slake their thirst at the re-discovered springs of knowledge.

Even so, there was only one serious rival to Salamanca. This was founded at Alcala de Henares in the first years of the sixteenth century by Cardinal Ximenes of Cisneros, Archbishop of Toledo and Chancellor of Castille. It appeared, because of its organization and intellectual orientation, to be a typical product of the new epoch: in contrast with the democratic spirit of Salamanca, its statutes provided for an authoritarian and centralized constitution, which found expression in the powers invested in the rector, who was nominated by the Archbishop of Toledo and represented the royal authority. Here education ignored civil law and was chiefly concerned with the study of theology (helped by the reform undertaken by Cisneros in the Spanish Church) and classic literature, including instruction in Greek, Hebrew, and philology. At the middle of the sixteenth century Madrid, only about twenty-five miles distant, became the capital city of Spain. Alcala benefitted from this proximity and the privileges granted to it by successive kings. Pupils flocked to it, and around the college of St Ildefonse, the nucleus of the new university, arose others built by the principal monastic orders. In half a century the little medieval town, hemmed in by ramparts of brick, became, in the words of Erasmus, 'the treasury of all the sciences', and its fame spread throughout Spain and even beyond its frontiers.

Though they did not attain the glories of the two great rival universities, others had their special character and vitality. Saragossa attracted students from Aragon; Valencia specialized in the study of medicine; and, in Castille itself, the nearness of Salamanca did not eclipse Valladolid, which even surpassed its neighbours in the study of Roman and Spanish law. On the other hand most of the minor universities, born in the enthusiasm of renascent humanism, had no more than a precarious life. The diplomas, which certain of them bestowed at a reduced fee in order to attract a regular clientèle of students, were disparaged, and the three rural (*silvestres*) universities of Siguenza, Onate and Osuna were, from the seventeenth century, the butt of many a joke. 'Where, then, did you do your studying?' asks the worthy and indignant Sancho Panza, having been appointed governor of the isle of Barataria, to the doctor who was charged with looking after his health, and who, in the name of Hippocrates, forbade him all the tastiest dishes on the table. 'Excellency,' replies the doctor, 'I am a graduate of the University of Osuna. . . .'[1]

The diversity of origin of the universities – pontifical or royal creation, municipal initiative or private foundation – explains the lack of uniformity in their internal organization. However, the influence of tradition imposed similar methods of teaching and the same hierarchy of university rank. Moreover, Salamanca, by virtue of its antiquity, continued to enjoy a real moral ascendancy, and certain of the articles of its 'constitutions', either spontaneously or by royal decree, had been copied by other centres of learning. Furthermore, she continued to benefit from a clear numerical superiority by the influx of students from all parts of Spain: more than 7,000 in 1584, whereas the more aristocratic Alcala never had more than 2,000 at the very height of its fame. For all these reasons Salamanca tended to impress its particular style on university life. Thus the phrase 'student of Salamanca' doubtless meant in real life as well as in the literature of the time, the very embodiment of the student's way of life.

For the student a university is not only a place of learning: it is, one can say, his property, by virtue of the rights granted to him which, in large measure, put it under his authority. The 'pragmatic' of Santa Fé, enacted by the Catholic Kings in 1492, had confirmed the immunity of students from ordinary civil law and subjected them only to the jurisdiction of the 'theological professor', who was nominated by the Pope, and whose duties included the protection of the rights and privileges of all students, among them exemption from military service and from all taxes affecting his person and his goods.

This 'rector', responsible for the general welfare of the university community and for administering its finances, was elected for one year only, by a committee made up half of professors and half of students appointed by their fellows. He himself was always a student and, in order to enhance, by the lustre of this birth, the prestige of the office, they usually chose the scion of one of the great families. Thus it was that Gasper Guzman d'Olivares, destined to become the all-powerful minister of Philip IV, was at the beginning of the seventeenth century elected 'rector of Salamanca.

As for the professors, they were chosen, not by their peers, but by the students themselves, at a public meeting at which the candidates for each chair were examined. Every precaution was officially taken to prevent canvassing or corruption from falsifying these elections. 'We direct,' said the Catholic Kings, in a decree of 1494, 'that every person attached to our universities, or exterior to them, no matter what his status, condition or eminence may be, shall not have the audacity publicly or privately to suborn those who have to elect a candidate for a new chair, or to make presents to the students who have to cast their votes; or to act on them by entreaty or by threat, whether directly or through hirelings.' In specifying, in the following year, the limits of application of this edict, the sovereigns indicated some of the practices currently in use: the formation of 'parties' in favour of different candidates; promises of presents of silver, or of 'mules, slaves, jewellery, or parcels of land to buy votes, or to obtain the withdrawal of certain candidates'.[2] All in vain; the renewal of the same edicts by Philip II and Philip III is evidence enough of their inefficacy. There were too many students for whom daily existence was a constant problem and who did not know if they would have food for the morrow for them not to be influenced when offered a present or an invitation to a lavish meal, or some other generous inducement. There was only one solution, that which Philip IV adopted in 1624: the appointment of professors to Salamanca, Valladodid, and Alcala by the Council of Castille, choosing them for their qualifications and academic merits only.

Generally speaking education had remained faithful to medieval practice both in its syllabus and in its methods of teaching: the faculty of arts where logic, rhetoric, and natural science were taught opened its doors to the more specialized subjects: theology, civil and canon law, and medicine. Each professor 'read' his lessons (hence the name 'reader' by which he is sometimes called) or dictated them to his pupils. There remained, however, for the tutors an obligation which, to some extent, mitigated the too exclusively dogmatic nature of an *ex cathedra* education: this was to 'put his back against the pillar' (*asistir al poste*), that is to say, to await his pupils after class in the cloisters of the university, where they could have any clarifications which they liked to ask. These *ex cathedra* tuitions were far more informal than they used to be. This remote reminder of the Aristotelian Porch offered the student the opportunity of close intellectual contact with his teacher, which could be most rewarding. Thus Enrique de Guzman, writing an impersonal guide for his son who was then about to begin his studies at Salamanca, does not fail to enjoin him to derive the greatest benefit from them: 'As one comes out of a class, it is necessary to go to the cloister and hear the questions put by his fellow-scholars to the master at the pillar in order to get one's difficulties solved, and to understand the subject better, which will encourage him to study with care so that he too can argue with the master.'[3]

In the first part of the sixteenth century the influence of humanism and, especially, the considerable influence of Erasmus had widened the intellectual horizon and had set on foot a new spirit, in reaction against scholastic formalism. But, after the reign of Philip II, the fear that these 'novelties' might threaten religious orthodoxy stirred up a sharp distrust of everything that was not in keeping with tradition. The proceedings taken by the Inquisition against certain professors at Salamanca – including Fray Luis de León – were ample warning to those who showed some independence in their scholastic work. The full bloom of enlightenment of the first three-quarters of the previous century was followed by a contraction marked by a return to the letter of the old laws, which insisted that each professor must lecture in the spirit of the teacher whose name was given to the professorial chair: St Augustine, St Thomas, Duns Scotus, to which was added, at the beginning of the seventeenth century, the name of the Jesuit, Suarez. Violent quarrels were the result. Both in their teaching and in the public 'disputes', masters belonging to different monastic orders blindly followed the opinions of St Augustine, of St Thomas or of Suarez, depending on whether they were Augustinian, Dominican or Jesuit. Even over the most futile questions the fury of the debate degenerated into unthinkable excesses. Barrionuevo recalls that: 'Between the Augustinians and the Trinitarians of Salamanca great debates have taken place. They came to blows, punching and kicking each other. The point in question was whether Adam remained incomplete when God removed one of his ribs and if it was with flesh alone that he filled up the cavity from which he had taken it.'[4]

The public debates at which masters and doctors confronted each other, egged on by the *vitores* ('bravoes') of their students, were red-letter days in university life, on a par with the examinations for the degrees of bachelor, licentiate, and doctor. Their conferment gave place to rejoicing in which everyone in the town joined, and each detail of the award was meticulously enumerated in the *Ceremonial*, which was the ritual of the university. The dramatist, Ruiz de Alarcón, who studied at Salamanca at the end of the sixteenth century, tells us that graduation was an expensive affair for the candidates: honorariums to the professor, to the beadles, and to the examiners themselves: tips to all those who in various ways had helped to make the show worthy of the graduation – the master of ceremonies, workmen who had the job of hanging tapestries on the front of the university, kettle-drummers, trumpeters, and bell-ringers. But the most expensive item without doubt was the cost of the banquet given to all the members of the faculty. Details of the menu and service are laid down in full in the *Ceremonial:*

'The salads must consist of various kinds of fruit, vegetables, citrates, preserves, sugared almonds, preserved cherries, eggs, and other titbits which go to make a "salade royale". . . After the salad, eggs are served. . . . After the eggs comes a dish of game – whatever is best in the season, such as partridge and poults, chicken, pigeons "*à la neige*", and other things which have the best and most delicate taste. There follows a dish of chicken hash, served with slices of bacon and sausage, pieces of rabbit and veal, with roundels of lemon and other seasoning. . . . Then comes the fish course, which must be of the choicest to be found in season, such as salmon, ell or dorado. . . . Next there must be a dessert, which normally consists of eggs *à la royale*. Sometimes blancmange is served, but as this dish is becoming less expensive, it is necessary to add another. . . . To end the meal one is offered cheese and Seville olives, bonbons of anise, and half a pound of wrapped comfits, with wafers and toothpicks.'[5]

But, as Alarcon points out, the cost of a degree of licentiate is relatively cheaper than that of a doctorate. For this highest university honour – which carries with it ennoblement – the ceremonial prescribed was a ritual as brilliant as it was ruinous for the laureate.

On the eve of the investiture there is a *paseo* (procession) in which all the masters and doctors are expected to take part. In a long procession, headed by trumpeters and drummers, the masters of ceremony are followed by the professorial staff in full dress of black, fringed hat, black robes trimmed with white lace, and covered by a cape, the colour of which denotes the different faculties: masters of arts in blue capes; theologians in white, physicians in yellow, canonists in green, and jurists in red. Then, accompanied by the dean, the rector, the beadles, and the professor sponsoring the new graduate, came the candidate, mounted on a richly caparisoned steed, dressed in velvet or silk, and wearing sword and dagger at his side. Finally, the students, along with the artisans and townfolk, brought up the rear of this long cortège, which proceded through the narrow streets of the city from the house of the laureate to the university, where a light meal and various delicacies were provided by the future doctor.

The next day begins with an interrogation of the candidate by one of his teachers in the grand hall of the university. Then, by a custom no doubt harking back to the gibes which greeted the conquering hero as he mounted the steps to the Capitol in ancient Rome, the comrades of the new graduate bombard him with highly derogatory comments on his person and talents. But a panegyric by one of those present quickly heals the wound which the gibes have opened. The procession then leaves the university and goes to the cathedral or to some other place for the final act. The new doctor there receives the insignia of his degree, which he hands over to his sponsor, and dons the doctorial cap. Then, seated in a chair, he takes the oath and reads the opening words of the Gospel according to St John: '*In principio erat verbum . . .*', to which all present listen kneeling.

When the ceremony was over, the rejoicings began and, as was customary in all great celebrations, there was a *corrida* in which at least five bulls must be put to death. It was in vain that Pope Sixtus V, recalling the general excommunication issued by Pius V against all clerics who attended these bloody spectacles, again condemned the professors of Salamanca, a condemnation which applied 'equally to professors of sacred theology as to professors of civil law, who are not only unashamed to be seen at the bull-fights, but have the temerity to affirm and teach in their lectures that clerics wearing their holy orders are guilty of no sin in this respect...' The attraction of these traditional fêtes proved stronger than the threats of spiritual punishment. In a reply addressed to Sixtus V, and bearing the signature of Fray Luis de Léon, the Assembly asked the Pope not to enforce a measure 'which would be prejudicial to the peace and good order of this seat of learning'.[6]

169

Now all that remained for the new graduate was to count the cost of the disbursements which represented the high dignity he had acquired, and which, in addition to the high costs of staging a *corrida*, included a whole series of gifts, details of which were fixed by the constitution and traditions of the university: fifty florins to the dean and to the sponsor, two gold pieces to each doctor, 100 silver reals to the beadle and to the college notary; and, on top of all this, were presents in kind: pairs of gloves, bags of sugar, and three brace of chickens for each, without counting the 'sweeteners' and the delicacies used during the *corrida*. The cost was so great that sometimes several students arranged to have their doctor's degrees conferred on the same day so as to share the expenses among them, an economy which was offset by the obligation to make an even braver show and to provide a larger number of bulls, ten or more. . . .

The organization of Salamanca has been defined as 'the students' democracy'. But the equality of principle which conferred on all students the benefit of common privileges, and the chance of participating directly in the recruitment of their own masters did not do away with class distinctions. It was not only the sons of the nobility and of the wealthy bourgeoisie who came to sit on the wooden benches of the lecture rooms. A great many families of modest means managed, at the cost of great sacrifice, to send a boy to fight for an honour which would earn for him an ecclesiastical benefice or the chance to enter, as a *letrado*, the civil service. And so, under the short cassock (*loba*) and the square cap, which made up the normal uniform of the students, their social lives, in fact, displayed a wide disparity.

At the top of the pyramid of this society was the son of an illustrious family. He would arrive, with numerous servants, and would take up residence at a house specially purchased or leased for him. Thus, Gaspar de Guzman came to Salamanca in 1601 accompanied by a preceptor, a tutor, eight pages, three valets, four footmen, a chef, and several grooms and servants; he rode to lectures on horseback, with his household cortège, who waited at the gate of the university to escort him back to his home. . . .

Equally favoured were those who had been admitted to an 'upper school' (*Colegio Mayor*). These 'upper schools' were founded by prelates or pious people who were anxious to give poor students the opportunity to pursue their studies secure from financial worries. In the second half of the sixteenth century, however, they turned away from their original purpose and became of an increasingly aristocratic character because of the manner by which they secured the recruitment of 'bursars'. This recruitment tended to become more and more selective, for there was a tight solidarity uniting the 'collegiates', who aimed to monopolize the best appointments both in the Church and in the state. They had at court their patrons (*hacedores*), chosen from amongst the most influential 'old boys' who undertook to look after their interests when it came to the securing of a benefice or some high office, and who, in return, obtained for their relatives and protégés admission to the 'Major Colleges'. Even within the university the collegiates were a group apart. When a new teacher was to be elected, they voted in a body for the candidate coming from their ranks. They had nothing but contempt for the bursars of the 'Minor Colleges' (*Colegios menores*), whose numbers increased as the 'Major Colleges' ceased to fulfil their original function, and in defiance of the earlier statutes which forbade students to wear ornate gowns, they now flaunted mantles made of costly and splendid materials.

But for the most part, the students lived outside the colleges and away from the material security which they were afforded there. University authorities endeavoured to help them with their difficulties, especially as to their lodgings, exercising careful supervision of the 'housemasters', that is, the owners of boarding-houses officially recognized as suitable for scholars. A regulation issued at Salamanca in 1534 not only set standards for these hostels but also charged the landlords to keep an eye on the morals and the studies of their guests. Doors were to be shut each evening at half-past seven; they were to do a round of the rooms, each morning and evening, to see that no one was missing; to make sure they attended the classes laid down in the syllabus; to prevent futile discussions between the students, and on the other hand to organize sessions in which the students could mull over the lessons of the day; and, finally, to prohibit absolutely card-playing and dicing, on pain of immediately losing the licence granted by the university.[7]

As far as food was concerned, these 'housemasters' were obliged to provide a pound of meat a day for each student–half a pound at breakfast and half a pound at dinner – together with hors d'œuvre, a dessert, and a 'reasonable' quantity of bread and wine, without counting the extras customary on the days of the major feasts of the year.

We do not know if the scholastic and moral clauses remained in force for any length of time or whether the diet prescribed in other universities was as generous as that at Salamanca. What is certain is that these 'housemasters' acquired an invidious reputation as 'soup merchants', more interested in economizing on food than in improving young minds, and that they make stock characters in the satirical literature of the time. The full force of Quevedo's flashing wit was deployed in describing the visit paid by Don Pablos of Segovia to the house of one of them, the licensee Cagra, nicknamed 'Valiant-for-Fasting', who was particularly anxious that his guests should not suffer from the effects of overeating.

'After the *benedicite*, wooden bowls were served containing a soup so clear that, in seeking to sup it, Narcissus would have run as great a peril as in looking at himself in the pool. I was fascinated by the skinny fingers of the guests as they fished for an orphaned split-pea, at the bottom of the bowl. At each mouthful, Cagra would exclaim: "Nothing like a good home-made soup. It is well said that all else is a sin and an 'indulgence'." After the feast, he would go on: "Now my lads, take some exercise for a couple of hours so that what you have eaten doesn't upset you." '

An empty belly seemed to be an essential for the exercise and observance of this diet. 'I would have explained,' said Pablos, 'this fundamental principle to the others, but I was so famished that I gulped down the rest of my words. . . .'[8]

All the same, the students were assured of a roof over their heads and food of sorts. Their state was sumptuous compared with that of the *capigorristas*, that is, the poor students who, in place of the ample cloak, wore a simple cape, which gave them little protection from cold weather, and a *gorra* (a sort of cap) instead of the 'square'. For them, existence was a daily problem. Obviously they could ask their parents for help, but these had already bled themselves white in order to send their sons to the university, and the student waited impatiently for the courier who perhaps would bring further money. But such windfalls were rare, and he had to console himself by burning the family letter, so full of good advice but devoid of money, and by chanting with his comrades the *Paulina*, a parody of the Lord's Prayer: 'Inhuman and cruel parents, fathers who do not send us our daily bread, may you suffer each week our daily hunger, and, as this paper burns, may the money which you refuse to send us change to ashes in your coffers. Amen.'

Some students found other ways of raising funds. They worked as servants for their more affluent friends, who had their own houses or hired apartments, and divided their time between the daily chores and the study of Aristotle and St Thomas. Others became waiters in some tavern or – worse – worked in the kitchen. The final step down was to get a mendicant's certificate (for that profession was controlled), and Charles V and his son, Philip II, both laid down conditions under which students might thus perform: 'Students can ask for alms under licence from the rector of their university, or, failing that, from the ecclesiastical court of their diocese.'[9] They would then have the right, along with other licensed beggars, to go to the soup kitchens (*sopa boba*) which the monks opened daily in front of their monasteries, after having prolonged the agony of hunger of their guests by the saying of grace.

This student hunger, all-consuming and never satisfied, is indissolubly linked, in all the literature of the time, with the idea of university life. 'If hunger and the mange,' says Cervantes, 'were not so closely identified with students, there would be no more agreeable way of life or of passing one's time, for virtue goes hand in hand with pleasure and one's youth is spent in learning and in amusing oneself.'[10] But the fun helped one to forget the hunger: Mateo Aleman asks:

'Is there a more beautiful life than that of the student? Is there a happier one? Is there any kind of amusement which is denied to students? Are they diligent? Then they will meet their like. Are they spoilt children? They will not lack companions. . . . Where else can one find such excellent friends? . . . O, sweet student life! To play the fool, dressed up as a bishop:[11] to buy votes on election days; to support one's compatriots through thick and thin; and to pawn all that one has until the messenger and the money arrive, not before time; something pledged with the pastrycook, and something else with the grocer: the works of Duns Scotus with the man who sells fritters; Aristotle's with the wine-merchant; to have one's coat of mail hidden under the mattress, one's sword under the bed, and one's buckler being used as a lid for the slop-pail in the kitchen. . . . Is there a confectioner's shop where we did not have our bill put on the "slate" when our pockets were empty?'[12]

The ragging of freshmen – a tradition faithfully adopted by the new university of Alcala – was in doubtful taste and was sometimes extremely rough. The freshman (*novato*) was immediately spotted because of the prim and proper way in which he wore his new gown and square cap. He would be immediately surrounded by a group of 'old hands' who would ask him with mock kindliness: 'Well then, you've left mama and papa? You didn't cry surely? . . . What a magnificent gown! It looks strong enough' – and someone would try to tear the sleeve. 'And what a lovely cap!' – the cap would be tossed from hand to hand, until, its four corners all squashed in, it was roughly crammed back over the ears of its owner.[13] But this was only the beginning. Pablos of Segovia tells us about the next stage of the initiation (*novatada*):

'I entered the main court [of Alcala University], and I had hardly set foot in it, then various scholars stared at me and said, "Look, a new boy!" I laughed to make them think that they were mistaken, but in vain. . . . There must have been about a hundred round me. They began to sniffle and reading their lips, I could guess what was to happen. One of them, a lad with a bad cold, spat a huge gob at me. I shouted: "By God you'll . . ." but I got no further.[14] A veritable torrent of spittle rained on me. I hid my face in a fold of my cloak, but they all made me their target, and they were all crack shots. I was constellated with white from head to foot, and I looked like the spittoon of some old asthmatic.'

This practice of *sacar nevado* ('making as white as snow'), according to contemporary evidence, was followed by even more disgusting pleasantries which might be carried on for several days. Finally, this initiation would be brought to an end by a meal which the freshman had to provide for the 'bloods', who would toast him with, 'For he's a jolly good fellow! He's one of us now. Let him forthwith enjoy all our privileges: may he get the mange and die of hunger like the rest of us!' He could henceforth join in all the fun and the squabbles offered by this new world, which, to quote Cervantes, was 'amiable, fantastic, intrepid, free and easy, amorous, spendthrift, diabolical, and amusing'. This was the world of the student.

The diversions were not only those offered by a university calendar, plentifully strewn with festivals; there were also those which were specifically forbidden by academic rule: cards, dice and, above all, amorous adventures. Such regulations were more easily honoured in the breach than the observance. For the *galanteo de monjas* was an accepted practice in Salamanca and other university towns, where certain students pursued amorous casuistry in the parlours of the convents, which were more numerous than the colleges. But, away from the constraining shelter of the wicket-gate, 'young ladies' of slightly skittish virtue and all ready to console the students for the many vexations of their existence, abounded in all the university towns. Though their favours were venal, they nevertheless gave rise to rivalries which sometimes ended in duels, in brawls, and even in murder. Guzman of Alfarache was not the only one to hide his sword under the bed, and many a student wore a coat of mail under his gown, and dagger and sword at his side, when he went out at night.

Another cause of friction was the existence of various 'nations', or factions of students, who came from the different provinces of Spain. Disputes might arise over the election of a new master, each 'nation' backing its own compatriot, but more often the trouble started because the factions were always mocking and jeering at each other. A frivolous quarrel arises between two students belonging to different 'nations' and, when their respective friends join in, a battle ensues which is ended only with the arrival of the common enemy: the gentlemen of the watch, who were born enemies of the students. They treated the young men with even less sympathy because of their privileges which protected them from the ordinary processes of the common law. Such privileges gave rise to abuses which, in 1645, were denounced by a royal commission set up to study the problem: 'One finds, in the registers of the universities, the names of people over the age of twenty who have no intention of pursuing their studies and never, in fact, do so. Their sole purpose is to act the bully and lead a disorderly and immoral life, tending thereby to corrupt the students of tender age.' In consequence, the commission proposed a tightening of discipline, insisting that all undergraduates should attend all their lectures and should learn to speak Latin: otherwise they would be handed over to the *corrégidor*, that is, the ordinary courts of law, and treated as vagabonds.[15]

The citizens of Salamanca, like those of Alcala, were victims of these excesses. They clearly knew that almost all the livelihood of the town depended on the presence of the university, and that its printing house, its bookshops, its boarding-houses, and the whole of its trade would cease but for the large student population. But how to tolerate not only the shop-lifting (Pablos of Segovia, a student at Alcala, boasted that he was a past master in this art), but also the house-breaking, the seduction of girls, and other 'pranks' of the same order? On various occasions, the citizens sided with the police against the students, and criminal justice did not hesitate – in spite of the famous university *fueros* – to hang some of the ring-leaders to re-establish law and order.[16]

Without doubt such excesses and the vigorous measures of the authorities contributed to the waning of academic life at the beginning of the seventeenth century. But the real causes were intellectual: Spain's increasing introversion ever since the time of Philip II: hostility to all new ideas, and a regression to the methods and the spirit of scholasticism, after the flowering of the first half of the sixteenth century had withered away. Finally, there was the ever-increasing challenge of the Jesuit colleges which attracted the better elements of high society in Spain. The foundation of the Imperial College of Madrid in 1625, despite the protestations of Salamanca, Alcala, and other great universities, seemed, from this point of view, to be an event of special significance. A splendid era in university life had indeed ended; but the place which it held in the most celebrated authors of the time remains the most eloquent witness to the part which the universities had played in the spiritual formation of those things which made the Golden Age so illustrious.

II

Without doubt Lope de Vega is our best guide to the world of letters, not only because of the exceptional scope and genius of his work, but also because his life epitomizes all the triumphs and, above all, the hardships of the writer, and we cross the battlefields on which were fought the literary struggles of the time. The very existence of so extraordinary a personality in the Golden Age sheds a curious light on certain moral deviations of the entire social structure.[17]

Coming from a doubtless ordinary family which originated in the Montaña (that is, the Asturias), Lope Felix de Vega Carpio did not escape from the snobbery of the time. Although his father was only an 'embroiderer' (or, more precisely, the owner of an embroidery workshop, and benefiting from certain privileges attaching to a profession considered to be particularly honourable), he sought later, as his literary reputation began to grow, to assume the prestige of noble birth connected with his second patronymic, that of Bernardo del Carpio – the conqueror of Roland at Ronceval, according to Spanish legend – from whom he took his coat of arms (also legendary) with its blazon of nineteen turrets.

He went first to a Jesuit school in Madrid, in 1572, when he was eleven years old. His precocious talents brought him the patronage of Jerome de Manrique, a high ecclesiastical dignitary, later to become Bishop of Cartagena. Thanks to him, the young Lope was admitted to Santiago, one of the 'Major Colleges' of Alcala, and his future seemed assured: to take holy orders and to live – like his enemy Gongora – on the income from a prebend or an ecclesiastical benefice. But did he merely frequent the courts of the university? His name is not in the matriculation register which has survived for this period, but, without doubt, he knew all about the life of students, their freedoms, comradeship, and pleasures which are eulogized in *Guzman de Alfarache*. In any case, he left Alcala without graduating and for several years little is known of him. It seems that he led a life of adventure in the company of strolling actors and actresses, and during this period he began his career as playwright and seducer.

He next appeared in Madrid in 1583, linked with a group of young men who formed a Bohemian set, bent on pleasure, but also hankering after danger and glory. An opportunity arose: a naval expedition to subdue the Azores, who refused to accept their seizure by Spain from the Portuguese. Lope de Vega set sail from Lisbon with a few friends, but the success of the campaign did not encourage him to take up a military career. When he returned to the capital it was to the Muses – and particularly to Melpomene – that he dedicated himself. To Jerome Velazquez, the manager of a theatrical company, he supplied a number of plays, which established his reputation and, at the same time, made money for

M

Velazquez. But when Lope offered his plays to the impresario, he had an ulterior motive. He was after Jerome's daughter, Elena, already married to an actor but separated from him, and, aided and abetted it seems by her mother, he made an easy conquest. Too easy in fact: taking advantage of Lope's absence in Seville, the fair lady found a richer and more powerful protector. Lope avenged himself, not only by shifting his allegiance from Velazquez to a rival producer, but also by writing atrociously violent satirical verses about Elena and her family:

> The lady sells herself to any buyer.
> She is put up for auction. Who will buy?
> Her father bargains; she says not a word.
> Her mother decks her out to walk the streets.[18]

But the actors retaliated by charging the writer with defamation. Lope was arrested during a performance in the very theatre in which he had come to show his defiance. He was interrogated. He contemptuously denied every charge. He was given a heavy sentence: eight years' banishment from Madrid and two years of exile from the 'kingdom' (that is, all territories under the sovereignty of Castille).

He was given two weeks to leave Madrid: just time enough for him to make himself guilty of another equally grave crime – an abduction. Lope had already consoled himself for the perfidy of Elena, and had become suddenly infatuated with a young middle-class girl, Isabella de Urbina, whose parents would never have agreed to a marriage with a penniless poet. But, aided by a constable, whom he had persuaded to go to the girl and make the dreaded pronouncement 'In the name of the Inquisition . . .' (an injunction which no one dared disregard), Lope got Isabella out of the house and eloped with her to Valencia. But the risk was great. For abduction was punishable by death and justice could hunt down the wanted man throughout Spain. It was necessary, then, to flee. Then the unhappy and pregnant Isabella was sent back to Madrid, though it is true Lope had arranged to marry her by proxy. But where to hide himself? Luckily for Lope the whole of Spain was at that time in the grip of a religious and patriotic fervour. The 'Invincible Armada', sworn to destroy the might of England, was gathering its ships in Lisbon and volunteers streamed in from every direction to take part in this great enterprise. Lope decided to rejoin his squadron. Surely this was the way, first to be forgotten, and then to return covered with glory to ask for the amnesty which they could not deny to one who had helped in a victory for Spain?

The outcome, as one knows, was quite different from his expectations, and Lope de Vega, aboard the *San Juan*, could win none of the laurels acquired by Cervantes in the battle of Lepanto fifteen years earlier. So he went back to Spain and made a secret journey through Castille to Valencia where he again joined his wife Isabella, the marriage by proxy having meanwhile expunged the accusation of abduction.

The people of Valencia had a passionate love for the theatre, and it was a boon to the *corral de la Olivera* (the Olivaire Theatre) to have this 'manufacturer' of plays whose reputation was already widely known. As far as Lope was concerned, he enjoyed all the pleasures offered to him by a city reputed to be the gayest and friendliest in the whole of Spain.

Despite the distractions of the capital of the Levant, Lope was determined to return to Castille. His term of exile from the 'kingdom' expired in 1590. Unable to go to Madrid (from which he had been banished for eight years), he travelled to Toledo and became the personal servant (*criado*) and secretary of Francisco de Ribera. Next year, however, he obtained by chance the patronage of a man of far greater importance, Diego Alvarez of Toledo, Duke of Alba, who took him to Alba de Tormes, where he normally lived. Alba is only a small town, but Salamanca, which was quite near, offered to an old student of Alcala the lively ambiance of university life. Lope found frequent opportunity for escapades and amorous adventures. Meanwhile, at Alba de Tormes, the Duke of Alba held his little court in his palace, with an 'academy' at which poetry contests between members of the household were held.

Five years passed thus. They were productive years from the literary point of view, until Lope had a brush with the Duke and left the palace to return to Toledo. He returned alone, for his wife Isabella had died a little while before. But there was another misfortune which perhaps affected him even more: the death of the Princess Catherine of Savoy, daughter of Philip II, which caused the immediate closure of all theatres, and then, as a result of the urgent intervention of a group of theologians, a complete ban on theatrical productions, which were held to be no more than schools of immorality (1598).

How then to live henceforth? He could no longer count on selling his pieces to the directors of companies. As to booksellers, they paid so badly for works of prose and verse that the less said the better. Clearly it was time to find another patron, and luckily Lope met the Duke of Sarria (later Count of Lemos and the patron of Cervantes). Lope became his secretary, with the special task of drafting his love letters. At the same time Lope dreamed of exploiting his own amours, or at least their possibilities. He therefore paid court to Juana de Guardo, the daughter of an extremely rich wholesale grocer, specializing in contracts for the revictualling of the city of Madrid, from whom one could hope for a handsome dowry in compensation for his daughter's ugliness. Despite the opposition of her father, insensible to poetry's charms, Lope – who could not resist the idea of seduction – brought the matter to a head, with disastrous results: his father-in-law refused to give his daughter a dowry. For his part the poet, it is true, lost no time in consoling himself for the lack of Juana's charms. He had not been married for three months when he began courting an actress who was 'resting', one Micaela de Lujan, aged about twenty-seven or eight, beautiful, witty, but already married to a mediocre actor, by whom she had three children. No sooner had the conquest been achieved than the Duke of Sarria ordered Lope to accompany him to Valencia to attend the great celebrations in honour of the marriage of Philip III to Margaret of Austria. There were many attractions: a 'combat of Shrovetide against Lent', bull-fights, jousting, and tournaments (where Lope intervened to deliver a poem on 'The Champions', and a panegyric of the sovereign). He had time all the same to forget Micaela and to indulge his sexual appetite, and a son (who later became a monk) was born of a brief liaison with a Valencian woman.

When he returned to Toledo, Micaela's husband had just departed for America, and his wife yielded to her passion for Lope so that for several years she divided her time between her two households, the legal and the illegal, and enriched both with children. But the reopening of theatres, decreed in 1600 by Philip III, induced Micaela to go on tour, and, to find her again, her lover made various journeys to Granada and Seville, where the literary world of Andalusia generally hailed him as the most celebrated of Spanish dramatists. But there were some who were jealous of him, and they belittled his poems, and, with better reason, condemned him for his private life. On the frontispiece of his book of poems, *El peregrino en su patria* (*The Pilgrim in His own Country*), Lope had an engraving of the famous escutcheon of the nineteen towers of Bernardo del Carpio, which provoked his rival poets, and especially Gongora, to sarcasm:

> Dear Lope, let your way of life erase
> The nineteen towers from your coat of arms.
> The breath of scandal is a gale, no doubt,
> But hardly strong enough for all those windmills.[19]

The revival of theatrical activity giving Lope the chance to sell his *comedias* again, he left the service of the Duke of Sarria. But he soon found a new patron, the Duke of Sessa, a young man of twenty-three, an amateur of both verse and women with as much passion but less talent than our poet. For the rest of his life Lope remained the Duke's 'Secretary of Affairs of the Heart', charged with writing, in the affected and artificial style which was fashionable, letters addressed to his lights of love.

Meanwhile, Lope broke off relations with Micaela de Lujan (leaving her with several children), and in 1610 moved to Madrid, where he bought a little house with a flower garden in French Street. His reputation as dramatist and poet was then at its peak, moving Cervantes to remark: 'He reigns supreme over all the dramatists of Spain.' There was not a theatre in the peninsula which did not produce his plays, and the expression '*That's as good as Lope . . .*' came to signify 'the very best'. But it was at this moment that Lope seemed to want to withdraw from the world and to become reconciled to God. From 1608 he added to his name the title 'familiar of the Holy Office', and, as such, he took part in 1624 in a procession which ended with the death of a 'false Christian' accused of sacrilege. He had also joined the Brotherhood of the Slaves of the Holy Sacrament of 1609 and, three years later, published his *Four soliloquies of Lope de Vega and tears which he shed before the Crucifix, begging God's forgiveness for his sins: a work of extreme importance to every sinner who wishes to turn away from vice and to begin a new life.*

A new life? The death of his legal wife, the unhappy Juana, in 1613 seems to have made up his mind for him. In 1614, at the age of fifty-two, he decided to become a priest and actually took holy orders in Toledo. But on the very day of his ordination he went to live with a new mistress, another actress, Jeronima de Burgos,

181

whom he had got to know in the previous year, a few days before Juana's death.

Such was the scandal that the new priest – who in addition continued to conduct the amorous correspondence of the Duke of Sessa and, moreover, joined him in his romantic adventures – was unable to find a confessor. Jeronima was soon succeeded by another actress, Lucia de Salceda, whom Lope himself referred to in his letters as 'The Madcap' (la Loca). Without beauty or wit, she yet held him completely in thrall. Unable to live without her, he rejoined her at Valencia (under the pretext of going to see his son, the monk), and went with her on tour.

Only a still more ardent passion could set him free from 'The Madcap'. In 1617 he made the acquaintance of a young lady, Marthe de Nevares. She was twenty-six years old and married to a greybeard (but wasn't Lope himself . . .?) who had given her several children. She was beautiful, very cultured, a poetess in her leisure time, faithful to her husband – or at least wanting to be. It was by virtue of his cloth and priestly dignity that Lope insinuated himself into her household as a 'spiritual guide'. She soon became pregnant and, pressed by Lope, brought an action for divorce against her husband. The husband died, having given his name to the last-born child, and Marthe went to live in French Street. There she gave birth to two daughters, who were not only illegitimate but also 'sacrilegious', since their father was a priest regularly saying Mass at the convent of the Magdalen.[20]

However, his renown was such that the scandal was condoned, and Lope was called upon to take part in the most solemn official ceremonies. In 1620 the city of Madrid invited him to preside at a 'tourney of poets' to celebrate the beatification of its patron, St Isidorus. The best poets of Spain came to participate in the contest, and later one of them, Calderon de la Barca, was, after Lope, to reign sovereign over the world of drama. Two years later St Isidorus was canonized and there were more festivities and a new literary joust, in which 132 poets took part. Lope took the first prize, the others going to Calderon and Guillen de Castro. In the same year the municipality of Madrid organized another poetical tourney to mark the canonization of St Theresa, which took place in the centre of the royal palace in the presence of the king and queen. The Madrid News reported that: '. . . Lope de Vega Carpio was secretary of the gathering: there is no need to say more to signify that the occasion was successful in every respect.'[21] Other honours came to him from the Vatican: Pope Urban VIII named him as doctor of theology of the *Collegium sapientiae*, and bestowed on him the cross of the order of St John of Jerusalem.

He was then, as his biographer Montalban puts it, the richest and the poorest man of his time. Rich in the production of a literature prodigious in its scope and variety: poor, because from all in their payment for the pieces which he sold to them at the price this output he drew an income insufficient to support his illegitimate family. For the managers of theatrical troupes, whose life was precarious, and often finished up in bankruptcy, were irregular in their payment for the pieces which he sold to them at the price – a very high one – of 500 ducats. On top of this the complete lack of copyright put Lope at the mercy of plagiarists and plunderers. A certain Luis Ramirez de Arellano, a former scholar of Alcala and possessed of an amazing memory, made a speciality of learning the gist of the plot of a play, and then, by listening to two or three performances, putting it on paper and selling it. Lope protested in vain and took the man to court; but the judges held that the fact of registering a text in a man's memory could not be counted as a theft.

Lope needed more resources, and it was to the Duke of Sessa that he turned again and again, asking him for the loan of a horse and carriage, for clothes for his daughters, sometimes for money, no doubt in dignified terms. But what lowers him in our eyes is, for example, his request to be taken on as the Duke's private chaplain and to 'say Mass for him every day for a modest fee'. That he himself bitterly resented this bondage is proved by the advice he gave his son in dedicating a book to him:

' . . . if your nature inclines you to the writing of verse (which God forbid), take particular care that this is not your main attainment. . . . Look for no other example than mine own, because, even if you live to be full of years, you will never render as many services to your country's rulers as I have done to deserve honours. And, as you are aware, all I own is a poor little house, a humble bed, a meagre table, and a tiny garden whose flowers distract me from my worries.'

The young Lope did not follow in the footsteps of his father. Falling out with him, he embraced a military career and was killed in the Castillian Indies. Of the two daughters who remained with him (both, of course, born 'father unknown'), one took the veil in the convent of the Holy Trinity in Madrid. The other, Maria Antonia, brought up as Lope's 'niece', continued to be his only joy after her mother, Marthe de Nevares, had become blind, then mad, and died in 1632. But Nemesis would not permit this Don Juan, this sacrilegious poet and ravisher of women, to end his days in peace. In 1634, Maria Antonia, a willing victim, was abducted by Christopher Tenorio of Villalta, carried off, as Isabella of Urbina had been carried off by her father. A few months later (August 1635), the familiars of the Holy Office, and Knights of St John and all the priests of Madrid, carried Lope de Vega Carpio, the 'Phoenix of the Poets', to his last resting-place.

The life of Lope de Vega is the prime example of the condition of the writers of those days. He was the recognized 'purveyor' of all the theatrical companies in Spain for more than twenty years. But he could keep going only through the patronage of certain great noblemen. No writer could earn a living by his pen alone, and those who had no chance of obtaining a generous patron or of drawing some income from a benefice or other job in the church (such as Gongora, prebend of the chapter of Seville) had to demean themselves by seeking work unworthy of their genius. Thus Cervantes was a 'purveyor for the navy'. In this office, accused of embezzlement, he got to know the prisons of Seville, which he found less comfortable than the convict prison in Algiers to which he had been introduced during his career as a soldier.

Meanwhile, in singular contrast to the poverty of the writers, literature was becoming increasingly important in Spain. It became 'a general activity in which everyone takes part and which affects the lives of all the world'.[22] This was particularly true of poetry, to which people of all classes became devotees, from the grandee to the student and the simple artisan. Spain was inundated with poets and versifiers in search of a rhyme – and a publisher.

The taste for poetry and literary debates found expression, towards the end of the sixteenth century, in the 'academies', whose numbers were multiplied at the beginning of the following century. They were generally under the patronage of a man of great distinction, and the king himself presided over 'The Palace Academy'. These centres brought together writers, wits, and those grandees who were not content merely to inhale the poetic incense burnt in their honour, but often joined the ranks of the versifiers themselves. Everyone came to seek applause and fame, either by reading his more recent compositions, or by throwing off some ingenious impromptus, in the form of sonnets, songs, and ballads.[23] A jury had the task of awarding the palm to the winners of the jousts, but Cervantes offered this advice to a young poet: 'Always aim at the second prize, for the first will be awarded through favouritism and the "quality" of the competitor; the second is gained on merit.' There were many who did not take this good advice. Some lost their tempers when their poetry was not appreciated, and there was trouble at what should have been a peaceful contest. Lope de Vega, writing to the Duke of Sessa in 1612, says:

'No one speaks to me about anything but the academies where the gentlemen and many of the poets compete. At the Academy of Parnassus, Soto, a licentiate and a native of Granada, and the famous Luis Velez had a rare poetic set-to, which led to their brandishing the buckler and waiting for each other at the street door. Never did Mars behave so naughtily towards those young ladies, the Muses.'[24]

We have seen the importance of the poetry 'jousts' organized for the beatification of St Theresa and St Isidorus, in which the most famous poets of Spain took a part. This kind of gathering became a regular feature of fêtes held in the big cities, and also in quite small towns and villages. Estebanillo Gonzalez recalls that, when he passed through a small hamlet where they were preparing a 'battle of Christians versus the Moors',[25] he saw a notice fixed to the door of the church saying that

' . . . twenty-four prizes would be awarded for the twenty-four best sonnets extolling and describing a rose which is in bud at dawn, in bloom at noon, and withered at twilight. . . . The prizes included belts, gloves, purses, and a pair of coloured garters. When we arrived for the prizewinning, there were more than twenty sonnets by students or persons of quality who had come to see the fête.'

True poetry had little to gain from this orgy of versification in which verbal ingenuity was more esteemed than inspiration. But this cleverness in the use of words gained ground in the two schools of poetry, which, especially between 1610 and 1650, divided the Spanish literary world: 'culteranism' and 'conceptualism'. The former sought to create an original poetic language with a vocabulary enriched by Latin syntactical forms and searching for the most subtle and fine-drawn modes of expression. The other school was concerned to explain all the complexity of ideas and concepts by the clever manipulation of parallels and antitheses and finally pushing beyond the bounds of common sense.

In the long run, both these schools reached a more or less identical result: the creation of an artificial language deliberately divorced from common usage, where hermeticism and preciosity became fused. The friction between these two schools, and the attacks of their common adversaries, would have been less intense if personal insults had not been joined to their rivalry. Never has the *genus irritabile vatum* showed itself more peevish than in the literature of the Golden Age, in which polemical controversy, both in poetry and prose, played so large a part. As we have seen, Lope de Vega was the favourite target of his rivals and his private life offered a splendid ground from which to attack. But he always fired back, aiming particularly at Gongora, the undisputed head of the school of 'culteranism' since the publication of *Solitudes* (1614). Lope attacked him in a parody, in the style of the *cueto*, implying that he was a 'butcher of words':[26]

> Ines, I by thy bright orbs murdered am,
> Since first you that mournful day beheld,
> Done by thy fault to death with torment cruel.

Quevedo is even more biting, when he puts these words into the same mouth of a 'prebendary' of Seville, accused – despite his ecclesiastical rank – of being a half-converted Jew:

> I'll send you my verses well and truly larded,
> So you'll not savour them, my dear Gongora.

But despite the attacks against the master and his disciples, the mischief only increased, and there was not a poetaster who did not claim to have outdone his rivals in verbal refinement and obscure profundity. In an Aragonese village where Estebanillo Gonzalez paused for a rest, he tried in vain to understand the sonnets which had been sent in for the poetry prize; baffled he asked one of the students there if these poems had been written in Chaldean or Aramaic.

'I got the reply that he dared not give a straight answer. But he did say that he had presented one of the fruits of his own genius, which he hoped would win him the first prize. And, even if he had been able to explain the meaning of this poem, he made no effort to do so, because all that seems to count in writing verse these days is to *gongorize* with bombastic elegance something which is meaningless, both to the author who wrote it and to the curious who read it. For the poet who would debase himself by the use of such platitudes as writing the word "bread" for "bread", or "wine" for "wine", would lose his reputation immediately; he would be exactly right for writing couplets for the blind.'

Having delivered himself of his verdict, Estebanillo decided to take part in the contest himself, and, on a table in the inn to which he had fled post-haste, he wrote a sonnet[27] in the current style, and nailed it to the door of the church. 'I had just done this when a crowd gathered, avid to read it, praising it aloud, and not understanding a word. Over thirty copies were made of it. Certain judges from the Academy who happened to be present gave me the garters, of which I have spoken, as a prize. Now, I suppose I shall be hailed as a second Gongora.'

Reasonable people naturally rebelled against these abuses of a language which was of use only to the initiates. One of the characters in *The Traveller's Guide* asks,

'And what should we say about the sort of talk which these writers have invented: so difficult and so obscure that nobody really understands what is meant? This style of writing, against all the rules of the old style, places the noun two leagues away from its adjective, and the subject ten lines apart from its verb. . . . This cipher-talk is full of Greek words and Spanish-Latinisms and is only a fourth cousin to our national language. These writers will, within the next fifty years, poison the pure tongue of the Castilian language, unless the government either forbids their drivel or establishes a new vocabulary.'[28]

Although the academies were largely responsible for these excesses, a 'burlesque academy', established in the palace of Buen Retiro in 1637, took delight in denouncing and parodying the style of royal decrees and the poetic flatulence from which the country was suffering and making fun of the habits and the jealousies of the literary 'tribe':

' Don Apollo, by the grace of poetry, King of the Muses, Prince of the Dawn, Count and Seigneur of the Oracles of Delphi and Delos, Duke of Pindus, Archduke of both slopes of Parnassus, to all epic, lyric, tragic, comic, dithyrambic, and dramatic poets, etc. . . . salutations and peace.

'Know that, being aware of the great confusion and damage which have up to now beset those who make our rhymes and verses, and the excessive number of those who, without fear of God and their own consciences, compose, write, and make verses by stealing and plundering, by day and by night, the styles, ideas, and manner of writing of their elders, adapting the centos borrowed from other people, and committing all sorts of frauds and trickeries in their verses, being desirous of remedying this state of things, by these presents command and ordain:

'Firstly: that everybody shall write in Castilian words, without introducing words from foreign languages, and that those who introduce into their verses extravagant statements and hyperboles shall be deprived of their status as poets by the Academy, and, in the case of the repetition of the offence, shall have all their verses confiscated.

'*Item*, that the oldest poets assume the task of giving alms in the form of sonnets, songs, roundelays, and ballads, and all sorts of verse to the foolish poets, and to collect from the streets all those who have fallen ill or lost their senses through reading the *Solitudes* by Don Luis de Gongoron, and that, outside the gates of the Academy, they shall distribute a soup made from the surplus poetry to be found there.

'*Item*, that poetry in the Moorish style shall be baptized within forty days, on pain of being exiled from the kingdom.

'*Item*, that the poet who enters the service of a *grand seigneur* may be justly allowed to die of hunger.

'*Item*, that no poet shall be so bold as to dare to speak ill of his fellows more than twice a week.[29]

But both protest and parody were powerless against a literary vogue which invaded the whole of Spain, during the first part of the century, and even contaminated men like Quevedo who had fought so stoutly against it. Despite the 'pragmatic' burlesque made by the Palace Academy, poets continued to starve, to seek the patronage of the mighty, and to go on tearing at each other's reputation with sharp teeth.

CHAPTER TEN

MILITARY LIFE

The prestige of Spanish arms. Recruitment and strength of the armed forces — The military career. The life and adventures of Captain Alonso de Contreras – A soldier's temperament: gallantry, endurance, pride and boasting – The loss of morale. 'The Life and Great Exploits of Estebanillo Gonzales.'

When Pierre Brantome, gentleman, writer, and hero-worshipper, heard in 1566 that the Duke of Alba's army, coming from Italy, was going to cross Lorraine in a punitive expedition against the Flemish rebels, he went post-haste to see

'. . . this fine company of gallant and valiant soldiers on the march . . . all were seasoned veterans, so well appointed as to uniforms and arms that one took them for captains rather than private soldiers. . . . One would have said that they were princes, so stiff they were and so arrogantly and gracefully they marched.'

In effect, after the campaigns in Italy, during which 'the furious dash' of the French made little impression on their stolid regiments, the Spanish soldier won unequalled fame, a reputation which remained untarnished until the first part of the seventeenth century.

However, not all those who fought under the colours and for the cause of the Catholic king were Spaniards. A considerable proportion were foreign mercenaries (mostly German and Irish), who were engaged for a particular campaign, or subjects of the king of Spain from the Italian vice-royalties, which during the Golden Age had given some remarkable captains to the Spanish armies, such as Alexandre Farnèse and Ambrosio Spinola. Spain provided only the nucleus of this military force, to which her soldiers gave the example of bravery, endurance, and especially arrogance.

The old medieval principle by which a nobleman was obliged to serve the king by providing him with troops was still in force. Sometimes a noble on his own account would enlist as a private soldier. But such cases were exceptional, and the nobility, now become courtiers, tended more and more to withdraw from military service. If we except the penal impressment of convicts to row the galleys of the king, and, in exceptional cases, the raising of troops imposed on the municipal authorities in the face of imminent danger to the nation, the Spanish army was made up of volunteers, who thus constituted a standing army endowed with all the military virtues – and some of the vices.

The captain who had received a special commission from the king had to form his own unit of which he would be the leader. So he 'planted his pikestaff' and hoisted his banner in the towns and villages assigned to him, and having literally 'drummed up' a crowd, he tried to raise some volunteers. When there were insufficient numbers, all methods – promises, stratagem, force – were considered fair (as was the case in other countries of Europe) to induce men to join the army. In 1639 the *News* of Madrid announced:

'A lady of good family, the mistress of an officer, was horsewhipped for helping him to recruit soldiers. She enticed the poor beggars by offering them food; she then, by a trick, shut them up in a cellar and kept them there without food until they had signed on and received their pay; in this fashion, she has already netted no end of men.'[1]

On the other hand, amongst those who were voluntarily sworn in in the presence of registrar or notary, more than one only just touched the book intending to desert at the first opportunity. Thus it was no easy matter for the captain to get his men together, a little under strength, to the appointed rallying place, generally a port from which they would embark for one of the battlegrounds outside the peninsula.

On the way, the recruits were instructed in the way to handle the pike, the arquebus, and the musket, the standard equipment of the infantry: and more exceptionally the long lance, with which the cavalry was armed. For the cavalry consisted mainly of foreign mercenaries, while Spain provided most of the foot-soldiers who formed the effective force of the *tercios*. Each *tercio* consisted of a dozen companies of 200 to 250 men under the command of a camp master.

But the shortage of money from which the monarchy suffered did not permit Spain to maintain all the effective forces permanently under the colours, and normally meant not only the end of the mercenaries' contracts, but also the dissolution of certain companies whose captains were retired until the renewal of military activity or a threat to some part of the empire necessitated another call to arms.

There was an extraordinary discrepancy between the extent of the possessions of the Catholic Kings, with the multiplicity of the land and sea fronts thus exposed to enemy attack, and the smallness of the effective forces on which their defence rested. Under Philip IV, at a time when Spain had to face the rebellious Flemings of the United Provinces, as well as the French and English, they never numbered more than 100,000 men, including the foreign mercenaries. It was therefore necessary constantly to switch troops from areas not immediately under attack to reinforce those which appeared to be immediately threatened. A large part of the energy and the resources of the Spanish monarchy were used up in the struggle against her most redoubtable foe, against whom there could be no assured and lasting victory: distance.[2]

But what ample scope for adventure was offered by the immensity of the battlefield and in the variety of countries from the West Indies to Germany and to the Ionian Sea, wherever the might of Spain held sway! Innumerable autobiographical accounts have preserved for us the memory of the adventurous life of a soldier, but none is more expressive than that left by Captain Alonso de Contreras. There is no rhetoric, no striving for effect in the account of his life: Contreras contents himself with telling plainly what he did and saw, relating with equal candour his crimes and his exploits, and there is about his narrative a feeling of complete authenticity.[3]

Alonso was born in Madrid in 1582, of a very humble family:

'My parents were "Old Christians", without any taint of Jewish or Moorish blood, without condemnation from the Holy Office. They were married, according to the rites of our Holy Mother Church, for twenty-four years, during which they had sixteen children. When my father died there were eight left, six boys and two girls, and I was the eldest.'

At the school to which he was sent, the young Contreras killed one of his schoolfellows with blows from a knife, to avenge the humiliation which he had inflicted on him. Justice intervened and, taking his age into account, was content to send him into exile at Avila for a year. When he returned to Madrid, even though he had declared his wish to become a soldier, his mother apprenticed him to a goldsmith. Now, from the very first day, his master's wife insisted that it was his job to pump water, but his pride revolted and he ran away. He mixed with rogues and vagabonds and with the women of bad character who followed – as with all the armies of the time – the troops of the Archduke Alber who were on their way to Flanders. By chance he got a job as scullion with the Archduke's French chef, and this enabled him to embark at Barcelona for the port of Savona. This journey gave him his first taste of the realities of war:

'Before we made landfall, we seized a ship, whether Turkish, Moorish or French, I do not know (for there was, I believe, a war being waged), but it gave me great pleasure to see the cannons firing at each other.'

From Savona, the Archduke and his forces reached the Franche Comté, where other formations had assembled. Alonso, who was then fourteen, noticed among the soldiers other youngsters no older than himself, and he asked the head cook to release him from his duties so that he could bear arms, but his request was refused. So Alonso went direct to the Archduke, who gave him written permission to enlist, even though the boy was under the required age. He joined a unit, and on the march to Flanders, though before they arrived, '. . . my corporal whom I respected as though he were the king himself, told me to follow him one night on orders from the captain. So we deserted from the army, for he was hardly a lover of fighting. When dawn broke, we were five leagues from the army. I asked him where we were going and learnt that we were headed for Naples. . . .'

A deserter in spite of himself, Contreras had no difficulty in resuming his duties. From Naples, he went to Palermo where he became a 'page of the buckler' (shield-bearer) to a Catalan noble. It was just at this time that a fleet was being got together at Naples and in Sicily for an assault against the Turks in Morea. Alonso went aboard and took part in the attack on Patras: 'It was there that for the first time I heard bullets whistling past my ears, since I was standing in front of my captain, with my shield . . . ; we failed to take the town, but captured a good deal of booty and many slaves.' He left his Catalan the next year to enlist, not as a page, but as a soldier in another company. He went aboard one of the ships of war which pursued the Turks and made razzias on the coast of Barbary and the Levant.

'We took so many prizes that it would take far too long to describe them all. We returned so rich that I, a private soldier whose pay was only three crowns, even I, brought back three hundred crowns for my part, in clothing and silver. Moreover, when we returned to Palermo, the viceroy ordered that we should be awarded a further share of the booty and I got a hat crammed to the brim with double silver reals. But, in three days, I lost the lot gambling and in other dissipations.'

But these losses were soon, if temporarily, made good by other expeditions in the eastern Mediterranean:

'There was incredible plundering both on land and sea. We sacked the warehouses of Alexandretta, the port at which is collected all the merchandise which comes overland from the Portuguese Indies via Babylon and Aleppo. Great were the spoils which we brought back.'

But all was soon squandered 'in tavern or bawdy-house'.

Nevertheless, Alonso de Contreras was not one to be content with battle and pillage and then to spend all his gains on booze and other debaucheries. He took the opportunity to teach himself the art of navigation during his voyage in the Ionian seas, and started to make a *derrotero* (a nautical chart) which he gradually enlarged to include the whole of the Mediterranean, showing the best anchorages and the depth of water in the various ports.[4] His nautical knowledge was to serve him immediately when, because of 'an incident', he was obliged to quit the service of the viceroy of Sicily surreptitiously. During a brawl one of his companions killed an innkeeper in Palermo. The culprit and his friends sought sanctuary in a church, but were given to understand that they would all be hanged when they emerged. It so happened that the church was on the seafront; when night fell Alonso and his companions managed to slip out of their hiding-place, to commandeer a fishing-boat and, after rowing for three days, to reach Naples.

Learning of the circumstances in which they had fled from Palermo, the viceroy of Naples, who was even then forming a company to be put under the command of his son, welcomed the fugitives and authorized their engagement. But hardly had they done so than there was another brawl which ended in murder and two of Alonso's friends were hanged. Alonso himself took refuge in the house of a Knight of Malta who sheltered him, and then spirited him away on a ship bound for that island. Malta was not only a Christian outpost against the Turks: it was also an important base for the Spanish fleets operating in the eastern Mediterranean, and the Knights had need of good sailors to man their galleys. So Contreras joined the service of the Grand Master of the Order, the Frenchman, Alof de Vignacourt, and took part in a number of naval engagements, the descriptions of which constitute a vivid document on what were the conditions of war at sea.

'As night fell, we saw what appeared to be a very large ship, which indeed it was. We followed in her wake so as not to lose her and, when it was completely dark, we overtook her. With our cannons ready for action, we called out: "What manner of ship are you?" to which they replied: "A ship that sails the high seas . . . !" And as she was also ready and lacked nothing that a ship should have (she carried more than 400 Turks and was well furnished with artillery), this ship let fly with a broadside which sent seventeen of our men to another world, and wounded a number of others. We replied with our guns, which were not less effective. They we boarded her, and the fight was hard, for they captured our forecastle and it was not easy to hurl them back on to their ship. Thus the night passed, and at daybreak we attacked again but she would not give in. Our captain then had recourse to an effective measure. He left on deck only those needed to conduct the battle and had all hatches closed, so that only two courses of action were left: to fight or to jump into the sea. The battle was relentless; we captured their forecastle and held it for some time, but we were thrown back. Then we unhooked our grapples to continue the battle with cannon-fire, since we were better sailors than they and had better artillery. The fight lasted all day long and when night came, the enemy endeavoured to reach the land which was close by, and, following her, we found ourselves side by side near the shore. When the next day dawned, the feast of Our Lady of the Conception, our captain gave orders that all the wounded should be taken up on deck to die there, saying: "Tonight

we will sup with Christ – or in Constantinople." We had as chaplain a Carmelite priest to whom the captain said: "Brother, give
us your blessing for this is our last day." The good brother did so,
and when it was done, the captain ordered our ship to go alongside
the other which was quite close. When we boarded her, the battle
which ensued was extremely fierce and even if we had wanted to
break it off, we could not, for from the other ship they had thrown
an anchor attached to a long chain over us so that we could not
free ourselves. The fight lasted for more than three hours before
we realized that victory was coming our way, for the Turks, seeing
themselves so near to land, started to jump into the water, not
realizing that we would fish them out again. Victory assured, we
took the Turks as slaves and looted their ship to our great profit.
Below decks there were more than 250 dead whom they had
not thrown overboard lest we should see the number of their
casualties.'

The military valour of Contreras, coupled with his nautical
knowledge, brought him swift advancement. The Grand Master
gave him a commission as captain in charge of 'intelligence mis-
sions' in the eastern Mediterranean. His mission was to discover the
plans and movements of the Turkish squadron which, each year,
made a tour of the islands of the Archipelago to collect the tribute
due to the Sultan: and sometimes, strengthened by flotillas from
Rhodes, Alexandria, and Syria, it went to Sicily and beyond in
order to pillage the Christian shores. But it would be possible to
understand the size of the proposed operation if one knew exactly
how many ships were at sea, and especially the quantities of provisions which they carried. There were more ways than one of
getting this information. One could slip, on a fast galley, into the
middle of Turkish waters, seize some of the merchant ships, and
find out from the crew and passengers, by torture if needs be, some
clues as to the movements from the ports whence they had come.
Another method would be to land on the Ottoman coast where one
might glean useful information from the Christian communities
living under the yoke of Constantinople. In this task, Contreras
proved to be of astonishing audacity. He advanced as far as Jaffa,
Acre, and Beirut, and not content merely to gather imformation,
he seized naval prizes here and there and made forays ashore.

An astonishing exploit carried his reputation to its peak. In

Malta they got wind of the fact that the Grand Turk was fitting out an armada, but 'they did not know for where, which gave them great concern'. However, spies had learned that the Jewish tax-collector, charged with raising the funds necessary for the expedition (especially at the expense of his co-religionists), lived in a fortified house five miles from Salonika. 'The Knights ordered me to kidnap him, as if it were as easy as buying a few pears from the market.' All the same, he sailed with seventeen picked men, on a frigate which took him as far as the Gulf of Salonika. He landed a little distance from the house, and blew up the gate with explosives. He then seized the Jew, his wife, and two children, and took them back to the ship, and put out to sea just as 400 Turkish cavalry arrived on the beach. 'The Jew offered me anything I wished if I would set him free. I could easily have accepted this offer but did not wish to do so for he went on to tell me that this fleet had been assembled to sail against the Venetians and that the Turks were demanding a million sequins under threat of seizing Candia, an island as big as Sicily, in the waters dominated by the Turks.'

On the way back, Contreras, learning from some Greek seamen that Soliman, the Bey of Khioz, had left the island, abducted his concubine – 'of Hungarian birth and the most beautiful woman I ever saw' – and took her back to Malta with him. 'I learned later,' he wrote, 'that because I had made her my mistress, the Bey had vowed to impale me the day he laid hands on me. . . . When I reached Malta, I was well received as can be imagined, for at the news I bore everybody calmed down, and they stopped bringing over the foot-soldiers whom the knights had recruited in Naples and in Rome.'

To the glory was added the booty. In 1601, an expedition to Platza, in Morea (Peloponnesus), yielded a catch of 500 captives, as many men as women, among whom was the governor of the place, his wife and children, as well as horses and thirty pieces of artillery. These prisoners sold as slaves fetched a good price, for the order of Malta bought them for one hundred crowns apiece, 'taking the good with the bad'. As for the naval prizes, they represented a fortune, for the ships carried all the merchandise from the Orient and the Far East. But money slipped through the fingers of Contreras and his comrades and flowed into the hands of the *quiracas* (the lasses) of Malta, 'who are so pretty and so artful that they soon became mistresses of all that the knights and soldiers possessed'. For his own mistress, Contreras set up house in grand style. Alas! on his return from his triumphant expedition to Salonika he found her locked in her house with one of his comrades. 'I had at him with my sword and left him within an inch of death; and, as soon as he recovered, he quitted Malta, from fear that I really would kill him.' As regards the girl, she ran away, and 'even though she sent me a thousand apologies, I never met her again, for, as there were so many to choose from, I quickly found a replacement – even the more easily as I was sought after as a man of importance'.

This vexing episode, however, seems to have turned our hero against Malta. After a final expedition to the Barbary Coast, from which he returned with fourteen slaves and a cargo of cloth 'big enough to stock a shop', he asked the Grand Master for his discharge and the latter regretfully granted his request. He set sail for Spain. In 1603 the court was at Valladolid, and, having learned that a new 'batch of officers' was being chosen, he submitted his record to the council of war. But he only succeeded in being given the commission of *alférez* (lieutenant) under the orders of a captain whose mission was to levy men in Estremadura and conduct them to Portugal.

On the way he had a strange adventure. His party halted for the night at Hornachos, a huge market-town whose inhabitants were all Moriscos with the exception of the priest. The soldiers were billeted with one of the citizens, and some of them, rummaging in their host's cellar in search of victuals, discovered three whitewashed tombs. They went to their *alférez*, told him what they had seen and suggested that they should rob these graves of the jewels which the Moors customarily buried with them. But on scratching the whitewash with a pike, Contreras discovered that what appeared to be tombs were in fact cases full of arquebuses and balls, 'which gave me great satisfaction to think that with these weapons I could arm my company, and that people would have more respect for us, for as we only had swords, and some not even those, we lacked sometimes in self-respect'. Alonso then went to the quartermaster (the official responsible for the equipment of the troops) and ordered him to keep his mouth shut, so that the proper steps could be taken against the possible danger of a Moriscan uprising.

Contreras and his party pressed on, and some days later when his captain tried to steal his mistress – a prostitute – he ran his sword through that officer's body. Sentenced to death for the attempted murder of his captain ('The greatest crime,' said he, 'that one can commit in the army is to lack respect for one's superior officer. . . .') he went as a prisoner to Madrid, and appealed to a higher court which acquitted him. But when he returned to Badajoz, of the one hundred men he had raised there were now no more than twenty. On the remainder of the march there were several more desertions and he arrived in Lisbon with only fourteen men and a drummer. . . . He did not board the ship for fear of again coming under the command of the officer whom he had wounded, and, with the king's permission, he departed once more for Palermo. There the viceroy of Sicily, having heard of his exploits in the service of the Order of Malta, put him in charge of new expeditions on the sea off the Levant and the Barbary coast.

His reputation and his gift for seduction won him the love of a rich Spanish lady, the widow of a magistrate, who consented to marry him, '. . . despite the fact,' he says, 'that I was only a soldier who owned no more than four ruffs and that my pay was but twelve *sous*'. But within a year of the marriage he discovered that his wife was having intimate relations with one of his friends: 'I found them together one day, and they died. God has them in heaven if in that supreme moment they repented.'

Once again he took the road to Spain, seeking yet again a commission as captain; but, frustrated by all the applications and delays which were imposed on him, he made a sudden and surprising decision: to become a hermit and to end his days in solitude. 'I bought the necessary tools of the trade: a hair-shirt and a scourge; some homespun from which one makes frocks, a sun-dial, many books of penitence, some seed, a skull, and a small hoe.' Then, armed with the panoply of the perfect hermit, he went to Aragon and installed himself in a little hermitage which he built for himself on the slopes of Moncayo, near the town of Agréda where there was a Franciscan monastery.

'I attended mass at the monastery every day; on Saturdays I went to the town and begged for alms. I would accept no money, only some oil and bread and garlic, with which I kept myself going. Each Sunday I went to confession and received Holy Communion. I was called Fra Alonso de la Madre de Dios, and sometimes the monks would ask me to eat with them hoping to persuade me to become a monk. I was never more joyful than on Palm Sunday. And I swear that if I had not been arrested and taken off the way I was, I would still be there today.'

But one fine day, in 1608, Fra Alonso saw climbing up to his hermitage a troop of armed men, who without giving him any explanation tied him up and carried him off to the neighbouring town, where the corregidor informed him that he had learnt that Alonso had wanted to proclaim himself 'King of the Moriscos' and start a general uprising. The accusation was obviously absurd; it had been made out of spite by that quartermaster whom he had told about the finding of the chests full of guns in Hornachos several years earlier, and who, to cover up his own failure to provide the party with proper equipment, had now denounced him. Contreras was interrogated and submitted to torture, but ended by being cleared of all charges. To compensate him for his ordeal and for not being given the captain's commission for which he had asked, he was given a letter addressed to the Archduke Charles, governor of Flanders, which contained a request by the king of Spain that he should entrust Contreras with a new company.

He thereupon embarked at San Sebastian and reached Brussels, where he was warmly welcomed by the Archduke and promised the first captaincy that became available. . . . But two years passed and nothing happened. Tired of waiting (especially as the assassination of Henry IV had produced the threat of war, which many thought to be imminent) and having heard that a chapter general of the order of Malta was to be held in the near future, Alonso asked for his discharge so that he could return to the island and claim some recompense for his past services. He travelled through France disguised as a pilgrim and, going via Naples and Palermo, arrived in time for the chapter general. He was admitted as a 'servant-at-arms' after they had, by unanimous decision, dispensed with the proofs of nobility normally required when a man asked to join the order. This was indeed an exceptional distinction for the boy of humble origin who, fifteen years earlier, had left Madrid to become a scullion. Yet he was eager to return to Spain, 'whereupon everyone showered good wishes on me, some with envy, some with sympathy'.

But his temperament remained the same; jealous of a married woman, he wounded her with two sword cuts, and only his belonging to the order of Malta saved him from the jurisdiction of the ordinary criminal courts which had laid its hand upon him once before. By way of Genoa, Rome, and Naples he returned to Malta, where he found, at long last, the captain's commission that the king of Spain had conferred on him; but, in addition, the king asked the Grand Master to allow Contreras to return to his service. Back in Spain, after receiving many orders and counter-orders, Alonso was ordered to Cadiz to take two hundred men aboard ship and go to the relief of Puerto Rico, then being threatened by the Dutch fleets. This was a perilous task, for if it was not easy to recruit men; it was much more difficult to make them embark on a ship bound for the Indies. All the preparations, therefore, were made secretly, '. . . otherwise not a single man would have stepped aboard, for the soldiers of that garrison and its fleet are the slyest ruffians from Andalusia'. Induced to go aboard by surprise 'the soldiers realize that they have been pressed before really understanding what was happening'. It now remained to forestall the risk of mutiny, which the arrogant behaviour of the soldiers towards the captain made likely. Having assured himself of the loyalty of a dozen reliable men, Contreras cut down with a single slash of his sword the first man who dared to raise his voice, and order was restored.

After about forty days at sea the galleon reached Puerto Rico, where the governor congratulated Contreras on having escaped the famous pirate, Walter Raleigh, who was roving in that area, and begged to be given forty men to reinforce the defences of the island. . . . 'But not a single man wanted to land. They all cried out at the thought of remaining there, and for good reason, for that would mean being marooned for ever.' So those destined to stay were chosen by lot. Fifty others were landed at San Domingo, where Contreras built a small fort at the entrance to the harbour. Another fortification, built in four days, was established in Cuba, and ten men were left to man it. . . . Then, having sunk a ship belonging to Raleigh's squadron, the galleon set sail for Spain. They were scarcely back in Cadiz when news was received that some 30,000 Moors had laid siege to the fortress of La Mamora on the coast of Africa. Contreras asked for the command of the relief expedition. He raised the enemy's blockade and entered the harbour, where he was received 'like the dove after the Flood' by the governor. Contreras delivered reinforcements and munitions to the town, which persuaded the Moors to open negotiations.

The governor of Andalusia, the Duke of Medina Sidonia, bade him take this happy news to Madrid himself, and he had the honour of personally giving to King Philip III an account of the successful outcome of the enterprise. As a reward for his exploits, and because of his naval experience, he applied for the rank of admiral, that is commander-in-chief of a fleet; but once more the palace officials delayed the fulfilment of the promise made to him. He had to content himself with the privilege of 'raising a company' in the capital itself (a thing which had never been done before) and putting his men aboard ships whose mission was the supervision of the Strait of Gibraltar and the protection of the galleons, laden with silver, which arrived from America. But he fell ill, and was put on the reserve. Returning to Madrid, without any resources, he was sheltered and fed by Lope de Vega, who had never set eyes on him before, but welcomed him with the words: 'Sir Captain, a man must share his cloak with men such as you!' and he dedicated to him a play, *The King Without a Kingdom*, inspired by his alleged Morisco royalty.

Through his persistence, Alonso managed to persuade the war council to send him to Sicily where the viceroy appointed him to the governorship of Pantellaria, 'an island situated almost on the Barbary coast', which overlooked the Straits of Sicily and guarded it with 120 men. After three months he obtained the viceroy's permission to go to Rome, where he had an audience of the Pope. He explained all that he had done in defence of the Faith, and received a 'brief' from His Holiness addressed to the order of Malta, giving him an exemption from the conditions of residence normally required in order to become a knight and to obtain a commandership. Then, armed with this precious document, he returned to Malta where he was invested as a 'Knight of Justice' with all due solemnity.

Invested with this resounding title, he returned to Naples, the viceroy of which, the Duke of Monterrey, had taken a liking to him and appointed him governor of Aquila, a town in which brigands and influential families made the law. Contreras was charged with restoring law and order, and exacting obedience to the king of Spain and to his representative. After a few had been tried and

hanged, despite all intervention, his authority was quickly established. But the implacable justice which he imposed caused so
much ill-feeling that Monterrey was obliged to recall him after
three months. As compensation he granted him command of a
company of cavalry, and Contreras, at the head of his troop with
his full retinue, took part in a general review of all the cavalry of
the kingdom of Naples.

'Poor as I was, I had my livery worn by two trumpeters and four
lackeys; they were dressed in scarlet uniforms faced with silver,
with cross-belts and plumes, and over their uniforms, capes of the
same colour. . . . My horses (five in all) had their saddles trimmed
with silver braid, with pistols showing at their saddle-bows.'

But as the Duke of Monterrey had refused to grant a captain's
commission to one of his brothers (who had, like him, led a warlike
and adventurous life), Contreras left his service. Once again he
was in danger of finding himself without either employment or
resources, when he heard the news that the Grand Master of Malta
had accorded him a commandership in Spain, with the income
which it carried. He therefore set sail for Spain, on what was
without doubt his last voyage, for his autobiography abruptly
ends at this date (1633).

Such a career seems so fantastic that one would be tempted to
doubt its authenticity; but, quite apart from Lope de Vega's long
dedication in *The King Without a Kingdom* (in which there are
allusions to certain exploits of Contreras not reported in his autobiography), the Spanish archives have preserved many documents
which corroborate his story – in particular the nautical *derrotero*
which he had devised and lent to the Archduke Philibert of Savoy,
who kept it, together with a plea addressed in 1623 to King
Philip IV, in which he had set down a record of his previous
service.

Other Spanish soldiers of the Golden Age have left similar
accounts of their lives, which, though less astonishing than that of
Alonso de Contreras, echo and corroborate the account he gives of
the military life.[5] One such was Diego Duque de Estrada, of a noble
family, who escaped from the prison at Toledo where, at the age
of thirteen, he had been locked up for the murder of one of his
friends, and sought refuge in the army. When he returned to
Madrid he became known as much for his poetic talents as for his

amorous adventures; having assassinated a rival, he was sentenced to be hanged. He managed to escape again, reached Italy, then Transylvania, where he became a gentleman-in-waiting at the semi-oriental court of the Ban, and fought against the Turks. Later he went to Germany, entered the service of the emperor, a cousin of the king of Spain, during the Thirty Years War, and became the governor of a province of Bohemia. Returning to Rome, he underwent a spiritual crisis, and joined the order of St John of God, and went on to found monasteries in Sardinia. A French attack on the island in 1637 made him take up arms again. He repulsed the invaders, and then returned to the monastic life, and ended his days in the cloister.[6]

In Diego de Estrada's memoirs of his adventurous life there is a most significant anecdote. After leaving Transylvania he went to Vienna, where he was presented to the emperor Ferdinand who asked him who he was: ' "A soldier of fortune," I replied. He wanted to know what I had done in my military career; I replied "Soldier" and that all the rest was included in that word.' No other answer could better have illustrated the spirit of these soldier-adventurers, who considered themselves above the common herd, and who, wherever they went, in Italy, in Flanders, in Germany, and even in Spain, were accustomed to speaking with authority.

The Spanish soldier carried to a very high degree his sense of personal dignity, founded on faith in the warlike qualities which had made his reputation, and on a consciousness of serving, while fighting for the king, the greatest of all causes; that of God. Hence the concept that the profession of soldier in itself conferred a sort of nobility on those who bore arms:

> My lineage starts with me;
> For men are of more worth
> Who stablish a new line
> Than those who ruin one
> By earning ill-repute.[7]

In an epoch when armies had no regular 'uniform', the soldier, like the nobleman, sought to distinguish himself from the common man not only by the way he wore his sword but also by the richness, and sometimes by the extravagance, of his costume. Things were easier for him because the sumptuary laws, which limited the amount of money to be spent on clothes and forbade sartorial

excesses, did not apply to him. 'Never,' said a text at the beginning
of the seventeenth century, 'was there a strict ruling on the costume
and ornament of the Spanish infantry, for it was this which raised
the morale and dash which must possess the men of war.'[8] Thus the
long cloaks, the doublets, the hose and belts in vivid colours, often
embroidered with silver, and wide-brimmed hats adorned with
multi-coloured plumes were the outward signs of a soldier's quality.

This keen feeling of personal worth, however, of which the dress
was only a reflection, made it difficult for the officers to exercise
authority over the private soldiers, for, says Calderon in *The Siege
of Breda*:

> They would suffer all hardship in the assault
> But would suffer no man to shout them down. . . .

These martial qualities, and the merciless punishments meted out
to all for breaches of discipline under arms, were counterbalanced
by the freedom allowed to the men when they were off duty, a
tolerance whose limits were widely stretched.

The army was above all plagued by two things: gaming and
women. An anecdote of Alonso de Contreras gives some idea of the
lengths to which the passion for gaming could go. The capture of
an enemy ship in Turkish waters yielded such vast booty that the
captain of the victorious galley, in his men's interest, banned all
kinds of gaming, 'in order that each should return to Malta a rich
man'. To make assurance doubly sure, he had all the cards and dice
which he could find thrown into the sea. The crew then had the
idea of organizing a '*pari-mutuel*' of a very unusual kind. They
drew a circle on the deck, marking out the race-course; each man
took his own 'personal' louse and placed it in the centre of the
circle at the same time as his companions. The owner of the first
louse to overstep the circle swept the board. 'When the captain saw how determined we were,' Contreras comments, 'he let
us play as we pleased, so great a hold had gambling amongst the
soldiers.'

The royal government was also anxious to put an end to this
excessive gambling. An attempt was made to regulate gaming by
authorizing soldiers to play at cards and dice, but only in their own
guard-rooms, 'for, if soldiers go out to play elsewhere, this can lead
to grave consequences'. But this limitation remained a theory
only.[9]

As for the women who followed the camp, they were often the lawful wedded wives of the soldiers or officers, who brought their children along with them; but for the most part they were women of bad repute. They were given a sort of official status, since there were certain regulations fixing their numbers in proportion to the number of soldiers: generally, eight women to a hundred men. Thus an army on campaign, with the women, the children, the pedlars, and the rogues of all kinds who followed in its train, resembled an Arab caravan – a sight quite unworthy of a Spanish army of the period. But libertinism and prostitution, like the passion for gambling, were the cause of frequent quarrels which often ended in tragedy. The five or six murders of which Alonso de Contreras, an exemplary soldier, was guilty during the course of his career had no other cause.

It was a matter for grave concern that the licence accorded to soldiers was transformed not only into contempt, but also into all kinds of acts of violence against the civilian population. Already, during the reign of Philip II, the Ambassador of the Republic of Venice, Suriano, while praising the valour of the Spanish soldier, laid stress on the other side of the coin:

'The king of Spain possesses a nursery for young men, tough both in mind and body, disciplined, highly trained for battle, for long marches, and for assaults and the defence of places; but they are so insolent, so greedy for the property and honours of others, that one can but ask whether these brave soldiers would not have served their king better in some other capacity, and not been spoiled as they have been in recent times; for even though they have been the intruments of his victories, they have lost the king the affection and goodwill of his people by maltreating them.'[10]

Now, at the beginning of the seventeenth century, and particularly it seems after 1621, the year of the resumption of the war against the United Provinces, troubles were magnified by the increasing difficulty encountered by the Spanish government in recruiting and maintaining its troops. It was at this point that the expression 'To plant a pikestaff in Flanders' became a synonym for an enterprise that was nigh on impossible. The flow of volunteers became a trickle and the recruiting officers were obliged to accept all who presented themselves, especially the blackguards and vagabonds of whom the local authorities were glad to be rid in favour of the army. In an impoverished Spain, hunger became the best recruiting sergeant for the army, and there were many who signed on to earn, at least for a time, the bare necessities of existence. 'There is not a man, however lowly and humble,' wrote Estebanillo Gonzalez with irony, 'who, seeing that, because of his faults, there is no place for him in the world and that nobody will give him a crust of bread, but will seek the asylum offered to him in this sanctuary. . . .'

Officers became increasingly more interested in the quantity than in the quality of the men enlisted. The practice of 'false musters' (*plaza muertas*), common to all armies of the time, allowed an officer to draw pay and rations for the full strength of soldiers, who appeared on parade only on 'inspection' days. 'Our company,' says Estebanillo Gonzalez again, 'had an effective strength of sixty soldiers to mount guard, but 150 for review days.' So the real strength of the army was far less than the official number, and a *tercio*, which in theory had 3,000 men on its strength, could in fact seldom muster more than a tenth of this number.[11]

However, the royal government was unable to maintain even the reduced numbers of its regular forces, especially when they were in distant theatres of operations. The pay of a soldier (from four to six crowns per month for an ordinary soldier; fifty for a captain; 500 for a camp commandant in 1630) was so irregular that months could pass when neither the men nor the officers received a real. As for the rations, one can judge of them from a letter addressed from Flanders to the Count of Olivares, first minister of Philip IV, in 1629: ' . . . Soldiers are dying of hunger, going about half-naked, and begging for alms from door to door. . . . We have reached a point of extreme misery, destitution, and poverty, especially the Spaniards, who die off like flies, and not one from wounds.'[12]

One can understand, in these conditions, the difficulty of maintaining discipline among the troops, and the all-too-frequent cases of mutiny, which, especially in Flanders, endangered the previous successes of the Spanish forces. One can understand also that war feeds on war, that the soldier must live off the land that he occupies, be it friendly or hostile, and that pillage and the holding to ransom of the civil population are practices which were not only common but tolerated. In Spain, even the billeting of troops was a calamity for those towns and villages which had not obtained the privilege of being exempted, and the excesses committed by the troops concentrated in Catalonia to repel a French invasion were a determining factor in the uprising of Barcelona against the authority of the king of Spain in 1640.

Even Madrid, where the government usually forbade the army to take up quarters (with the exception of the Royal Guards), did not entirely escape these misfortunes, for the capital saw a constant stream of men cut off from the army: officers on the reserve who besieged the offices of the war council and the antechambers of the palace; private soldiers, discharged following the disbandment of their companies, or in the process of enlisting; the pensioners, real or fake, who solicited charity from passers-by, extolling their past feats of arms. Proteced from the civil law by the military *fuero*, some of them resorted to other 'exploits', as related by the *News* of Madrid:

'Not a day passes but people are found killed or wounded by brigands or soldiers; houses burgled; young girls and widows weeping because they have been assaulted and robbed: such is the confidence that the soldiers have in the war council. . . .'

'In Madrid in a fortnight, there were seventy dead and forty wounded in the hospitals, so many were the exploits of the soldiers.'[13]

More serious again for the king of all Spain than the excesses of individuals was the decline of the military spirit which took place at the same time. In an order of the day of 1632, the king admitted that: ' . . . The discipline of my armies has declined in all parts and, as a result, they no longer enjoy their former prestige.' The aristocracy itself refused to answer the call of the king, or deserted the ranks of the army, like the noblemen 'mobilized' in 1640 by Olivares at the time of the revolt of Catalonia.[14] Twenty years later when Luis de Haro hastened to the defence of Badajoz, besieged by the Portuguese ' . . . only about fifteen to twenty reliable men followed him, the others refusing to leave the court, relishing its pleasures above valour in battle and the honour of the country'.[15]

The decadence of military virtues, contrasted with the arrogance of the soldier and the crimes of which he was guilty, explains the disrepute which began to attach to the military life, and gave birth,

13. The relief of Cadiz, by Zurbaran

14. The Surrender of Breda

not only among foreigners, but also in Spain itself, to the character of the *fanfarrón*, cowardly and boastful, a figure more redoubtable in his handling of the bottle and the virtue of young girls than in facing the enemy:

> I know how to steal hens and chickens,
> And give full welcome to a fallen girl,
> To bring the good cards back into play,
> And in combat and battle to show
> My foe a clean pair of heels,

said the soldier in a play by Tirso de Molina. Even Lope de Vega who, as we have seen, was a great admirer of the heroism of Alonso de Contreras, has this piece of dialogue in one of his plays, the action of which takes place in Palermo:

> Who are these? Men of good repute?
> – Soldiers and Spaniards they be,
> Compact of words and boasts and lies,
> Arrogance, bluster, and foul deeds.

It is not, however, in these mockeries that we must seek the most significant evidence of the decline of the military spirit, but in the picaresque romance *Estebanillo Gonzales*.[16] *The Life and High Adventures of Estebanillo* is a sort of antitheses – one might almost say a parody – of the life of Alonso de Contreras. The contrast is even more striking because, although Estebanillo has obviously romanticized certain of his adventures to the point of burlesque, the two characters had had a real existence, with many things in common. Both had wandered over Europe under the Spanish banner, and both had taken part in some of the great military episodes of their time. But, whereas one is the epitome of all the heroic virtues put at the service of an ideal, the other takes upon himself the task of denigrating, depreciating, and ridiculing everything which had been done, for a century, to the glory and honour of the armies of Spain.

Born in Rome in 1608 of a Spanish father, Estebanillo ran away, as Alonso had done, from the shop where he had been apprenticed, and at thirteen became a standard-bearer in a company raised at Messina. But his ambition was the reverse of that of the young Contreras. The latter had given up his safe job as a scullion in order to take up arms; the former discarded his standard to become assistant cook on a ship carrying his company to fight the Turks,

o

for he explained, 'I was so neutral in this business that my only thought was to fill my belly, having my stove as my crossbow, a long spoon as my pike, and an old cauldron as my piece of naval artillery.'

This idyllic existence was short-lived; he was sacked by the captain. Estebanillo then tramped across Italy, trying different jobs – which always ended in the sack, for stealing – and finally, finding himself without resources, he re-enlisted. But when he heard that his *tercio* was on the way to Flanders, 'riding the mules of St Francis' (i.e. on foot), he deserted with fifteen of his comrades to go and look for a place in another company, which he abandoned after a few days to go home to Spain. Successively a pilgrim of 'St James', an actor and a vendor of nostrums, he eventually arrived in Andalusia and, for a time, lived on the fat of the land, until the day when his company set out on the march. As they went through a forest Estebanillo and some fifty of the soldiers 'chucked' the officer who commanded them: 'We left him on his own, with only a banner, the drummer, the lieutenant, and a sergeant, as well as the young boys who carried the baggage.' This particular officer lacked understanding; he did not know how to alleviate the fatigues of his men, ' . . . not realizing that it is easy to find an officer, but very difficult to muster fifty men. . . .' This facility allowed Estebanillo to play this trick each time he was short of money.

Threatened with prison in Malaga for some misdeed, he managed to board a ship bound for France (then at war with Spain). How should he live in this unknown country? 'I met a sergeant in a village who asked me if I would like to be a soldier and serve "His Most Christian Majesty". I, suffering from such acute pangs of hunger that I would have served the Grand Turk for a square meal, said "Yes".' Estebanillo was then incorporated into an army which faced the Spaniards in the *compté* of Nice; he lost not a moment in deserting to the other side, and so signed on for a new engagement. But his regiment was ordered to the north, to Germany, where he would have to fight. To avoid further risks Estebanillo hit on the safe solution: he resumed the office of cook which he had held at the beginning of his 'military' career.

Thus he was in a safe position to witness one of the military exploits which marked the last decades of the might of Spain: the battle of Nordlingen, in which the troops of Philip IV crushed the redoubtable Swedish army which Gustavus Adolphus had forged. But, if his account is about the way his comrades covered themselves with glory, his real motive is to glorify himself for having taken no part, and for being always as far as possible from where the grapeshot rained down. On the eve of the battle, sensing that the clash between the two armies would be very savage, he started by concealing himself in the carcase of a horse. Then fearing that he might be spotted, he took advantage of darkness to sneak further from the field of battle. 'I met my captain who asked me: "Why don't you take a pike and die in the defence of the Faith, or give the victory to your King?" I answered him: "If his Majesty waits for what I give him, he'll catch it!"'

And when his captain was carried back, mortally wounded after having fought with great valour, Estebanillo drew this cynical conclusion from the episode: 'They brought him to the town, where, *because he had not been as wise as me*, he returned his soul to his Creator.'[17]

The victory at Nordlingen (1634) came at the very time when Alonso de Contreras, the incarnation of the spirit of heroism, ended his military career. When, fifteen years later, Estebanillo wrote the story of his adventures, in which he delighted in displaying his cowardice and indifference to a cause for which his comrades were shedding their blood, the battle of Rocroi (1643) delivered the final blow to the myth of Spain's invincibility. The contrast between these two men is symbolic: Alonso de Contreras chose a military career at the end of the reign of Philip II at a time when Spain, undermined at home, was still dominant in Europe. It was a Spain not only ruined, but also doubting itself, which is reflected in the derision of Estebanillo Gonzalez.

A contemporary Spanish historian asks:

'What happened to those kings from whom the fastness of a palace, or from the shelter of a monastery governed the world? What became of those great captains of war who conquered kingdoms and worlds? What of the *heroic story*, written with the blood of our soldiers and sailors on the Garigliano, at Oran, Pavia, Tunis, at Otumba and in Peru, at Lepanto and at St Quentin? *The epic was finished. The picaresque romance was at its apogee.*'[18]

CHAPTER ELEVEN

THE PICARESQUE LIFE

The Picaro *and the picaresque world. The picaresque romance as a social document — Picaresque fauna and its variety: beggars, swindlers, killers, and prostitutes — The geography of* Picaresca *— Picaresque philosophy and its significance in Spain in the Golden Century.*

It was in 1599 – a year after the death of Philip II – that the term *picaro* makes its first appearance in Spanish literature to describe *Guzman de Alfarache,* in which Mateo Aleman related his life and adventures. The word had a dazzling future; not only did the 'picaresque' romance enjoy undiminishing success for half a century in Spain, but the *picaro* became like the *hidalgo,* one of the characteristic types of Spanish society of the Golden Age, as reflected in its literature. It is not easy, however, to give an exact equivalent of this word, for the variety of literary incarnations are charged with so many different meanings and nuances. The best translation remains without doubt the one given to it by contemporary French writers, especially Chapelain – as excellent an authority on Spain as he is execrable as a poet – who translated Mateo Aleman's romance under the title: *The Scoundrels, or The Life of Guzman de Alfarache, a Mirror of Human Life.*[1]

Nevertheless, one must distinguish between the *picaro* glorified by literature and the picaresque society in which he evolved. The *picaro* type, cynical, amoral, antisocial, was not an evil-doer nor even a professional 'rogue'. But the hazards of life, and above all the refusal to conform to the conventions which a normal society imposes, made him find his *milieu* among those who lived on the fringe of that society; a region infested by every sort of vagrant and scoundrel, ranging from the harmless beggar to the swindler, from the professional thief to the hired killer and the common assassin. But, if the *picaro* was at home in this world, he disdained to join its ranks permanently, and his adventurous and most vagabond life, with brief intervals of stability, allowed him to watch, to judge, and to depict the other social groups. In this sense the picaresque romance can well be said to be a 'mirror of mankind'.

But what is the value of the image it gives us? It appears to us to be essentially realistic, since the writer is supposed to relate all the vicissitudes of his existence, hiding nothing and not letting himself be blinded or hindered by the prejudices and conventions which appertain to rank, to fortune or to good sense. Must we then see in such a scene not only an authentic picture, but perhaps the only true picture of society at that time?

Such an interpretation is contradicted by the fact that the picaresque romance became a true literary *genre*, the archetype of which was the *Lazarillo de Tormes*, preceding *Guzman* by half a century. Although the word *picaro* does not appear, none the less it served as the model for all later work, as much for its auto-biographical form as for its background. In the story of his 'fortunes and adversities' Lazarillo leads the reader through the society of his time, presenting his successive masters, amongst whom stands out the *hidalgo*, who, with the same stereotyped traits, reappeared in most of the later romances.[2]

As generally happens in questions of imitation and literary evolution, the significant features of the model, often discreetly indicated, were accentuated to the point of over-writing and cari-catured in subsequent works. The tribulations suffered by the young Lazare are a mere trifle compared with the innumerable adventures of the picaresque heroes of the following epoch – *Guzman de Alfarache, Marcos de Obregon, Pablos de Segovia, Estebanillo Gonzalez*, and many others – each writer seeming to outdo those who had preceded him in the multiplication and odd-ness of the episodes. If many of these, taken in isolation, preserve a certain stamp of authenticity, their cumulative effect becomes improbable and suggests that the author is more anxious to divert his readers in the approved manner than to give an exact portrait of social reality in those days. Furthermore, how can one believe that, in a society where the moral values of honour and the faith permeated the mind, the picaresque world with its gallery of characteristic types – cheats, prostitutes, ruffians, complaisant hus-bands, and corrupt magistrates – could maintain such a position? Many sound judges have refused to give any documentary value to this literature as a social record of the period.[3]

But such a conclusion goes too far. There is too much non-literary evidence for anyone to dismiss the picaresque novel as simple fiction. It is a fact, to begin with, that the autobiographical form which it normally adopts often corresponds to real life. If the author has evidently not know all the tribulations attributed to his hero, he has frequently led like him an adventurous life which has given him intimate knowledge of the social *milieu* in which the action of the novel is set.

Mateo Aleman, author of *Guzman*, was the son of a surgeon at the prison of Seville, which gave him the chance to study, from an early age, the vagabond world of which this great Andalusian town was in some ways the capital. After having led the tumultuous life af an impoverished student at Salamanca and Alcala, he went off to seek his fortune in Italy. Then he returned to Spain where certain regrettable happenings enabled him, this time as an inmate, to get to know the rigours of a prison cell, before he embarked for the Castillian Indies to die in Mexico. *The Diverting Voyage* (*El viaje entretenido*) is the story, romanticized, of the life of the author, Augustin de Rojas: a typical case of the authentic *picaro*. By birth *hidalgo*, the young Rojas, at the age of fourteen, absconded from the stately home where he had been placed as a page, and headed for Seville. Necessity and the spirit of adventure inspired him next, like so many others, to join the army; he fought in France and was taken prisoner. Freed, he sailed away on privateering raids against the English, and then, after many voyages, finished up in Italy, where he led a vagabond existence for some time. On returning to Spain he was pursued by the law for murder, and found sanctuary in a church. He could leave it only thanks to the generosity of a woman who, beguiled by his good looks, ruined herself to put an end to the proceedings taken out against him. He then sank, with her, to the lowest *picaresca* level, living by begging and theft, all the while earning a little money by means of sermons which he composed for an Augustinian friar. . . . Next he joined a band of strolling players, and shared the hazards and hardships of their life until the government of Philip II ordered the closure of all theatres. Having become a shopkeeper in Granada, an amorous disillusionment decided him to become a hermit in the Sierra di Cordova. After some time he returned to 'civil' life, got married, underwent again some varied adventures which landed him back in prison, and ended his days as the clerk of the royal court of justice at Zamora, after having, he says, 'struggled for twenty-five years, for his great sins, in the sad camp of misery'.[4]

Many other cases could be cited: for example that of Vincente Espinel, author of *The Life of the Esquire Marcos of Obregon*, of which one could declare that 'knowing the facts about the life of the novelist, one could not say which is the more interesting for its picturesqueness and singularity: the adventures of Obregon, as narrated by Espinel, or the vicissitudes in the life of Espinel, as they are mirrored in *Marcos de Obregon*'.[5]

But more significant again than this total or partial identification of the author with his heroes is the coincidence of many features of picaresque fiction with the evidence of contemporary documents. Knowing the exasperating baroquism of Quevedo, his need to push caricature and satire to the extreme, one's credulity is strained by reading his description of the lives of these knights of the road. Among them Pablos de Segovia (*El Buscon*) lived for several weeks by begging and theft, endeavouring to preserve the dignity and outward appearance of a *hidalgo* by hiding, under an ample cape, garments made of *filthy rags*. As one of those who 'educated' Pablos said:

'We hold the sun to be our worst enemy, because he lays bare our darns, our rags, and our patches. . . . We have nothing on our bodies which has not previously been something else. . . . You see this doublet? Well, it was a pair of breeches, daughters of a cloak, granddaughters of a cowl . . . and, looking at my shoes, who would believe that they are next to the skin, without stockings or anything else in between? Who would imagine, when he sees this ruff, that I have no shirt? It is because, Mr Scholar, a gentleman can do without almost anything, but to be without a starched ruff . . . never!'

It is a burlesque description which it is difficult to take literally. One reads, moreover, in a letter from a Jesuit father to a colleague:

'Three or four days ago in Madrid a man was arrested who, that morning, was dressed in rags and feigned to be crippled and sick, begging for alms with great cries and lamentations for fully an hour. Then he returned to his dwelling, ate and reclothed himself splendidly in silk, and combed his hair neatly. He had a good demeanour, and off he went for a stroll, dressed up to the nines. He did not lack curious neighbours, however, who asked themselves how he managed to live. They spied on him one morning

215

when he went out, and in the evening, thus discovering his "dodge". They notified the *alcalde* who came at once to arrest him. When they went to his house, they found a beautiful bed, a chest full of fine linen, and other clothes of silk, all new; his ragged clothes were in one corner, elsewhere a table and two chairs and a little book in which he entered each day what he collected in alms, and how he spent it. He was persuaded to confess without difficulty, and declared that he *had adopted this way of life to avoid the pitfalls of those who wander about and live in brilliant style, having neither rent nor source of income, working at night on unguarded houses, laying hands on anything which was not locked up.*'[6]

This testimony confirms and enriches that of Quevedo.

It is not, then, possible to deny all documentary value to the picaresque novel. But one must consider whether the picture it gives of Spanish society is not systematically distorted, as, in another diametrically opposed sense, the picture of a society completely dominated by a feeling of honour which was presented at the same time by the Spanish theatre in its finest productions was also distorted. It is, then, the weight of the other sources, of a purely historical character, that we must look to as a confirmation on which we can rely. Now these sources abound in the form of *relaciones* or *avisos* and private correspondence, reports of legal proceedings, royal decrees, political and economic tracts; all of which attest not only to the numerical importance of the beggarly class but also to the marked tendency to the 'picarization' of certain sections of Spanish society quite foreign to this class.

This social deterioration, well understood by the most perspicacious contemporaries, stems from many causes in the material and moral spheres. In the material sphere, it is the impoverishment of Spain, the consequence of an economic decline, the manifestations of which one has seen elsewhere: peasants driven from their lands, labourers without work, ruined artisans swelling the flood of human flotsam coming to try its luck in the big cities, or, at the very least, to live off them by begging. Among the other elements which came to swell the picaresque tribe, two have particular importance: soldiers and students. Alongside the disabled and infirm soldiers who solicited public charity by displaying their wounds, there were all those – and they were very numerous – for whom the military life and the picaresque life constituted alternate stages of one and the same existence, as was the case for Estebanillo Gonzalez. Hunger – or the need to escape from justice – obliged them to enlist; they deserted at the first opportunity in order to resume, far away from the scene of their earlier exploits, their shabby practices, made even more despicable by their army experiences.

As for the student world, it was in constant touch, one might say, with the underworld and there was scarcely a picaresque here who did not recall his happy sojourn at Alcala or Salamanca. There is ample proof that it is not merely a question of literary fashion, evoking picturesque descriptions of student life: numerous were the young men, from humble and unpretentious families, who, having set out to gain the degree which would allow them to escape from their original backgrounds, acquired at the university or in its surroundings only a taste for a 'free' life and, at the same time, a contempt for manual work.

This contempt for manual skills and, in a more general way, for productive activities explains how the picaresque world attracted to a far from negligible extent a number of recruits from the impoverished petty nobility, and from many of those who, rightly or wrongly, pretended to the rank of *hidalgo*, preferring 'glamour' rather than applying themselves to a form of livelihood which would lower them in the eyes of the world as well as in their own. A contemporary Spanish historian who keenly investigated the sources of the mentality of the Spaniard of the Golden Age, poses these questions:

'Could it be that the *picaro was not a creature of pure fiction*; could it be that the *picaresca*, which had not created these archetypes out of nothing, would have been conceived in any other country but ours? Could they have been born to a people with a well-developed economic life, had there not been such social disparity between the powerful and the masses whom fortune had disinherited; where the obverse and the reverse of the social life did not offer so violent a contrast as that to the south of the Pyrenees? *For in Spain we lacked a bourgeois conscience capable of offering an ideal life different from the herioc ideal and its picaresque reverse.*'[7]

The most diverse elements – among which we must not forget certain renegades from the cloister – contributed, then, to the breeding of the picaresque 'fauna', with which contemporary writers amuse themselves occasionally by classifying the specimen into genera and species. In order of increasing obnoxiousness, the lowest is the beggar, who also belonged to a category classified juridically. Begging was in fact recognized as a right for those who could not work (whom the law distinguished from the *ragos*, who refused to work). The 'recognized' beggar was obliged to hold a 'licence' furnished by the priest in his place of origin, which allowed him to beg for alms in the locality and for six leagues around.[8] Among them there was a privileged class: the blind, who had the monopoly of reciting or 'chanting' the prayers which were intended to preserve individuals and the community from all manner of maladies and calamities. In certain towns the blind were grouped in brotherhoods, whose statutes, officially recognized by the municipal authorities, protected their rights. The statutes of the brotherhood of Madrid assured to their members, in addition to a monopoly of orisons, that of the selling of 'gazettes', gossip sheets, and almanacs; in Saragossa it was laid down that, if a blind man having regular clients fell ill,

'. . . in order that the goodwill of these aforesaid parishioners should not be lost, the stewards of the confraternity are to have the said prayers chanted in the said houses by other members of the brotherhood . . . and the money received for the said prayers shall serve to support the sick man while his illness lasts, and afterwards he shall retrieve his parishioners.'[9]

But the bogus blind men, like the bogus cripples, swarmed in the big cities, importuning passers-by at the crossroads and the faithful at the doors of the churches, with their groans and their entreaties, and sometimes with their insults. A work at the beginning of the seventeenth century dedicated to King Philip III, *A Discourse on the Protection due to the Genuine Poor and on the Abatement of Pretenders*, estimated the number of those who lived in Spain on public charity at 150,000, the great part of them being frauds.[10] It describes several of the 'dodges' used by those shamming illness and infirmity – such as 'amputating' an arm, or covering their bodies with faked scars, or giving themselves a cadaverous pallor, and tells the story of the beggar who played the part of a dying man in Atocha Street in Madrid. While he simulated the agony of dying, his companions put a candle between his hands and made a collection for his burial. Unfortunately for them there happened to be passing a doctor, who stopped and felt the pulse of the sick man, who promptly leapt to his feet and made off as fast as his legs would carry him.

The sham blind, sellers of pious prayers, can be compared with the bogus pilgrims who betook themselves or pretended to be on their way to the shrine of St James of Compostella, begging alms from the inhabitants of the towns and villages through which they passed. Many came from France, Germany, and elsewhere, but there were among them also a good number of Spaniards. Between two periods of service in the army, Estebanillo Gonzalez turned pilgrim, 'to feast at all hours, and not to fast all the time'. He joined forces with a Frenchman and a Genoese, both, like him, past masters in the art of dodging work.

'Having replenished our flasks discreetly, we began our pilgrimage with such fervour that on the day we tramped the most we never went more than two leagues, so as not to make hard work of an amusing diversion. On the road we harvested the fruit of lonely vines, we captured orphan chickens, and, with pleasantries on our lips, proceeded on our way loaded with money and with alms. . . .'

A degree above those who lived by begging came the *picaros*, who, with the aid of a little work sufficient to keep them from the offence of vagabondage, applied themselves to scrounging and petty theft; such as the *pinches de cocina* (scullions), who could always find enough to feed themselves and their friends plentifully at the expense of the kitchens where they were employed, and the *esportilleros* (street porters and errand boys), who being responsible for delivering to the homes of customers goods of all kinds, pinched anything that could be hidden easily under their clothes. Alongside them were the pedlars (*buhonero*), a calling carried on for some time by Estebanillo after being, he says, 'degraded' from his status of pilgrim, and investing his capital in the purchase of knives, combs, rosaries, needles, and other shoddy wares, which he sold in the streets of Seville, an obligatory stage in every picaresque life.

The passion for gaming which ravaged every class was a sure source of revenue for those who knew how to exploit it. Authorized gaming-houses were in existence (generally licensed to disabled veteran soldiers in lieu of a pension), but far more numerous were

219

the gambling-houses (*garitos*), where professional gamblers lay in wait to fleece too gullible clients. Sometimes they formed themselves into groups, in which each member of the gang had his special job. First, Quevedo tells us, there was the 'fixer' (*fullero*), whose job was to prepare several packs of marked cards in case one of them should be discovered. Then came the 'ruffian', whose job was to vanish at the end of the game so that those who had been fleeced could never discover the trick. Lastly, there was the 'catcher' or tout, whose job was to entice into the gambling den the too gullible amateur, or the one who was too sure of himself.

At the summit of the picaresque hierarchy and dominating the rabble of those who lived by their wits by exploiting the charity, the credulity or the unwariness of others, were those who really constituted the 'dangerous class', which comprised the professional thieves and the assassins. Amongst these there were a great number of specialists, and Carlos Garcia, a contemporary of Philip IV, distinguishes among the thieves alone at least a dozen varieties, among them cutpurses, the *capeadores* (specialists in the theft of capes and mantles during the night), the *salteadores* (highwaymen), the 'ship-boys' (*grumetes*), so called because of their skill at climbing rope-ladders when robbing a house, the 'apostles' who, like St Peter, were furnished with a handsome bunch of keys; the 'satyrs', who rustled cattle from the fields, and even the 'devotees' – expert at breaking open church alms-boxes and stripping the precious ornaments from the statues of saints.[11]

The aristocracy of crime was composed of the 'heroes' (*valentones*) and the 'killers' (*matones*), who sported a uniform rather like that of a soldier (many had formerly been soldiers): a hat with a large brim, sometimes trimmed with feathers, a leather doublet (often hiding a coat of mail), and a long sword thrust into the belt. They worked for a 'fee', hiring out their services to those who wanted to rid themselves of some importunate person by means of a quarrel opportunely provoked, or by a murder pure and simple. But admiration for their personal courage lent them a prestige which outlived them, if by chance their crimes led them to the scaffold, and if they still retained up to their last moment the courage for which they were known during their lives. Perez Vasquez de Escamillo and Alonso Alvarez de Soria, two notorious bandits hanged in Seville during the sixteenth century, are remembered by posterity because of their bravery and the arrogance with which they faced their execution; their memory was immortalized by Lope de Vega. And Quevedo, who mentions Escamillo in his *Buscon*, was no doubt inspired by these 'exemplary' episodes when he made the hangman describe to Pablos of Segovia the last moments of his father:

'Your father died, a little more than a week ago, with more courage than one could believe possible in this world. I speak as the man who hanged him. He was mounted on a donkey which took him to the scaffold without his putting a foot in the stirrup, and because of his bearing and the crucifix which was carried before him, there was not a soul who judged that he deserved to be hanged. He went with a very easy air, looking up at the windows, and saluting courteously those who had left their shops to see him pass. Twice he straightened his moustaches. He besought his confessors to compose themselves and praised them for speaking so beautifully. Arrived at the foot of the gibbet, he put his foot on the ladder and mounted it, neither slowly nor on all fours, and, finding a rung broken, he turned to the officials and asked them to replace it for the next man, for not everyone had the same guts as he. I cannot tell you how good an impression he made on everybody present. Once aloft, he sat down, threw behind him the folds of his cape, took the rope and placed it exactly upon his Adam's apple. Then, seeing the theatin brother preparing to preach, he said: "Father, I pray you dispense with your sermon. Give us a little of the *Credo* and let us have a speedy end to it all." So saying, he let himself fall without crossing his legs nor making a single gesture, and he maintained such a dignity throughout that there was no man there who could have asked any more of him.'[12]

In the big cities, where the lowest of the low represented no small part of the population, thieves and assassins sometimes formed organized bands with their informers, their accomplices, and their 'fences'. Is it true that 'brotherhoods' of thieves, having their rules in imitation of the pious and charitable confraternities, really existed? Cervantes, in his 'exemplary novel', *Rinconete y Cortadillo*, sets the action in Seville in 1598. He shows us a confraternity placed under the supreme rule of Monipodio, the members of which were joined together in the furtherance of their 'trade'. Their devotional observances were very strict, and they dedicated a large part of their earnings to the saying of masses for their 'brothers' who had died on the scaffold. One might be tempted to attribute to the Cervantes imagination the amusing effects that he gets from this paradox, if it were not for a testimony dating from 1592, which seems to corroborate what he says. Luis Zapata wrote:

'In Seville there is, they say, a brotherhood of thieves, with its prior and its consuls, like a proper merchant guild; it has depositories, where they keep the proceeds from robberies, and a chest with triple locks, where they keep a record of what they steal and what they sell; from this they take their necessary expenses, and *also monies needed to buy people who would be useful, when it is a question of saving someone who finds himself in a troublesome situation.* They are very circumspect about the admission of new members; they accept only brave men, able fellows, *"old christians"; they welcome none who are not the servants of rich or influential people in the town, or officers of the law,* and the first thing they have to swear is that, even if they were to be cut into little pieces, they would suffer every torment, rather than give away one of their companions.'[13]

The allusion to the 'funds of corruption' which enabled bribery to be paid to people in positions where they ought to uphold the law, highlights the impotence of the authorities in putting a stop to certain excesses. It is undoubtedly difficult to believe the repeated claims of the picaresque novel, especially in *Guzman de Alfarache*, that all judges were venal and all the alquazils in league with the thieves. One cannot, however, fail to be impressed by the number of accusations of this sort which are sometimes confirmed by the authorities themselves. The *Santa Hermandad* and its *cuadrilleros* (gendarmes), responsible for law and order in the countryside, had a detestable reputation: 'If you have not committed any fault,' says Guzman, 'then God save you from the Santa Hermandad, for these "holy cuadrilleros" are almost all nasty fellows without hearts; and many of them would not hesitate to testify against you under solemn oath, because they have received money, or simply a jug of wine, to bear false witness.' We find the same charges in the deliberations of the municipality of Osuna, in Andalusia, which 'having considered the number of *cuaderillos* who go off without an order from their alcaydes and, furthermore, get mixed up in denunciations and other matters which have nothing to do with their business, resulting in great harm and trouble', the municipality forbade them to leave the town without the express permission of the judicial authorities.[14] The lack of confidence which the government had in its own judicial officers and the police is illustrated by the royal edicts of 1610 and 1613 forbidding these officials, on the one hand, to frequent taverns, and forbidding innkeepers and wine retailers, on the other, to advance them any money.[15]

It would be absurd, however, to generalize. It often happened that an *alcalde* took his office seriously, and really tried to purge the town of the most dangerous villains. For those who fell into the hands of the law, punishment was merciless, and the spectacular character given to the execution of sentences was intended to increase the exemplary effect. The condemned man, garbed in a sort of white tunic and wearing a blue cap (a costume nicknamed 'the uniform of the Conception', the wearing of which secured heavenly indulgences for the wearer), made his last journey from the prison to the scaffold mounted on a mule or donkey, his hands bound to a crucifix, a halter round his neck, and flanked by two monks who exhorted him to die well. Before him went the town-crier, proclaiming his crimes and, behind him, on horseback, the alquazil who had captured him, as well as the judge who had sentenced him. The procession halted in front of every shrine or church on the way to recite a prayer. The execution once over (generally by hanging, beheading being the privilege of noblemen), the corpse was quartered and the quarters put on view at cross-roads and at the entrance to the town.

For those who knew that the police were looking for them there was only one haven: the inviolable sanctuary offered within the precincts of a church, often marked off by grilles or by chains. Such places thus became rendezvous for brigands who came to revictual their companions, now safe from the law, or for loose women, who turned a sacred place into a brothel.

Prostitution, in fact, held an important place in the picaresque world, for which it provided a source of revenue. The women, like the menfolk, were of various grades. The lowest were those women working in 'houses' (*mancebias*), whose activities had been regulated by Philip II in 1572 and 1575. Each *mancebia* was placed under the authority of a 'father' or a 'mother' recognized by the public authority, who, on taking charge, had to swear to obey the relevant royal decrees. They were forbidden to admit a married woman (still less, a young virgin), or a woman burdened with debts. They were likewise forbidden to lend money to their '*pension-naires*', as this could serve as a means of binding them indefinitely to their profession. Every week, the women had to be examined by a doctor; in cases of contagious disease, they were immediately sent to hospital.

The dress of the prostitutes was itself fixed by the regulations, copies of which had to be displayed in the 'house'. So that they should not be mistaken for respectable women, they were not allowed to wear trailing dresses, nor shoes with high heels, but a short red cloak thrown over the shoulders. They were denied the right to be accompanied by a page when they left the house, and to kneel on a hassock in church. The 'father' was responsible, under the authority of the municipal magistrates, for the orderly running of the establishment. Entry was forbidden to any man carrying sword or dagger; the tariff varied with the qualities and charms of the *pensionnaires,* and also according to requirements. A regulation affecting charges in the brothels of Aragon gives remarkable details: on the bed, half a real; in the bed, one real....[16]

The local authority also watched over the moral health of prostitutes; they were forbidden to ply their trade during Holy Week. Furthermore, during Lent, they were officially exhorted to repent; they were led into church where a preacher would deliver a fine sermon on the theme of the Magdalen. Then he would come down from the pulpit and offer them the crucifix saying: 'Behold the Lord; embrace Him.' If one of them did this she would be taken to a convent for repentant women; but the majority turned away to return to their 'work'.

Every town of any importance in Spain had one of these *puterias* some of which were particularly renowned, notably those in Valencia. 'There is in Valencia, as everywhere in Spain, but most delightful here,' writes Barthélemy Joly, 'a large and celebrated place full of girls dedicated to the public pleasure; there is a whole quarter of the city where they can ply their trade in complete freedom. The women are dirt cheap compared with the excessively high prices of other merchandise.'[17] This quarter consisted of rows of little houses, each surrounded by a garden, which were the property of the 'fathers' and the 'mothers' who installed the prosti-tutes in them. Seville had a quarter of the same sort, in the outer

15. Lope de Vega, by Obra de Caxes

16. Cervantes, by Juan de Jauregui

sanctuary of La Lagune, where the houses belonged partly to the municipality and partly to individuals – often persons of some note in the city – who appointed the brothel-keepers. The success of these establishments was considerable, if one can believe the contemporary accounts of Spaniards and foreigners alike. Enrique Cock, 'apostolic notary and constable of the Royal Guard' under Philip II, declared that 'the public *puteria* is so common in Spain that on entering a town, many people go there before going to the church'.[18] Another writer says, apropos the *mancebias* in the towns of Aragon, that the stream of low fellows is such that 'they fight at the entrance to keep their turn as though they were queuing for an audience with a prince or a judge. . . .'[19]

But prostitution overflowed its special 'reserves' and the Spanish language defined a whole hierarchy of those who took part in the traffic, from the street-walkers at street corners (*ramera, cantonera*), to the *dama de achaque*, who looked like an honest bourgeoise, to the *tusona* ('goldilocks', so called in allusion to the Golden Fleece, most illustrious of the orders of chivalry), who played at being the great lady, and, to enhance her 'respectability' – and her price – would employ a duenna to accompany her, or a pimp who pretended to be her squire. Certain picaresque novels have as the heroine one of these adventuresses, such as *La picara Justina*, or *Elena, Daughter of Celestine*, whose spirited demeanour and irresistible charm have been depicted by Salas Barbadillo:

'What a woman, my friends! If you had seen her going out, only one eye visible, with a cloak of Seville satin, a dark dress, with long sleeves, high-heeled shoes, walking with assurance and a long stride, I do not know which among you would have been virtuous enough not to follow her, if not with your legs, at least with your eyes, during the brief instant in which she crossed the road.'[20]

Like every 'circle', that of the *picaresca* had its own particular slang, the 'jargon of the brotherhood' (*jerga de germania*), the use of which served as a means of recognition among the vagabonds; for, says the attorney Chaves in his description of the prison at Seville, 'it is an outrage among these people to call things by their proper names'. The argot was notable for its taste for 'antiphrases' (the 'tavern' became the 'hermitage'), and for the metaphors with which it clothed the grim realities of life and death: the torture-chamber was called the 'confessional', where one was recommended not to 'sing' even if silence forced you to 'wed the widow' (the gallows), and led you to *finibus terrae*.

The picaresque world also had its own geography, and he was not a 'passed-out' *picaro* who had not graduated through the different stages before reaching 'the high places', whose reputation, doubtless due in large measure to literary works, spread throughout Spain. In Madrid the Place of the Blacksmiths (Herradores) and the Puerta del Sol were the principal rendezvous of the light-fingered gentry; in Segovia they met in the shadow of the Roman aqueduct, in the little square of the Azoguejo; Toledo was celebrated for its Zocodover (an old Arab bazaar), and Seville for its Arenal (Strand), which ran down to the Guadalquivir. But even their renown was eclipsed by the Potro in Cordova; it produced the fine flower of the *picaresca*. The very fact of having been born there was almost a sign of 'nobility', and it was there that Estebanillo Gonzalez came seeking recognition of his merits, for 'having been student, page, soldier, I lacked nothing but this degree to become a doctor of the laws of my chosen profession. . . .' It was, however, the little Andalusian port of Zahara, with its tunny-fishers, which was the supreme hide-out, the Mecca of the *picaro*, if one can believe Cervantes, who traces, in his *Illustrious Kitchen Maid*, the career and social progress of Diego de Carriazo:

'He learnt to play knuckle-bones in Madrid, écarté in the suburbs of Toledo and piquet in the barbicans of Seville, passing through all the grades of *picaro* to the summit where he found his mastership in the tunny-nets of Zahara, the end of the rainbow for all *picaros*. O *picaros* of the kitchen, dirty, fat, and shiny; bogus beggars and cripples, counterfeiters, cutpurses from Zocodover or other places in Madrid, braying prayer-mongers, street-porters of Seville, pimps of the lowest order, and all the teeming horde, rejoicing in the name – *picaro*! But do not call yourselves *picaros* if you have not served two terms at Tunnyfish Academy. Here one sings; there one blasphemes God; there they dispute and fight, and, everywhere they steal. It is there that liberty finds its true domain, and here flourish its golden "works". And here come many fathers of good families to look for their sons, *only to discover that the boy hates being snatched from this life as if he were being led to his death.*'[21]

We must make ample allowance for the 'poetic licence' which inspired the author of *Don Quixote* to write this enthusiastic evocation, but we cannot isolate from other eulogies of the picaresque life that are to be found in the literature of the time, and which eloquently testify to the attraction which the carefree life of the *picaro* had for many minds. It is one of the constantly recurring themes in *Guzman de Alfarache*, this 'compendium of the picaresque philosophy', whose author knew and never forgot, the miseries and the delights of that existence:

'O twice, thrice, and four times blessed art thou who risest up in the morning at whatever hour thou choosest, troubling thyself neither to wait upon anybody, nor to be waited upon, free to keep what thou hast without fear of losing it! At every festival, thou hast the best seat; in winter the sunshine, and in summer the shade. Thou layest thy table, thou makest thy bed wherever thou pleasest, and nobody questions thee. . . .'

Yet it was not all joy in this life; the *picaros* knew hunger and thirst, the scorching heat of summers and the rigour of winters without the shelter of a roof, and the last walk that they took was probably the one to the scaffold. What matters all that against the incomparable price of freedom? When Diego de Carriazo, the son, Cervantes tells us, of a noble family of Burgos, ran away from home to travel the world

' . . . he was so content with this carefree life that, despite all its troubles and miseries he never pined for the luxury of his parents' house. His foot-slogging never left him fatigued, and he complained of neither heat nor cold; for him, all the seasons of the year were as sweet as the gentle springtime; he slept as well in the hay as between the sheets; he burrowed into a heap of straw at an inn with as much pleasure as he would bed himself down between two fine sheets of Holland linen. . . .'

The picaresque philosophy goes much deeper than the rejection of and indifference to the comforts of a conformist existence; for these it has nothing but scorn. But what rights do the conformists claim to be superior to the *picaros*? In the name of their moral virtues? 'Everybody robs, everybody lies, everybody cheats; and worst of all are those who make a virtue of it,' replies *Guzman*. In the name of this honour, so greatly vaunted? A fine invention for the rich, for 'hunger and honour make very poor bedfellows'. And what is the value of the social distinctions which are so prized among men? Rich or poor, gentlemen or beggars, are they not all moulded from the same clay or rather from the same mud?

Across the irony and the sarcasm which are directed at the vain glories of the world, we can detect a *Vanitas vanitatum*, where one can find the reflection of the Spain which evolved between the reign of Philip II and his second successor, between Lepanto and Rocroi. Recalling the time of his youth, *Guzman* indicates that then the *picaros* were few in number; today, he says 'there is no profession more widespread, *or more glorified by so many* . . .'[22] It is clear that picarization not only manifests itself as a social factor, which more or less affects all classes, but it is also a state of mind; and in this latter aspect it appears as an attitude of disillusion and renunciation, a kind of weariness with the heriocs, the honour and the grand ventures which had so preoccupied the soul of Spain: 'Forget, forget these puffed-up giants,' cried Mateo Aleman, fifteen years before Cervantes unleashed Don Quixote for his assault on the windmills. . . .[23]

And so, if it is no more than a distorting mirror of the life and society of Spain during the Golden Age, the picaresque novel is nevertheless the expression of a Spain which, weighing the immensity of her efforts against the paucity of the results obtained, looks into her own heart, seeking her destiny.

BIBLIOGRAPHICAL NOTES

From the enormous bibliography in the Spanish language which covers our subject (and one must include in it all the dramatic and romantic literature of our epoch), we can select only a very small part. With reference to the details of the contents indicated in the chapter headings and in the bibliographical notes, we draw attention below to a number of general works which concern social life and its reflection in literature. We must also pay a special tribute to a series of studies in which José DELEITO PIÑUELA paints a sweeping panorama of *The Spain of Philip II*, studies which we have mentioned in the relevant chapters. The bibliographical notes acknowledge our great debt to this historian.

ALTAMIRA (Rafael): *Historia de España y de la civilización española*, 3rd edn, vol. III, 1913.

VICENS VIVES (José): *Historia económica y social de España*, vol III; *Imperio, Aristocrasia, Absolutismo*, 1st part by J. REGLA.

PALACIO ATARD (Vicente); *Derrota, agotamiento, decadencia de la España del siglo XVII*, 2nd edn, 1956.

DOMÍNGUES ORTIZ (Antonio): *Política y hacienda de Felipe IV*, 1960.

MOREL FATIO (Alfred): *L'Espagne au XVIe et au XVIIe siècle* (Heilbronn, 1878) and *Études sur l'Espagne*, First series, 2nd edn (1895), Part V: 'Don Quixote', considered as a critical portrait of Spanish society in the sixteenth and seventeenth centuries.

GONZÁLEZ PALENCIA (Angel): *La España del Siglo de Oro* (1940).

PFANDL (Ludwig): *Introducción al Siglo de Oro (Cultura y costumbres del pueblo español de los siglos XVI y XVII)*, trans. from the German (1929).

VALBUENA PRAT (Angel): *La vida española en la Edad de Oro según las fuentes literarias* (1943).

IGUAL ÚBEDA (Francisco): *El Siglo de Oro* (1951).

DEL ARCO (Ricardo): *La sociedad española en las obras dramaticas de Lope de Vega* (1942).

VILAR (Pierre): *Le temps du 'Quichotte'* (*Europe*, XXXIV, 1956, pp. 3–16).

ORTEGA Y GASSET (José) *Papeles sobre Velázques y Goya*. First part: *De la España alucinante y alucinada de Velázquez*, 1950.

CHAPTER 1: 'LETTER ABOUT A JOURNEY IN SPAIN'

There have been numerous accounts of travel in Spain in the sixteenth and seventeenth centuries, cf. FOUCHÉ DELBOSC: *Bibliographie des voyages en Espagne et au Portugal*, in the *Revue Hispanique*, vol. III, 1896 and FARENELLI: *Viajes por España y Portugal desde la Edad Media hasta el siglo XX* (1921), completed by a *Suplemento* (1930). The most important of these have been collected and published in Spanish by J. GARCÍA MERCADAL: *Viajes de extranjeros por España y Portugal*, 2 vols, Madrid, 1959.

Our 'letter' is chiefly inspired by the accounts of three French travellers who visited Spain between 1600 and 1659: *Voyage of Barthélemy Joly in Spain, 1603–1604* (B. Joly describes himself as 'Counsellor and Almoner to the King of France'), text published by the *Revue Hispanique*, vol. XX, 1909, pp. 460–618; *Voyage d'Espagne* (1655) by Antoine de BRUNEL (Brunel was a Protestant gentleman from the Dauphiné), text in *Revue Hispanique*, vol. XXX, 1914, pp. 119–376; *Journal du voyage d'Espagne* (1659) by François BERTAUT (Bertaut, brother of Mme de Motteville, was chief clerk to the high court of Rouen), text in the *Revue Hispanique*, vol. XLVII, 1919, pp. 1–319. All three were cultivated men, speaking Castillian, who frequently mentioned contemporary Spanish authors as proof of the intellectual radiance of the Golden Age.

The famous *Relations du voyage d'Espagne* of Mme d'Aulnoy, which had a lasting success and which helped to fix in French minds the 'traditional' Spanish traits, are in fact a far from reliable source. Apart from the fact that her journey was made appreciably later (1679–1681), the countess has not hesitated to flavour her description of Spanish life with piquant details of doubtful authenticity. But since her writing is largely inspired by the accounts of travellers who preceded her and, moreover, has drawn on the works of contemporary Spanish authors, her evidence can be used if it is corroborated by other sources. (The Duke of MAURA and A. GONZÁLEZ AMEZUA: *Fantasías y realidades del viaje a Madrid de la Condesa d'Aulnoy*, Madrid, undated, have partly re-established the testimony of Mme d'Aulnoy in face of criticism by Fouché Delbosc (ed. of the *Voyage d'Espagne*).)

1. This prefatory admonition is borrowed from B. JOLY (*Préface*) and from BRUNEL (chap. I, p. 124).

2. BRUNEL, chap. II; the collection of Inquisition dues is also referred to by Camille BORGHÈSE, whose journal of a voyage *Descripción del camino de Irún a Madrid* (the beginning of the seventeenth century) was published by MOREL FATIO: *L'Espagne au XVIᵉ et au XVIIᵉ siècle*, appendix IV.

3. B. JOLY, p. 528; BRUNEL, chap. XXVI.

4. On the Spanish postal services; cf. María MONTÁNEZ MATILLAS: *El correo en la España de los Asturias* (1953): *Le Journal de voyage* of Camille Borghèse gives details of the time taken on mule-back: from Irun to Pampelune, 2 days; from Pampelune to Burgos, 3 days; from Madrid to Escorial, 1 day. Brunel took ten days to make the journey from Irun to Madrid (84 leagues).

5. All travellers of all nationalities deplore the tiresome state of Spanish inns 'where you can find only what you bring with you'.

6. All this passage – including the quotation from *Guzmán de Alfarache* – is in B. JOLY, pp. 541–2.

7. The 'Éloge de l'Espagne' (*Laus Spaniae*), vaunting the fertility and abundance of the country, has been a traditional 'piece' to be found in every history of Spain since Isidore of Seville. *L'Histoire d'Espagne* by P. MARIANA (*Historiae de rebus Hispaniae*, Book XXV, Toledo, 1592–1595) is frequently cited by BERTAUT.

8. On the Castillian countryside, BERTAUT, p. 190. The number of sheep coming from France to Aragon is given by B. JOLY, pp. 501–2.

9. BERTAUT twice returns to his description of the *norias* which he saw in La Mancha (p. 57) and in Andalusia (p. 193).

10. A description by the Polish magnate Jacques Sobieski, who visited Spain in 1611. (GARCÍA MERCADAL: *Viajes . . .*, vol. II, p. 330.)

11. On the splendour of the kingdom of Valencia, B. JOLY, p. 507.

12. The testimony of Brunel, more than forty years after the expulsion, shows us the profound repercussion of this event, not

only on the material plane, but also on the Spanish soul. Cervantes saluted 'the historic decision of the great King Philip III', but the Valencian historian ESCOLANO, in his *Décadas de la historia de Valencia,* speaks of 'the beautiful garden of Spain turned into a dry and desolate steppe'. B. JOLY, who visited the region after the expulsion, mentioned the subterfuges of the Moriscos to evade the Christian discipline.

13. BERTAUT, who also speaks about the expulsion, numbers the exiles at 900,000. H. LAPEYRE (*Géographie de l'Espagne morisque*) has, on the basis of irrefutable documents, given a total of 270,000.

14. In 1619 SÁNCHEZ DE MONCADA wrote: 'The poverty of Spain is the result of the discovery of America', an idea already expressed in the reign of Philip II by the author of *Norte de Príncipes* (for a long time attributed to Antonio Pérez, adviser to the King).

15. BRUNEL, p. 153.

16. BRUNEL, chap. XIX. On Segovia, BERTAUT, p. 163.

17. Descriptions of Barcelona and Saragossa by B. JOLY (pp. 476–81 and 537); on Valencia, *ibid,* p. 515.

18. On the French established in Catalonia and Saragossa, B. JOLY, pp. 483 and 535–6. It is clear that the figures given by French authors have little in common with reality; but one finds similar figures in the works of contemporary Spanish authors. Certain towns gave the impression of being literally 'invaded' by the French; Seville, for example, where, according to the moderate estimates of A. DOMÍNGUEZ ORTIZ: *Los extranjeros en la vida española durante el siglo XVII,* there were about 12,000 out of a total population of 120,000.

19. On Spain's monetory system, cf. the final note of this chapter.

20. BRUNEL, chap. XXXVII.

21. '*Toda la inmundicia de Europa ha venido a España, sin que se haya quedado en Francia, Alemania, Italia, Flandes, cojo, manco, tullido ni ciego que no se haya venido a España*' (FERNÁNDEZ DE NAVARRETE, *Conservación de Monarquías 1626.*)

22. BRUNEL, p. 144. B. JOLY makes comments time and again about Spanish arrogance, especially among the artisans.

23. BRUNEL, chap. VI, pp. 143–4.

24. This expansion is referred to by B. JOLY. BRUNEL (chap.

XXV) insists on the differences of temperament between natives of the various provinces.

25. BERTAUT, p. 193. On the fiscal inequalities between different provinces, DOMÍNGUES ORTIZ: *Politica y hacienda da Felipe IV*, vol. III, chap. I.

26. Enrique COCK: *Anales del año ochenta y cinto* (in GARCIA MERCADAL: *Viajes . . .*, vol. I, p. 1303). Cock, 'His Majesty's Notary and Constable of the Watch', accompanied Philip II when the king attended the Cortes at Monzon, in Aragon (1585).

27. This fine parallel between France and Spain is borrowed at the end of the account of the voyage of Brunel (chap. XXXVIII, *passim*).

28. NOTE ON THE SPANISH MONETARY SYSTEM (*time of Philip III and Philip IV 1598–1665*).

Spain had two monetary systems: The territories of the kingdom of Aragon (Aragon, Catalonia, Valencia) counted, like France, in livres, sous, and deniers (1 livre = 20 sous; 1 sol = 12 deniers). The Castillian system was more complex: the basic unit was the *maravédi* and its multiple the real = 34 *maravédis*, large sums being expressed in ducats (1 ducat = 375 *maravédis*). Money in circulation consisted of: the *ochavo* worth 2 *maravédis*, the *cuarto* worth 4 *maravédis*, the *cuartillo* worth 8 *maravédis*.

Silver coins: the *real de a ocho* (the piece of eight) which had a nominal value of 8 reals or 275 *marivédis*; and its sub-multiples: pieces of four and of two, the real or the half-real.

Gold coins: the escudo (the crown), worth 340 *maravédis*.

In effect, the relative value of copper and silver coins was affected by the monetary manipulations which became increasingly frequent in the reigns of Philip III and IV, and caused an 'inflation' of copper money either by the massive minting of new coins or by the 'restamping' of those in circulation to which a higher nominal value was attributed above their intrinsic worth. It follows that the relation between silver coinage (represented by the eight-real piece, the value of which remained constant) and copper or nickel coins was falsified. The latter being legally over-valued, permitted foreigners to introduce copper coins (such as the French *liard*) and exchange them at a profitable rate against silver reals.

The consequence, for Spain itself, was a 'flight' of silver, and a 'premium' (*premio*) for white metal over copper, a premium which might reach 50 per cent: which meant that in paying a fixed sum (expressed in ducats), one had to give one and a half times more than the nominal value if payment was made in copper, instead of the nominal value itself if one paid in silver.

As a result, there are two different 'prices' for the same object, one corresponding to its value in silver, the other to its value in copper coin.

In these circumstances it is difficult to draft a 'table of prices' which would give an exact idea of economic reality and this is even more so because, although prices varied as a result of inflation (the over-valuation of copper money) and deflation (its reduction in value), salaries remained relatively stable, and their purchasing power was thus subject to wide fluctuations. The general trend was always unfavourable to the salaried class because, between 1620 and 1665, the inflationary tendency prevailed over the deflationary measures, often drastic, decreed by the sovereign. Thus, although prices rose by as much as 100 per cent during this period, any increase in salaries lagged far behind this rise in prices. One can estimate – very roughly – that daily earnings of 2 to 2½ reals represented a minimum 'living' wage.

CHAPTER 2: THE CONCEPTION OF LIFE

Three essential books present different points of view on the idiosyncrasies of the Spaniard and their reflection in history and social life: R. MENÉNDEZ PIDAL: *Los Españoles en la historia* (Col. Austral, 1951); C. SÁNCHEZ ALBORNOZ: *España, un enigma histórico*, 2nd edn, Buenos Aires, 1962); Américo CASTRO: *Réalité de l'Espagne* (trans. from the Spanish, Paris, 1963).

Among the many studies of the concept of honour are: A. CASTRO: *Algunas observaciones acerca del concepto del honor en los siglos XVI y XVII (Rev. de Filología española*, vol. III (1916); and *De la edad conflictiva. El drama del honor en España y su literatura* (1961); R. MENÉNDEZ PIDAL: *Del honor en el teatro espanol (España y su historia*, 1957, vol. II, pp. 357–94); GARCÍA VALDECASAS: *El hidalgo y el honor* (1948). On the deviations from this concept of honour: M. BATAILLON, introduction to the bi-lingual edition of *Lazarillo de Tormes,* and *El sentido del 'Lazarillo de Tormes'*, Paris, 1954.

On the prejudice of 'purity of blood': A. DOMÍNGUEZ ORTIZ: *La clase social de los conversos en Castilla en la Edad moderna* (1955); Albert A. SICROFF: *Les statuts de pureté de sang en Espagne aux XVIᵉ and XVIIᵉ siècles* (1955).

1. Mateo ALEMÁN: *Guzmán de Alfarache*, cited by MORENO BÁEZ, *Lección y sentido del 'Guzmán de Alfarache'*, pp. 162–3.

2. Alessandro TASSONI: *Filipicas* (*c.* 1602), in GARCÍA MERCADAL: *Viajes . . .*, vol. II, p. 10.

3. MOREL FATIO: *Études sur l'Espagne*, vol. I, p. 10.

4. Juan de PALAFOX: *Discurso . . . y comparación de España con las otras naciones*, cited by PALACIO ATARD: *Derrota y agotamiento*, p. 22.

5. GARCÍA MERCADAL: *Viajes . . .*, vol. II, p. 18.

6. This is the sub-title given by J. DELEITO PIÑUELA to the volume devoted to *La vida religiosa bajo el cuarto Felipe. Santos y pecadores*.

7. *Noticias de Madrid*, edited by GONZÁLEZ PALENCIA, pp. 31, 32, and 110.

8. *Relación de la cárcel de Seville*, attrib. to Christobal de CHAVES.

9. *Las Partidas*, book II, section XIII, article IV.

10. *La contienda de García de Paredes*, cited by VALBUENA PRAT: *La vida española en la Edad de Oro*, p. 20.

11. E. LAFUENTE FERRARI: *Vélazquez* (Skira), p. 60.

12. A letter by Andrés de Almansa y Mendoza, with commentary by ORTEGA Y GASSET: *Papeles sobre Velázquez*, pp. 204–6. On Rodrigo Calderón, cf. also MARANÓN: *El conde duque de Olivares*, p. 50.

13. *Las comendadoras de Córdoba*, cited by A. CASTRO; *La Edad conflictiva*.

14. VIEL CASTEL: *De l'honneur comme ressort dramatique dans les pièces de Calderón, Rojas etc.* (*Rev. des Deux Mondes*, 1841), passage cited by and commented on by R. MENÉNDEZ PIDEL: *Del honor en el teatro español*, *loc. cit.*, vol. II, p. 360.

15. LOPE DE VEGA: *La estrella de Sevilla*.

16. *Baltazar* GRACIÁN: *El criticón* (GARCÍA VALDECASAS), *loc. cit.*, pp. 215–16.

17. *Tradato compuesto por un religioso de la orden de los frayles menores aprobado por algunos reverendos padres y señores maestros en theología y juristas de la Universidad de Salamanca,*

Salamanca, 1586, cited by DOMÍNGUEZ ORTIZ; *La clase de los conversos* . . ., p. 227.

18. *Ibid.*, p. 152, note.

19. *Ibid.*, p. 208. Cazalla, canon of Salamanca, was one of the first adepts of the Reformation in Spain, and died at the stake.

20. Cf. the works of BATAILLON cited, especially the introduction to *Lazarillo*, p. 48 *et seq.* On *hidalguism* cf. also MOREL FATIO: *L'Espagne du 'Don Quichotte', Études sur l'Espagne*, vol. I, pp. 337–41.

21. Marqués del SALTILLO; *La nobleza española en el siglo XVIII, Rev. de Archivos, Bibliotecas y Museos*, vol. LX (1954), No. 2.

22. Barthélemy JOLY: *Voyage* . . ., p. 616.

23. DOMÍNGUEZ ORTIZ: *Orto y ocaso Sevilla*, p. 82.

24. SAAVEDRA FAJARDO: *Empresas* (1640).

25. *Guzmán de Alfarache, passim*, cited by MORENO BÁEZ: *Lección y sentido del 'Guzmán de Alfarache'*, pp. 139–40.

26. On anti-honour, personified by *Estebanillo González, infra* chap. X (*La vie militaire*), p. 278.

CHAPTER 3: MADRID, THE COURT AND THE TOWN

The 'gossip columns' (*Avisos, Noticias, Relaciones*) are an essential source for the knowledge of Madrilenian life, certain of them being in the form of 'annals': Luis CABRERA DE CÓRDOBA: *Relación de las cosas sucedidas en la Corte de España desde 1599 hasta 1614* (Madrid, 1857); León PINELO; *Anales de Madrid* (1598–1621), published by R. MARTORELL and TÉLEZ GIRÓN (1931); *Noticias de Madrid* (1621–1627), published by A. GONZÁLEZ PALENCIA (1942); *La Corte y la Monarquía de España, en los años 1636 y 1637 (colección de cartas publicadas por* A. RODRÍGUEZ VILLA (1886)); *Avisos* of José PELLICER (1639–1644), pub. in *Seminario erudito* (vols. XXXI, XXXII, and XXXIII); *Avisos* of BARRIONUEVO (1654–1658), pub. by A. PAZ Y MELIÁ; *Cartas de algunos Padres de la compañía de Jesús* (1634–1648), pub. by GAYANGOS (*Memorial histórico español*, vols. XIII–XIV).

One must add the works of contemporary '*costumbristas*' (painters of manners), especially LINÁN Y VERDUGO: *Guía y avisos de forasteros que vienen a la Corte* (about 1620), pub. by the *Real Academia española* (1923), and ZABALETA; *El día de fiesta por la manaña y por la tarde* (re-iss. in *Clásicos castellanos*, Madrid, 1948).

On the life at the court, DELEITO PIÑUELA: *El declinar de la monarquía española* (3rd edn, 1955), and *El rey se divierte* (1935); Martin HUME: *The Court of Philip IV and the decline of Spain* (1912); Gregorio MARAÑÓN: *El conde duque de Olivares o la pasión de mandar* (1st edn, 1936).

On Madrid and Madrilenian life: E. SÁINZ DE ROBLES: *Porqué es Madrid capital de España*; J. OLIVER ASÍN: *El nombre 'Madrid'* (1959); C. VINAS Y MEY: *Le estructura social-demográfica del Madrid de los Asturias (Rev. de la Universidad de Madrid,* vol. IV, No. 16) (1955); M. ESPADA BURGOS Y M. A. BURGOA: *Abastecimiento de Madrid en el siglo XVI* (1960); J. DELEITO PIÑUELA: *Sólo Madrid es Corte* (1953) and . . . *También se divierte el pueblo* (2nd edn, 1954).

1. A eulogy of the capital entitled *Sólo Madrid es Corte*, pub. by NÚÑEZ DE CASTRO in 1658.

2. *Archivo municipal de Madrid*, vol. XXVI, folio 168 vo.

3. *Relation du voyage d'Espagne*, ed. Carrey, pp. 175–6.

4. Cited by ORTEGA Y GASSET: *Papeles sobre Velázquez*, pp. 134–6.

5. BRUNEL: *Voyage d'Espagne*, chap. VI, p. 146.

6. GARCIA MERCADAL: *Viajes* . . . , vol. I, pp. 1178–9.

7. DELEITO PIÑUELA: *El rey se divierte*, pp. 183–90.

8. Cited by DELEITO PIÑUELA: *loc. cit.*, p. 215.

9. *Avisos* of BARRIONUEVO (cited by ORTEGA Y GASSET: *Papeles sobre Velázquez*, p. 191).

10. *Velázquez, documentos publicados por el C.S.I.C.* (1960).

11. MATÍAS DE NOVOA: *Historia de Felipe IV*, cited by DELEITO PIÑUELA, p. 142.

12. *Noticias* of Madrid, ed by GONZÁLEZ PALENCIA, p. 70.

13. *Relation du voyage d'Espagne*, p. 447.

14. *Cartas de los Jesuitas* (ORTEGA Y GASSET, *loc. cit.*, pp. 124–5).

15. BRUNEL: *Voyage d'Espagne*, pp. 155–6.

16. MARAÑÓN: *El conde duque de Olivares*, p. 95.

17. *Ibid.*, p. 208 and p. 98, note 29.

18. BRUNEL: chap. V, p. 141.

19. *Diario* of Camille BORGHÈSE (MOREL FATIO: *L'Espagne au XVIᵉ siècles*, p. 177).

20. Text of an ordinance in DELEITO PIÑUELA: *Sólo Madrid es Corte*, p. 128.

21. GARCÍA MERCADAL: *Viajes . . .* , vol. I, p. 142.

22. ESPADA BURGOS and BURGOA: *El abastecimiento de Madrid*, p. 16.

23. The municipal archives of Madrid contain much documentation relative to the *asiento de nieve* (the snow farm).

24. DOMÍNGUEZ ORTIZ: *Los extranjeros en la vida española durante el siglo XVII* (1960), p. 339.

25. LINÁN Y VERDUGO: *Guia y avisos de forasteros que vienen a la Corte. Novela y escarmiento sexto.*

26. Texts cited by DELEITO PIÑUELA: *La mala vida en la España de Felipe IV*, p. 95, and ORTEGA Y GASSET: *Papeles sobre Velázquez*, p. 185.

27. On the *mentideros*, DELEITO PIÑUELA: *Sólo Madrid es Corte*, chaps. XLI, XLII, and XLIII. Saavedra's text (*Idea de un Principe político cristiano*) comes from J. A. MARAVALL: *La philosophie politique espagnole du XVIIᵉ siècle* (trans. from the Spanish, 1955), p. 280.

28. BRUNEL: *loc. cit.*, p. 156.

29. Camille BORGHÈSE, *loc cit.*, and Fulvio TESTI, in GARCÍA MERCADAL: *Viajes . . .* , vol. II, p. 26.

30. See the full description in BRUNEL'S *Voyage*, pp. 176–9.

CHAPTER 4: SEVILLE, THE MIRROR OF THE INDIES OF CASTILLE

Santigo MONTOTO: *Sevilla en el Imperio, Siglo XVI* (Seville, undated); A.DOMÍNGUEZ ORTIZ: *Orto y ocaso de Sevilla* (Seville, 1946); On the commerce of the Indes, P. CHAUNU: *Séville et l'Atlantique*, vol. VIII, 1 and 2; A. GIRARD: *Le commerce français à Séville et Cadix au temps des Habsbourg* (1932). The ambience of Seville is conjured up in the important introduction by RODRÍGUEZ MARIN to the annotated edition of *Rinconete y Cortadillo* by CERVANTES. Cf. likewise VALBUENA PRAT: *La vida española en la Edad de Oro*, chap. V.

1. DOMÍNGUES ORTIZ: *Orto y ocaso de Sevilla*, chap. III.

2. *Toda España, Italia y Francia*
Vive por este Arenal
Porqpé es plaza general
De toda trato y ganancia.

3. On the atmosphere of waiting, B. BENNASSAR: *Facteurs sévillans au XVIᵉ siècle d'après leurs lettres marchandes, Annales E.S.C.*, vol. XII (1957), pp. 60–71.

4. Text cited by DOMÍNGUEZ ORTIZ: *loc. cit.* On the dangers of the shoals, cf. likewise P. CHAUNU, *loc. cit.* vol. VIII, 1, p. 239 *et seq.*

5. A. MORGADO: *Historia de Sevilla* (1587) cited by RODRÍGUEZ MARÍN, p. 11.

6. *Ibid.*, after Francisco ARINO: *Sucesos de Sevilla de 1592 a 1604.*

7. GONZÁLEZ CÉSPEDES Y MENESES: *Historias peregrinas y ejemplares* cited by VALBUENA PRAT: *loc. cit.*, p. 140.

8. BRUNEL: *Voyage*, p. 169. On the organization of fraud and Spanish complicity, GIRARD. *loc. cit.*, 2nd part, chap. IV.

9. *Suma de tratos y contratos*, cited by CARANDE: *Carlos V y sus banqueros*, p. 136.

10. *Y unas geadas que una grada*
Vale más que todo el mundo (TORRES NAHARRO, 1545).

11. On the construction of the *Lonja* J. M. de la PEÑA: *Guía del archivo de Sevilla* (pp. 27–30).

12. MORGADO: *Historia de Sevilla*, cited by ALTIMIRA: *Historia de España*, vol. III, p. 456.

13. Tomás del MERCADO: *Suma de tratos y cantratos*, book II, chap. 1.

14. DOMÍNGUEZ ORTIS: *La esclavitud en Castilla durante la Edad Moderna, Estudios de Historia social de España*, vol. II (1952). p. 63.

15. DOMÍNGUEZ ORTIZ: *loc. cit.*, pp. 401–2.

16. MORGADO: *Historia de Sevilla*, cited by RODRÍGUEZ MARÍN: *loc. cit.*

17. MORGADO: *ibid.* This appreciation of Lope de Vega figures in the *Dorotea*.

18. CÉSPEDES Y MENESES, cited by VALBUENA PRAT: *La vida española* . . ., p. 140.

19. DOMÍNGUEZ ORTIZ: *Orto y ocaso*, pp. 69–71.

20. *Rinconete y Cortadillo*, ed. RODRÍGUEZ MARÍN, *p.* PE....

21. The letter of Philip IV was written in 1643. Texts cited by HUME: *The Court of Philip IV*, pp. 374–5.

CHAPTER 5: URBAN AND RURAL LIFE

J. VICENS VIVES: *Historia económica de España* (1959); P. VILAR: *La Catalogne dans l'Espagne moderne*, vol. I (1962); H. LAPEYRE: *Une famille de marchands, les Ruiz* (1955); A. DOMÍNGUEZ ORTIZ: *La sociedad española en el siglo XVIII* (1955). (There are numerous references to the preceding century. We have not been able to make use of the work of the same author, *La sociedad española en el siglo XVII*, published after this book went to press.)

The *Relaciones de pueblos de España ordenadas por Felipe II* are an essential source for an understanding of rural life. Two volumes containing accounts of life in the provinces of Toledo and Madrid have been published by C. VIÑAS Y MEY and Ramón PAZ (1949 and 1955). N. SALOMON has made a study of the accounts relating to New Castille: *Les campagnes de Nouvelle Castilla à la fin du XVIᵉ siècle, d'aprèss les 'Relaciones topográficas'*. C. VIÑAS Y MEY: *El problema de la tierra en España en los siglos XVI et XVII* (1941), cites numerous documents. On the community customs J. COSTA: *El colectivismo agrario en España* (1915). On the rearing and transhumance of sheep, J. KLEIN: *The Mesta*. (1936).

On literature reflecting rural life. A. VALBUENA PRAT: *La vida española en la Edad de Oro*, chap. X, *La vida de aldea en el teatro de Lope de Vega*.

1. Text cited in full by Pedro RODRÍGUEZ CAMPOMANES, *Educación popular de los artesanos, Apéndice IV* (1776), pp. 216–21.

2. On the decline of Castillian towns, cf. the figures given by A. GIRARD: *La répartition de la population en Espagne dans les temps modernes* (*Rev. d'Hist. écon, et sociale*, 1929, pp. 347–62.

3. Cf. the significant particulars of different trades in Medina del Campo furnished by B. BENNASSAR, *Medina del Campo, un*

exemple des structures urbaines de l'Espagne au XVIᵉ siècle (Rev. d'Hist. écon. et sociale, 1961, No. 4).

4. A. RUMEU DE ARMAS: *Historia de la Previsión social en España* (1942), p. 231.

5. Álvaro CASTILLO: *Dette flottante et dette consolidée en Espagne de 1557 à 1600, Annales E.S.C.,* July–Aug. 1963.

6. For example, GONZÁLEZ DE CELLÓRIGO: *Memorial de la política necesaria y útil restauración de la República de España* (1600); LOPE DE DEZA: *Gobierno político de agricultura* (1618): CAXA DE LERUELA: *Restauración de la abundancia de España* (1631). Numerous references in VIÑAS Y MEY, *El problema de la tierra.*

7. DOMÍNGUEZ ORTIZ: *La sociedad española en el siglo XVIII,* p. 310.

8. *Ibid.,* pp. 335–6.

9. VIÑAS Y MEY, *loc. cit.,* pp. 68–9.

10. ÁLVAREZ OSORIO: *Discurso general de las causas que ofenden la monarquía,* cited by JUDERÍAS, *España en tiempos de Carlos II el Hechizado,* pp. 121–2.

11. SEMPERE Y GUARINOS: *Biblioteca española de economía política,* vol. III, p. lx.

12. Benito de PEÑALOSA: *Libro de las cinco exelencias del Español que despueblan a España* (DOMÍNGUEZ ORTIZ, *loc. cit.,* pp. 277–8).

13. JIMÉNEZ GREGORIO: *El pasado económico social de Belvis de la Jara lugar de la tierra de Talavera (Estudios de Historia social de España,* vol. II (1952), pp. 661 *et seq.*).

14. *Relaciones topográficas. Provincia de Madrid.* Replies by El Olmedo, Getafe, Alcorcón, Pezuela.

15. NAVARRETE: *Conservación de Monarquías (Biblioteca de Autores Españoles,* vol. XXV, p. 476.)

16. *Relaciones . . . Provincia de Madrid,* p. 18.

CHAPTER 6: THE CHURCH AND RELIGIOUS LIFE

J. DELEITO PIÑUELA: *La vida religiosa bajo el cuarto Felipe, Santos y pecadores* (1952); VALBUENA PRAT: *La vida española en la Edad de Oro,* chap. IV: *La vida religiosa.* On magic and sorcery, the Duke of MAURA: *Supersticiones de los siglos XVI y XVII y hechizos de Carlos II* (undated).

The work of the former secretary of the Holy Office of Spain, J. A. LLORENTE: *Histoire critique de l'Inquisition espagnole* (Paris, 1817), even though it is hardly 'critical', is none the less useful. Among innumerable works about the Spanish Inquisition, Sir Henry Lea: *A History of the Inquisition of Spain* (London, 1907. 4 vols.) gives the fullest account. On the prisons of the Inquisition, M. de la PINTA LLORENTE: *Las cárceles inquisitoriales*.

1. Cited by DELEITO PIÑUELA: *La vida religiosa*, p. 79.

2. AGUADO: *Política española para el más proporcionado remedio de nuestra monarquía* (1646), cited by DOMÍNGUEZ ORTIZ: *La sociedad española en el siglo XVIII*, p. 554.

3. B. JOLY, *Voyage*, p. 554.

4. Jacques SOBIESKI, in GARCÍA MERCADAL: *Viajes . . .*, vol. II, pp. 330–1.

5. Letter of Fray Hernando del Castillo, cited by N. LÓPEZ MARTÍNEZ: *La desamortización de bienes eclesiásticos* (*Hispania*, Madrid, vol. XXII (1962), pp. 230–50).

6. In his *Avisos* PELLICER calls the *galanteo de monjas* an 'abuse wrongly permitted in the kingdom of Spain and wrongly tolerated by the ministers spiritual and temporal'.

7. *Razones por qué no se publicó el decreto de que los frailes no hablen con monjas* (DELEITO PIÑUELA, *loc. cit.*, p. 131.

8. Cf. other examples mentioned by DELEITO PIÑUELA, p. 105 *et seq.*

9. ZABALETA: *Día de fiesta por la noche.* cited by PFANDL; *Introducción al Siglo de Oro*, p. 147.

10. B. JOLY: *Voyage*, p. 554.

11. PÉREZ DE HERRERA: *Discursos*, cited by DOMÍNGUEZ ORTIZ: *Los extranjeros en la vida española*, p. 340.

12. *Noticias de Madrid*, ed. GONZÁLEZ PALENCIA, p. 168 (Nov. 4, 1627).

13. Cf. *infra*, chap. VII, p. 150.

14. *Pragmatique* of 1647, renewed in 1665 and 1657.

15. B. JOLY: *Voyage*, pp. 556–7.

16. VALBUENA PRAT: *La vida española . . .*, p. 87.

17. *Ibid.*, pp. 90 and 102–3.

18. DELEITO PIÑUELA: p. 204.

19. On the affair of the convent of San Placido, DELEITO PIÑUELA, chap. XIII, and G. MARANÓN: *El conde duque de Olivares*, pp. 190–2.

20. GARCÍA NAVARRO: *Tribunal de superstición ladina* (1631), cited by MAURA, pp. 40–1.

21. MAURA, loc. cit., p. 63.

22. MAURA, loc. cit.: *Exorcismos,* pp. 149–75. The practice of exorcism was 'codified' in two treatises: Benito Remigio NOYDENS: *Práctica de exorcistas y ministros de la Iglesia* (middle of seventeenth century) and Luis de la CONCEPCIÓN: *Prácticas de conjurar en que se tienen exorcismos y conjuraciones contra los malos espíritus de cualquier modo existentes en los cuerpos* (1721).

23. On the allegations of 'sorcery' concerning Olivares, MARAÑÓN: *El conde duque de Olivares,* chap. XV: *Las hechicerías de Olivares.*

24. On this 'witch hunt', REGLA: *Hist. económ. y social de España,* vol. III, pp. 383–4.

25. On this point see M. de la PINTA LLORENTE: *Las cárceles inquisitoriales.*

26. Barthelémy JOLY has left a striking description of the *auto-da-fe* which he witnessed in Valladolid (*Voyage,* pp. 578–9).

27. ÁLVAREZ DE COLMENAR: *Les Délices de l'Espagne et du Portugal,* vol. V, pp. 896–7, cited by DELEITO PIÑUELA, p. 331.

CHAPTER 7: PUBLIC LIFE, FESTIVALS, AND POPULAR ENTERTAINMENTS

J. DELEITO PIÑUELA: *El rey se divierte* (1936) and ... *También se divierte el pueblo* (2nd edn., 1954; A. VALBUENA PRAT: *La vida española en la Edad de Oro,* chap. V, *Entretenimientos y fiestas.* On bull-fights: J. M. DE COSSIO: *Los toros, tratado técnico e histórico* (4 vols. 1960–1).

On the theatre and dramatic productions: H. MÉRIMEÉ: *Spectacles et comédiens à Valencia* (1580–1630), Paris–Toulouse, 1913; VALBUENA PRAT: *Historia del teatro español* (1956); Bruce W. WARDROPPER, *Introducción al teatro religioso del Siglo de oro* (*La evolución del auto sacramental, 1500–1648*), Madrid, 1953.

1. BRUNEL: *Voyage d'Espagne,* p. 105 (this reflection follows an account of the festivals of Corpus Christi): DELEITO PIÑUELA: *También se divierte el pueblo,* p. 15.

2. *La Gran Sultana* (cited by PFANDL: *Introducción al Siglo de oro,* p. 250, note).

3. *Vida política de todos los estados de mujeres* of Fray Juan de la CERDA (1599), cited by DELEITO PIÑUELA, p. 77.

4. P. MARIANA, *De espectaculis*, (1609), chap. XII.

5. BRUNEL, p. 202; the description of the Fête-Dieu (*Corpus Christi*) fills the whole of chap. XVIII.

6. *Estebanillo González*, chap. XII.

7. BRUNEL, chap. XVII.

8. The term *toreador* which has disappeared from Spanish usage (where it has been replaced by *torrero*) was commonly employed in the seventeenth century.

9. BRUNEL, p. 198.

10. On the 'corrales', DELEITO PIÑUELA: *También se divierte el pueblo*, pp. 170–239; *loc. cit.*, pp. 234–5.

11. DELEITO PIÑUELA: *También de divierte el pueblo*, p. 181.

12. BERTAUT: *Journal du voyage d'Espagne*, pp. 211–12.

13. On the significance of the *autos*, apart from the work by WARDROPPER, cf. BATAILLON: *Essai d'explication des autos sacramentales* (*Bulletin hispanique*, vol. XLVII (1940), pp. 193–212).

14. WARDROPPER: *loc. cit.*, p. 60.

15. S. MONTOTO: *Sevilla en el Imperio*, p. 273.

16. Hints appear of the *Comedia famosa de San Antonio Abad* of Fernando de Zárate, which Mme d'Aulnoy saw performed at Vitoria (MAURA–AMEZÚA: *Fantasías y realidades del viaje de la condesa d'Aulnoy*, pp. 33–5).

17. WARDROPPER: loc. cit., p. 39.

18.   . . . *sermones*
puestos en verso
representables cuestiones
de la Sacra Teología
que no alcazan mis razones
a explicar ni comprender
y al regocijo disponen
en aplauso de este día

(cited by WARDROPPER, *ibid.*, p. 21).

19. On the strolling players, N. SALOMON; *Sur les représentations théâtrales dans les pueblos, Bulletin hispanique*, vol. LXII, Oct.–Dec. 1960.

20. *Don Quixote*, II, XI. Ángulo el Malo was an impresario

contemporary with Cervantes; the '*Auto sacramental de las Cortes de la Muerte*' is a work by Lope de Vega (see the notes by RODRÍGUEZ MARÍN, vol. IV, pp. 243–4 of the new edition of *Don Quijote de la Mancha*, 1947–9).

21. COTARELO: *Bibliografía de las controversias sobre la licitud del teatro en España* (1904).

22. *Guía de los extranjeros, Aviso quinto.*

CHAPTER 8: DOMESTIC LIFE, WOMAN AND THE HOME

A. GONZÁLES DE AMEZÚA: *La vida privada española en el protocolo notarial* (1950); Ricardo del ARCO: *La vida privada en las obras de Cervantes* (*Revista de Archivos, Bibliotecas y Museos*, vol. LVI, 1950, No. 3); DELEITO PIÑUELA: *La mujer, la casa y la moda* (1954). On the position of women: P. W. BOWLI: *La femme dans l'Espagne du Siècle d'or* (La Haye, 1950) and Amédée MAS: *La caricature de la femme, du mariage et de l'amour dans l'œuvre de Quevedo* (1957).

1. Francisco LUQUE FAJARDO: *Fiel desengaño contra la ociosidad y los juegos* (early seventeenth century), cited by RODRÍGUEZ MARÍN, annotated edn. of *Rinconete y Cortadillo*, p. 40.

2. CONFALONIERI, cited by GARCÍA MERCADAL: *España vista por los extranjeros*, vol. II, p. 260. His account is confirmed by Camille BORGHESE and most of the travellers from abroad. Satirical literature and Spanish drama make frequent allusions to the 'dama pedigüeña' (beggar maid), who does not hesitate to beg, not only from her acquaintances, but also from complete strangers, 'trifling presents'.

3. RODRÍGUEZ VILLA: *La corte y la monarquía de España*, cited by DELEITO PIÑUELA: *La mala vida en la España de Felipe IV*, p. 83.

4. Fr. Luis de LEÓN: *La perfecta casada* (1583).

5. Mme d'AULNOY: *Relation du voyage d'Espagne*, p. 445; BERTAUT: *Voyage*, p. 207, had already made a similar remark.

6. BRUNEL, p. 157 and BERTAUT: *loc. cit.*, p. 207.

7. After a manuscript in the *Biblioteca Nacional* of Madrid, cited by DELEITO PIÑUELA.

8. B. JOLY tells of his indignation against the indiscreet Spanish use of chamber-pots (*Voyage*, p. 552).

9. F. SANTOS: *Dia y noche de Madrid. Discurso X.*

10. PFANDL: *Introducción al Siglo de oro,* p. 278.

11. Cf. other evidence of Spanish sobriety in DELEITO PIÑUELA, pp. 108–15.

12. ASTRAÑA Y MARÍN: *Lope de Vega,* p. 164 (after the *Relaciones* of Luis de CABRERA (1609)).

13. On the 'femmes savantes', P. W. BOWLI, chap. IV.

14. Cited by A. MAS, p. 77.

15. *Relation du voyage d'Espagne,* pp. 249–50.

16. ÁLVAREZ DE COLMENAR, cited by DELEITO PIÑUELA, p. 175. Mme d'Aulnoy had made the same remark.

17. RODRÍGUEZ VILLA: *La corte y la monarquía de España,* p. 144, after contemporary *Noticias.*

18. The comparison between the portrait of Marie-Anne of Austria, in the Prado museum, and those of the preceding queen, Isabella de Bourbon, is significant.

19. Text cited by the Duke of MAURA and GONZÁLEZ AMEZÚA: *Fantasías y realidades del viaje de la condesa d'Aulnoy,* pp. 264–6.

20. León PINELO: *Velos antiguos y modernos en los rostros de las mujeres; sus convencias y daños* (MAURA and G. AMEZÚA, *ibid.,* pp. 266–7).

21. On the '*fiebre cocheril*', DELEITO PIÑUELA (pp. 257 *et seq.*) has collected numerous references.

CHAPTER 9: UNIVERSITY LIFE AND THE WORLD OF LETTERS

On university life and the life of students, LA FUENTE: *Historia de las Universidades, Colegios y demás establecimientos de enseñaza de España,* 4 vols. (1884–9); G. REYNIER: *La vie universitaire dans l'ancienne Espagne* (Paris–Toulouse, 1902); J. GARCÍA MERCADAL: *Estudiantes, sopistas y pícaros* (1934); VALBUENA PRAT: *La vida española en la Edad de Oro,* chap. II: *El Estudiante. Las Universidades.*

On the literary tribe: C. VOSSLER: *Lope de Vega y su tiempo* (1934) and *Introducción a la literatura del Siglo de Oro* (1949); A. VALBUENA PRAT: *Literatura dramática española* (1930); L. ASTRANA MARÍN: *La vida azarosa de Lope de Vega* (2nd edn., 1941); José SÁNCHEZ: *Academias literarias del Siglo de Oro español* (1960); A. COMAS and J. REGLA: *Góngora, su tiempo y su obra* (1960); R. MENÉNDEZ PIDAL: *Culteranos y conceptistas* (*España y su historia*, vol. II, pp. 501–47).

1. On the proliferation of universities and the 'sylvan' universities, REYNIER: *loc. cit.*, 2nd part, chap. I and III.

2. Ordinances preserved in the *Novísima Recopilación de las Leyes de España*, book III, section 9, rules 3 and 4.

3. *Instrucciones que dio D. Enrique de Guzmán, conde de Olivares a D. Laureano de Guzmán*, in GARCÍA MERCADAL, *loc. cit.*, p. 71.

4. *Avisos* by Barrionuevo, Vol. II, p. 240, cited by ORTEGA Y GASSET, *Papeles sobre Velásquez*, p. 190.

5. *Ceremonial* of the University of Salamanca, chap. XVI (GARCÍA MERCADAL, *loc. cit.*, pp. 152–3).

6. *Ibid.*, p. 143 and REYNIER, chap. VII.

7. *Instrucción de los bachilleres de pupilos* (1538) in GARCÍA MERCADAL, loc. cit., pp. 83–5.

8. QUEVEDO: *La vida del Buscón llamado D. Pablos*, chap. III.

9. *Novísima Recopilación de las Leyes de España*, book I, section XII, rule 14.

10. CERVANTES: *Coloquio de los perros.*

11. *hacerse de obispillo* (to dress up as a bishop and play the clown): an allusion to a burlesque fête, similar to the Fools' Festival which had a place in the Middle Ages in certain churches in France, where students and clerks, bedecked with sacerdotal ornaments, parodied a religious ceremony.

12. Mateo ALEMÁN: *Guzmán de Alfarache*, 2nd part, book III, chap. V.

13. Jerónimo de ALCALÁ: *Alonso, mozo de muchos amos.*

14. *Guzmán de Alfarache*, chap. V.

15. LA FUENTE: *Historia de las Universidades*, section III, p. 95.

16. On the disorders caused by students, REYNIER, chap. IV, and GARCÍA MERCADAL, chap. XI: *Armas y reyertas.*

17. Among the many biographies of Lope de Vega, we have specially drawn on that of ASTRAÑA MARÍN: *La vida azarosa de Lope de Vega*. Cf. also G. LAPLANE: *Lope de Vega* (1962).

18. *Una dama se vende a quien la quiere*
    en almoneda está? Quieren comprarla?
    su padre es quien la vende que, aunque calla
    su madre la sirvió de pregonera.

19. *Por tu vida, Lope, que me borres*
las diez y nueve torres de tu escudo
porque, aunque todas son de viento, dudo
que tengas viento para tantas torres.

20. *. . . que está aforrado de martas*
anda haciendo magdalenos.

21. *Noticias de Madrid*, ed. GONZÁLES PALENCIA, p. 28 (June 26, 1622).

22. On this literary invasion and on the increasing ascendancy of formalism, ORTEGA Y GASSET: *Papeles sobre Velázquez*, pp. 208 *et seq.*

23. 'Romance' in the Spanish sense of the word: a short poem inspired by an heroic or epic theme; in a more general sense, a poem formed of octosyllabic verses.

24. This refers to the Academy of *El Parnaso* whose patron was Francisco de Silva (ASTRANA MARÍN, p. 234).

25. *Estebanillo Gonzáles*, chap. XII; cf. *supra*, p. 151.

26. The first quotation reads:
Ebúrnea de candor, fénix pomposa
débil botón, frondoso brujulea
zafir mendiga, armiño golosea
siendo dosel, tribuna vaporosa

27. *Guía para forasteros, Escarmiento IX.*

28. *Académie burlesque célébrée par les poètes de Madrid au Buen Retiro en 1637*, text transcribed in full by MOREL FATIO: *L'Espagne au XVIe et au XVIIe siècle*, pp. 602–84.

CHAPTER X: MILITARY LIFE

J. DELEITO PIÑUELA: *El declinar de la monarquía española* (3rd edn., 1955), part III: *La defensa nacional* (with an important bibliography); *Autobiografías de soldados. Estudio preliminar* by J. M. de COSSIO (*Biblioteca de Autores españoles*, vol. XC (1956); MOREL FATIO: *Soldats espagnols du XVIIe siècle* (*Études sur l'Espagne*, 3rd series).

1. *Noticias de Madrid* (1639). On the 'press-ganging' of recruits, GARCÍA MERCADAL: *Estudiantes, pícaros y sopistas*, pp. 216–18.

2. F. BRAUDEL: *La Méditerranée et le monde méditerranéen*

au temps de Philippe II, has shown how heavily the problem of distances and liaison weighed on the policies of Philip II: '. . . A good half of the decisions made by Philip II can be explained solely by the need to maintain the lines of communication, to secure transport, and to safeguard the indispensable carriage of treasure in every distant corner of his kingdoms' (p. 321).

3. *Vida del Capitán de Contreras (Autobiografías de soldados,* pp. 77–148). There is a good French translation of this with an interesting introduction by J. BOULANGER: *Les aventures du capitaine Alonso de Contreras* (1933). There is another edition published by *Revista de Occidente* (Madrid, 1943), with a prologue by J. ORTEGA Y GASSET.

4. This *derrotero*, now in the national Archives of Madrid (Ms. 3715 folios 1 to 107) and an essential document in support of the statements of Contreras, was published after his life in *Autobiografías de soldados* (pp. 149–235).

5. *Vida y trabajos de Jerónimo de Pasamonte (Autobiografías,* pp. 5–75); *Vida de Miguel de Castro, ibid.,* pp. 487–627.

6. *Memorias de D. Diego Duque de Estrada, ibid.,* pp. 251–627.

7. *Mi linaje empieza en mí*
   porque son mejores hombres
   los que sus linajes hacen
   que aquellos que lo deschechan
   adquiriendo viles nombres.

       (Mateo Fragoso: *Lorenzo me llamo*)

8. Manuscript of 1610, cited by DELEITO PIÑUELA: *loc. cit.,* p. 177. However, royal decrees in 1632 and 1652 aimed at making military costumes more uniform.

9. DELEITO PIÑUELA: *ibid.,* p. 209.

10. Evidence of Miguel Suriano, in GARCÍA MERCADAL: *Viajes . . .,* vol. I, p. 1140.

11. In 1653, 14 *tercio* regiments had only a total strength of 1553 men (DELEITO PIÑUELA, *loc. cit.,* p. 194 *et seq.*).

12. Letter of Carlos Corona cited by ALTAMIRA: *Historia de España,* vol. III, p. 297.

13. *Avisos* of Pellicer (June 14 and July 26, 1639).

14. On this episode, see DOMÍNGUEZ ORTIZ: *La movilización de la nobleza castellana en 1640,* in *Anuario de Historia del Derecho español,* vol. XXV (1955), pp. 799–823.

15. DELEITO PIÑUELA: *loc. cit.*, p. 199.

16. The biography of the author, verified by Willis KNAPP JONES on the basis of documents in the archives (*Estebanillo Gonzalez, Revue hispanique*, vol. LXXVII, pp. 201–45), confirms the accuracy of Estebanillo's 'statements of service' (including his desertions and enlistment in the French army.)

17. *Estebanillo Gonzalez*, book I, chap. VII.

18. This is the conclusion of DELEITO PIÑUELA in his book *El declinar de la monarquía española.*

CHAPTER 11: THE PICARESQUE LIFE

The principle picaresque romances have been conveniently assembled in *La novela picaresca española. Estudio preliminar, selección, prólogos y notas* by A. VALBUENA PRAT (Madrid, 1962). By the same author, *La vida española en la Edad de Oro*, chap. VII: *La literatura picaresca y su significación y fondo social.*

The problem of the documentary value and the ethical significance of the picaresque romance is the subject of a very important literary critique (cf. DELEITO PIÑUELA: *La mala vida en la España de Felipe IV*, pp. 117–18, notes, for works earlier than 1950). In the French language one can consult G. REYNIER: *Le roman réaliste au XVIIe siècle* (1914), and particularly M. BATAILLON: *Le roman picaresque* (1931), and the introduction to the bilingual edition of *Lazarillo de Tormes*. In Spanish: GONZÁLES PALENCIA: *De Lazarillo a Quevedo* (1946); MORENO BÁEZ: *Lección y sentido del 'Guzmán de Alfarache'* (1945).

On the picaresque world in the work of Cervantes, R. del ARCO: *La infima levadura social en las obras de Cervantes* and *La critica social en Cervantes* (*Estudios de Historia social de España*, vol. II (1952), pp. 209–326), and E. F. JARENO: *'El Coloquio de los perros' documento de la vida española en la Edad de Oro* (*ibid.*, pp. 327–64). The introduction and the notes by RODRÍGUEZ MARÍN in his critical edition of *Rinconete y Cortadillo* gather together a number of texts and documents which throw into relief the close parallel between the realities of picaresque life and its reflection in literature.

1. *Guzmán de Alfarache, atalaya de la vida humana* ('atalaya' in this sense means a watch-tower or observatory). The two parts

of *Guzmán* were published by Chapelain in 1619 and 1620 (that is, about twenty years after the appearance of the Spanish work).

The discussions about the significance of the picaresque romance are mainly centred around *Guzmán*, the veritable 'bible' of the picaresque (at the same time it was its first authentic literary expression). MORENO BÁEZ, *loc. cit.*, describes it as a work typical of the baroque spirit issuing from the counter-Reformation; J. A. VAN PRAAG: *Sobre el sentido del 'Guzmán de Alfarache'* (*Estudios dedicados a Menédez Pidal*, vol. V (1954), pp. 282–306), who, on the contrary, sees in it a significant manifestation of the state of mind of the 'new Christian', full of rancour against the society in which he lives. Neither the one nor the other interpretation seems to us to be convincing.

2. On *Lazarillo* as the forebear of the picaresque novel, cf the works cited by M. BATAILLON.

3. This is the position of GONZALEZ PALENCIA: *De Lazarillo a Quevedo*. On the difference between the spirit of *Lazarillo* and that of *Guzmán de Alfarache*, BATAILLON, introduction to the bilingual edition of *Lazarillo de Tormes*.

4. Abridged biography of Agustín de Rojas, in DELEITO PIÑUELA: *La mala vida*, pp. 157–8.

5. The introduction to the *Vida del Escudero Marcos de Obregón* by Vincente Espinel ('*Las cien mejores obras de la literatura española*', vol. 35) by Ignacio Bauer. On the authenticity of the adventures of Estebanillo González, cf. note 17 of the preceding chapter.

6. *Cartas de los jesuitas,* cited by ORTEGA Y GASSET: *En torno a Velázquez*, p. 148.

7. Claudio SÁNCHEZ ALBORNOZ: *España, un enigma histórico*, vol. I, chap. IX, p. 573 (the italics are ours).

8. *Novísima recopilación de las leyes de España*, book I, section XII, rule 6 *et seq.*

9. RUMEU DE ARMAS: *Historia de la previsión social en España*, chap. XIV, pp. 270–1.

10. *Discurso del amparo de los legítimos pobres y recucción de los fingidos* by PÉREZ de HERRERA (1598), cited by R. del ARCO: *Cervantes testigo social*.

11. Cited by DELEITO PIÑUELA: *La mala vida*, pp. 136–7.

12. *La vida del Buscón,* book I, chap. VIII.

13. Luis ZAPATA: *Miscelánea* (1592), re-issued in *Memorial histórico español*, Madrid, 1852, vol. XI.

14. *Rinconete y Cortadillo*, ed. RODRÍGUEZ MARÍN, p. 56, note 2.

15. VALBUENA PRAT: *La vida española* . . ., p. 188.

16. Ricardo del ARCO: *La infima levadura social en la obra de Cervantes*, p. 222.

17. B. JOLY, *Voyage*, p. 518.

18. Enrique COCK, in GARCÍA MERCADAL: *Viajes* . . ., vol. I, p. 1047.

19. GARCÍA MERCADAL: *España vista por los extranjeros*, vol. III, p. 15 *et seq.*

20. *La hija de Celestina* (*La novela picaresca española*, p. 886).

21. *La Ilustre Fregona* (*ibid.*, pp. 150–1).

22. M. BATAILLON: *Le roman picaresque*, p. 16.

23. Cited by VALBUENA PRAT: *La vida española en la Edad de Oro*, p. 154. On the 'picarization' of Spanish society, M. BATAILLON, *loc. cit.*; on the atmosphere of 'disenchantment', P. VILAR: *L'Espagne du 'Quichotte'* (*Europe*, vol. XXXIV, pp. 3–16).

INDEX